U·X·L Encyclopedia
of Biomes

Second Edition

U·X·L Encyclopedia of Biomes

Second Edition VOLUME 1

Marlene Weigel

U·X·L

A part of Gale, Cengage Learning

GALE
CENGAGE Learning

Detroit • New York • San Francisco • New Haven, Conn • Waterville, Maine • London

GALE
CENGAGE Learning™

U·X·L Encyclopedia of Biomes
Marlene Weigel

Project Editor: Madeline Harris

Editorial: Kathleen Edgar, Debra Kirby, Kristine Krapp, Kimberley McGrath, and Lemma Shomali

Composition: Evi Abou-El-Seoud

Imaging: Lezlie Light

Manufacturing: Wendy Blurton

Product Design: Jennifer Wahi

Product Management: Julia Furtaw

Rights Acquisition and Management: Dean Dauphinais and Robyn Young

For product information and technology assistance, contact us at
Gale Customer Support, 1-800-877-4253.
For permission to use material from this text or product, submit all requests online at **www.cengage.com/permissions**.
Further permissions questions can be emailed to
permissionrequest@cengage.com

Cover photographs: Image copyright 2009: Debra Hughes (tree icon), Alexander Kolomietz (beach scene), Sergey Popov (baracudas), Snowleopard1 (frog), Chee-Onn Leong (tall pines), Sigen Photography (desert), and Oksana Perkins (pond and mountains), all used under licence from Shutterstock.com. Polar bear and fall leaves images © 2009/Getty Images.

While every effort has been made to ensure the reliability of the information presented in this publication, Gale, a part of Cengage Learning, does not guarantee the accuracy of the data contained herein. Gale accepts no payment for listing; and inclusion in the publication of any organization, agency, institution, publication, service, or individual does not imply endorsement of the editors or publisher. Errors brought to the attention of the publisher and verified to the satisfaction of the publisher will be corrected in future editions.

Library of Congress Cataloging-in-Publication Data

U-X-L encyclopedia of biomes / [editor] Marlene Weigel. -- 2nd ed.
  p. cm. --
  Includes bibliographical references and index.
  ISBN 978-1-4144-5516-7 (set) -- ISBN 978-1-4144-5517-4 (vol. 1) -- ISBN978-1-4144-5518-1 (vol. 2) -- ISBN 978-1-4144-5519-8 (vol. 3) -- ISBN 978-1-4144-4426-0 (e-book)
  1. Biotic communities--Juvenile literature. I. Weigel, Marlene. II. Title: Encyclopedia of biomes.
  QH541.14.U18 2009
  577.8'2--dc22

  2008014502

Gale
27500 Drake Rd.
Farmington Hills, MI, 48331-3535

978-1-4144-5516-7 (set)
978-1-4144-5517-4 (vol. 1)
978-1-4144-5518-1 (vol. 2)
978-1-4144-5519-8 (vol. 3)

1-4144-5516-X (set)
1-4144-5517-8 (vol. 1)
1-4144-5518-6 (vol. 2)
1-4144-5519-4 (vol. 3)

This title is also available as an e-book.
ISBN-13: 978-1-4144-4426-0 ISBN-10: 1-4144-4426-5
Contact your Gale, a part of Cengage Learning, sales representative for ordering information.

Printed in China by China Translation & Printing Services Limited
1 2 3 4 5 6 7 13 12 11 10 09

Table of Contents

U•X•L Encyclopedia of Biomes: Volume 1

Reader's Guide

This second edition of U·X·L Encyclopedia of Biomes offers readers comprehensive, easy-to-use, and current information on twelve of Earth's major biomes and their many component ecosystems. Arranged alphabetically across three volumes, each biome chapter includes: an overview; a description of how the biomes are formed; their climate; elevation; growing season; plants, animals, and endangered species; food webs; human culture; and economy. The information presented may be used in a variety of subject areas, such as biology, geography, anthropology, and current events. Each chapter includes a "spotlight" feature focusing on specific geographical areas related to the biome being discussed and concludes with a section composed of books, periodicals, Internet addresses, and environmental organizations for readers to conduct more extensive research.

Additional Features

Each volume of *U·X·L Encyclopedia of Biomes* includes color maps and at least 60 photos and illustrations pertaining to each biome, while sidebar boxes highlight fascinating facts and related information. All three volumes include a glossary, a bibliography, and a subject index covering all the subjects discussed in *U·X·L Encyclopedia of Biomes.*

Note

There are many different ways to describe certain aspects of a particular biome, and it would be impossible to include all of the classifications in *U·X·L Encyclopedia of Biomes.* However, in cases where more than one classification seemed useful, more than one was given. Please note that the classifications represented here may not be those preferred by all specialists in a particular field.

Every effort was made in this set to include the most accurate information pertaining to areas and other measurements. Great variations exist in the available data, however. Sometimes differences can be accounted for in terms of what was measured: the reported area of a lake, for example, may vary depending upon the point at which measuring began. Other differences may result from natural changes that took place between the time of one measurement and another. Further, other data may be questionable because reliable information has been difficult to obtain. This is particularly true for remote areas in developing countries, where funds for scientific research are lacking and non-native scientists may not be welcomed.

The U•X•L editors would like to thank author Marlene Weigel for her work on the original edition of this title. We also thank contributing writer Rita Travis for her work on the Coniferous Forest, Grassland, Tundra, and Wetland chapters. All the entries were updated by Lubnah Shomali for this new edition, and we relied heavily on our expert, Dr. Dan Skean, of Albion College to provide academic insight and additional feedback.

Comments and Suggestions

We welcome your comments on this work as well as your suggestions for topics to be featured in future editions of *U•X•L Encyclopedia of Biomes* Please write: Editors, *U•X•L Encyclopedia of Biomes,* U•X•L, 27500 Drake Rd., Farmington Hills, MI 48331-3535; call toll-free: 1-800-877-4253; fax: 248-699-8097; or send e-mail via www.gale.cengage.com.

Biomes of the World Map

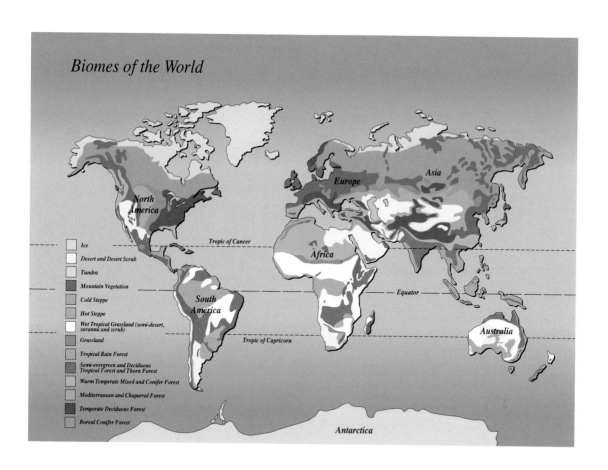

Biomes of the World

Ice
Desert and Desert Scrub
Tundra
Mountain Vegetation
Cold Steppe
Hot Steppe
Wet Tropical Grassland (semi-desert, savanna and scrub)
Grassland
Tropical Rain Forest
Semi-evergreen and Deciduous Tropical Forest and Thorn Forest
Warm Temperate Mixed and Conifer Forest
Mediterranean and Chaparral Forest
Temperate Deciduous Forest
Boreal Conifer Forest

North America
South America
Europe
Asia
Africa
Australia
Antarctica

Tropic of Cancer
Equator
Tropic of Capricorn

Words to Know

Abyssal plain: The flat midportion of the ocean floor that begins beyond the continental rise.

Acid rain: A mixture of water vapor and polluting compounds in the atmosphere that falls to Earth as rain or snow.

Active margin: A continental margin constantly being changed by earthquake and volcanic action.

Aerial roots: Plant roots that dangle in midair and absorb nutrients from their surroundings rather than from the soil.

Algae: Plantlike organisms that usually live in watery environments and depend upon photosynthesis for food.

Algal blooms: Sudden increases in the growth of algae on the ocean's surface.

Alluvial fan: A fan-shaped area created when a river or stream flows downhill, depositing sediment into a broader base that spreads outward.

Amphibians: Animals that spend part, if not most, of their lives in water.

Amphibious: Able to live on land or in water.

Angiosperms: Trees that bear flowers and produce their seeds inside a fruit; deciduous and rain forest trees are usually angiosperms.

Annuals: Plants that live for only one year or one growing season.

Aquatic: Having to do with water.

Aquifer: Rock beneath Earth's surface in which groundwater is stored.

Arachnids: Class of animals that includes spiders and scorpions.

Arctic tundra: Tundra located in the far north, close to or above the Arctic Circle.

Arid: Dry.

Arroyo: The dry bed of a stream that flows only after rain; also called a wash or a *wadi*.

Artifacts: Objects made by humans, including tools, weapons, jars, and clothing.

Artificial grassland: A grassland created by humans.

Artificial wetland: A wetland created by humans.

Atlantic blanket bogs: Blanket bogs in Ireland that are less than 656 feet (200 meters) above sea level.

Atolls: Ring-shaped reefs formed around a lagoon by tiny animals called corals.

B

Bactrian camel: The two-humped camel native to central Asia.

Bar: An underwater ridge of sand or gravel formed by tides or currents that extends across the mouth of a bay.

Barchan dunes: Sand dunes formed into crescent shapes with pointed ends created by wind blowing in the direction of their points.

Barrier island: An offshore island running parallel to a coastline that helps shelter the coast from the force of ocean waves.

Barrier reef: A type of reef that lines the edge of a continental shelf and separates it from deep ocean water. A barrier reef may enclose a lagoon and even small islands.

Bathypelagic zone: An oceanic zone based on depth that ranges from 3,300 to 13,000 feet (1,000 to 4,000 meters).

Bathyscaphe: A small, manned, submersible vehicle that accommodates several people and is able to withstand the extreme pressures of the deep ocean.

Bay: An area of the ocean partly enclosed by land; its opening into the ocean is called a mouth.

Beach: An almost level stretch of land along a shoreline.

Bed: The bottom of a river or stream channel.

Benthic: Term used to describe plants or animals that live attached to the seafloor.

Biodiverse: Term used to describe an environment that supports a wide variety of plants and animals.

Bio-indicators: Plants or animals whose health is used to indicate the general health of their environment.

Biological productivity: The growth rate of life forms in a certain period of time.

Biome: A distinct, natural community chiefly distinguished by its plant life and climate.

Blanket bogs: Shallow bogs that spread out like a blanket; they form in areas with relatively high levels of annual rainfall.

Bog: A type of wetland that has wet, spongy, acidic soil called peat.

Boreal forest: A type of coniferous forest found in areas bordering the Arctic tundra. Also called taiga.

Boundary layer: A thin layer of water along the floor of a river channel where friction has stopped the flow completely.

Brackish water: A mixture of freshwater and saltwater.

Braided stream: A stream consisting of a network of interconnecting channels broken by islands or ridges of sediment, primarily mud, sand, or gravel.

Branching network: A network of streams and smaller rivers that feeds a large river.

Breaker: A wave that collapses on a shoreline because the water at the bottom is slowed by friction as it travels along the ocean floor and the top outruns it.

Browsers: Herbivorous animals that eat from trees and shrubs.

Buoyancy: Ability to float.

Buran: Strong, northeasterly wind that blows over the Russian steppes.

Buttresses: Winglike thickenings of the lower trunk that give tall trees extra support.

Canopy: A roof over the forest created by the foliage of the tallest trees.

Canyon: A long, narrow valley between high cliffs that has been formed by the eroding force of a river.

Carbon cycle: Natural cycle in which trees remove excess carbon dioxide from the air and use it during photosynthesis. Carbon is then returned to the soil when trees die and decay.

Carnivore: A meat-eating plant or animal.

Carrion: Decaying flesh of dead animals.

Cay: An island formed from a coral reef.

Channel: The path along which a river or stream flows.

Chemosynthesis: A chemical process by which deep-sea bacteria use organic compounds to obtain food and oxygen.

Chernozim: A type of temperate grassland soil; also called black earth.

Chinook: A warm, dry wind that blows over the Rocky Mountains in North America.

Chitin: A hard chemical substance that forms the outer shell of certain invertebrates.

Chlorophyll: The green pigment in leaves used by plants to turn energy from the sun into food.

Clear-cutting: The cutting down of every tree in a selected area.

Climax forest: A forest in which only one species of tree grows because it has taken over and only that species can survive there.

Climbers: Plants that have roots in the ground but use hooklike tendrils to climb on the trunks and limbs of trees in order to reach the canopy, where there is light.

Cloud forest: A type of rain forest that occurs at elevations over 10,500 feet (3,200 meters) and that is covered by clouds most of the time.

Commensalism: Relationship between organisms in which one reaps a benefit from the other without either harming or helping the other.

Commercial fishing: Fishing done to earn money.

Conifer: A tree that produces seeds inside cones.

Coniferous trees: Trees, such as pines, spruces, and firs, that produce seeds within a cone.

Consumers: Animals in the food web that eat either plants or other animals.

Continental shelf: A flat extension of a continent that tapers gently into the sea.

Continental slope: An extension of a continent beyond the continental shelf that dips steeply into the sea.

Convergent evolution: When distantly related animals in different parts of the world evolve similar characteristics.

Coral reef: A wall formed by the skeletons of tiny animals called corals.

Coriolis effect: An effect on wind and current direction caused by Earth's rotation.

Crustaceans: Invertebrate animals that have hard outer shells.

Current: The steady flow of water in a certain direction.

Dambo: Small marsh found in Africa.

Dark zone: The deepest part of the ocean, where no light reaches.

Deciduous: Term used to describe trees, such as oaks and elms, that lose their leaves during cold or very dry seasons.

Decompose: The breaking down of dead plants and animals in order to release nutrients back into the environment.

Decomposers: Organisms that feed on dead organic materials, releasing nutrients into the environment.

Deforestation: The cutting down of all the trees in a forest.

Dehydration: Excessive loss of water from the body.

Delta: Muddy sediments that have formed a triangular shape over the continental shelf near the mouth of a river.

Deposition: The carrying of sediments by a river from one place to another and depositing them.

Desalination: Removing the salt from seawater.

Desert: A very dry area receiving no more than 10 inches (25 centimeters) of rain during a year and supporting little plant or animal life.

Desertification: The changing of fertile lands into deserts through destruction of vegetation (plant life) or depletion of soil nutrients. Topsoil and groundwater are eventually lost as well.

Desert varnish: A dark sheen on rocks and sand believed to be caused by the chemical reaction between overnight dew and minerals in the soil.

Diatom: A type of phytoplankton with a geometric shape and a hard, glasslike shell.

Dinoflagellate: A type of phytoplankton having two whiplike attachments that whirl in the water.

Discharge: The amount of water that flows out of a river or stream into another river, a lake, or the ocean.

Doldrums: Very light winds near the equator that create little or no movement in the ocean.

Downstream: The direction toward which a river or stream is flowing.

Drainage basin: All the land area that supplies water to a river or stream.

Dromedary: The one-humped, or Arabian, camel.

Drought: A long, extremely dry period.

Dune: A hill or ridge of sand created by the wind.

Duricrusts: Hard, rocklike crusts on ridges that are formed by a chemical reaction caused by the combination of dew and minerals such as limestone.

Ecosystem: A network of organisms that have adapted to a particular environment.

Elfin forest: The upper cloud forest at about 10,000 feet (3,000 meters) which has trees that tend to be smaller, and twisted.

Emergents: The trees that stand taller than surrounding trees.

Epiphytes: Plants that grow on other plants with their roots exposed to the air. Sometimes called "air" plants.

Etermy: A current that moves against the regular current, usually in a circular motion.

Elevation: The height of an object in relation to sea level.

Emergent plants: Plants that are rooted at the bottom of a body of water that have top portions that appear to be above the water's surface.

Emergents: The very tallest trees in the rain forest, which tower above the canopy.

Engineered wood: Manufactured wood products composed of particles of several types of wood mixed with strong glues and preservatives.

Epilimnion: The layer of warm or cold water closest to the surface of a large lake.

Epipelagic zone: An oceanic zone based on depth that reaches down to 650 feet (200 meters).

Epiphytes: Plants that grow on other plants or hang on them for physical support.

Ergs: Arabian word for vast seas of sand dunes, especially those found in the Sahara.

Erosion: Wearing away of the land.

Estivation: An inactive period experienced by some animals during very hot months.

Estuary: The place where a river traveling through lowlands meets the ocean in a semi-enclosed area.

Euphotic zone: The zone in a lake where sunlight can reach.

Eutrophication: Loss of oxygen in a lake or pond because increased plant growth has blocked sunlight.

Fast ice: Ice formed on the surface of the ocean between pack ice and land.

Faults: Breaks in Earth's crust caused by earthquake action.

Fell-fields: Bare rock-covered ground in the alpine tundra.

Fen: A bog that lies at or below sea level and is fed by mineral-rich ground-water.

First-generation stream: The type of stream on which a branching network is based; a stream with few tributaries. Two first-generation streams join to form a second-generation stream and so on.

Fish farms: Farms in which fish are raised for commercial use; also called hatcheries.

Fjords: Long, narrow, deep arms of the ocean that project inland.

Flash flood: A flood caused when a sudden rainstorm fills a dry riverbed to overflowing.

Floating aquatic plant: A plant that floats either partly or completely on top of the water.

Flood: An overflow caused when more water enters a river or stream than its channel can hold at one time.

Floodplain: Low-lying, flat land easily flooded because it is located next to streams and rivers.

Food chain: The transfer of energy from organism to organism when one organism eats another.

Food web: All of the possible feeding relationships that exist in a biome.

Forbs: A category of flowering, broadleaved plants other than grasses that lack woody stems.

Forest: A large number of trees covering not less than 25 percent of the area where the tops of the trees interlock, forming a canopy at maturity.

Fossil fuels: Fuels made from oil and gas that formed over time from sediments made of dead plants and animals.

Fossils: Remains of ancient plants or animals that have turned to stone.

Freshwater lake: A lake that contains relatively pure water and relatively little salt or soda.

Freshwater marsh: A wetland fed by freshwater and characterized by poorly drained soil and plant life dominated by nonwoody plants.

Freshwater swamp: A wetland fed by freshwater and characterized by poorly drained soil and plant life dominated by trees.

Friction: The resistance to motion when one object rubs against another.

Fringing reef: A type of coral reef that develops close to the land; no lagoon separates it from the shore.

Frond: A leaflike organ found on all species of kelp plants.

Fungi: Plantlike organisms that cannot make their own food by means of photosynthesis; instead they grow on decaying organic matter or live as parasites on a host.

Geyser: A spring heated by volcanic action. Some geysers produce enough steam to cause periodic eruptions of water.

Glacial moraine: A pile of rocks and sediments created as a glacier moves across an area.

Global warming: Warming of Earth's climate that may be speeded up by air pollution.

Gorge: A deep, narrow pass between mountains.

Grassland: A biome in which the dominant vegetation is grasses rather than trees or tall shrubs.

Grazers: Herbivorous animals that eat low-growing plants such as grass.

Ground birds: Birds that hunt food and make nests on the ground or close to it.

Groundwater: Freshwater stored in rock layers beneath the ground.

Gulf: A large area of the ocean partly enclosed by land; its opening is called a strait.

Gymnosperms: Trees that produce seeds that are often collected together into cones; most conifers are gymnosperms.

Gyre: A circular or spiral motion.

Hadal zone: An oceanic zone based on depth that reaches from 20,000 to 35,630 feet (6,000 to 10,860 meters).

Hardwoods: Woods usually produced by deciduous trees, such as oaks and elms.

Hatcheries: Farms in which fish are raised for commercial use; also called fish farms.

Headland: An arm of land made from hard rock that juts out into the ocean after softer rock has been eroded away by the force of tides and waves.

Headwaters: The source of a river or stream.

Herbicides: Poisons used to control weeds or any other unwanted plants.

Herbivore: An animal that eats only plant matter.

Herders: People who raise herds of animals for food and other needs; they may also raise some crops but are usually not dependent upon them.

Hermaphroditic: Term used to describe an animal or plant in which reproductive organs of both sexes are present in one individual.

Hibernation: An inactive period experienced by some animals during very cold months.

High tide: A rising of the surface level of the ocean caused by Earth's rotation and the gravitational pull of the sun and moon.

Holdfast: A rootlike structure by which kelp plants anchor themselves to rocks or the seafloor.

Hummocks: 1. Rounded hills or ridges, often heavily wooded, that are higher than the surrounding area; 2. Irregularly shaped ridges formed when large blocks of ice hit each other and one slides on top of the other; also called hammocks.

Humus: The nutrient-rich, spongy matter produced when the remains of plants and animals are broken down to form soil.

Hunter-gatherers: People who live by hunting animals and gathering nuts, berries, and fruits; normally, they do not raise crops or animals.

Hurricane: A violent tropical storm that begins over the ocean.

Hydric soil: Soil that contains a lot of water but little oxygen.

Hydrologic cycle: The manner in which molecules of water evaporate, condense as clouds, and return to Earth as precipitation.

Hydrophytes: Plants that are adapted to grow in water or very wet soil.

Hypolimnion: The layer of warm or cold water closest to the bottom of a large lake.

Hypothermia: A lowering of the body temperature that can result in death.

Insecticides: Poisons that kill insects.

Insectivores: Plants and animals that feed on insects.

Intermittent stream: A stream that flows only during certain seasons.

Interrupted stream: A stream that flows aboveground in some places and belowground in others.

Intertidal zone: The seashore zone covered with water during high tide and dry during low tide; also called the middle, or the littoral, zone.

Invertebrates: Animals without a backbone.

Kelp: A type of brown algae that usually grows on rocks in temperate water.

Kettle: A large pit created by a glacier that fills with water and becomes a pond or lake.

Kopjes: Small hills made out of rocks that are found on African grasslands.

Labrador Current: An icy Arctic current that mixes with warmer waters off the coast of northeastern Canada.

Lagoon: A large pool of seawater cut off from the ocean by a bar or other landmass.

Lake: A usually large body of inland water that is deep enough to have two distinct layers based on temperature.

Latitude: A measurement on a map or globe of a location north or south of the equator. The measurements are made in degrees, with the equator, or dissecting line, being zero.

Layering: Tree reproduction that occurs when a branch close to the ground develops roots from which a new tree grows.

Levee: High bank of sediment deposited by a very silty river.

Lichens: Plantlike organisms that are combinations of algae and fungi. The algae produces the food for both by means of photosynthesis.

Limnetic zone: The deeper, central region of a lake or pond where no plants grow.

Littoral zone: The area along the shoreline that is exposed to the air during low tide; also called intertidal zone.

Longshore currents: Currents that move along a shoreline.

Lowland rain forest: Rain forest found at elevations up to 3,000 feet (900 meters).

Low tide: A lowering of the surface level of the ocean caused by Earth's rotation and the gravitational pull of the sun and moon.

Macrophytic: Term used to describe a large plant.

Magma: Molten rock from beneath Earth's crust.

Mangrove swamp: A coastal saltwater swamp found in tropical and subtropical areas.

Marine: Having to do with the oceans.

Marsh: A wetland characterized by poorly drained soil and by plant life dominated by nonwoody plants.

Mature stream: A stream with a moderately wide channel and sloping banks.

Meandering stream: A stream that winds snakelike through flat countryside.

Mesopelagic zone: An oceanic zone based on depth that ranges from 650 to 3,300 feet (200 to 1,000 meters).

Mesophytes: Plants that live in soil that is moist but not saturated.

Mesophytic: Term used to describe a forest that grows where only a moderate amount of water is available.

Mid-ocean ridge: A long chain of mountains that lies under the World Ocean.

Migratory: Term used to describe animals that move regularly from one place to another in search of food or to breed.

Mixed-grass prairie: North American grassland with a variety of grass species of medium height.

Montane rain forest: Mountain rain forest found at elevations between 3,000 and 10,500 feet (900 and 3,200 meters).

Mountain blanket bogs: Blanket bogs in Ireland that are more than 656 feet (200 meters) above sea level.

Mouth: The point at which a river or stream empties into another river, a lake, or an ocean.

Muck: A type of gluelike bog soil formed when fully decomposed plants and animals mix with wet sediments.

Muskeg: A type of wetland containing thick layers of decaying plant matter.

Mycorrhiza: A type of fungi that surrounds the roots of conifers, helping them absorb nutrients from the soil.

Neap tides: High tides that are lower and low tides that are higher than normal when the Earth, sun, and moon form a right angle.

Nekton: Animals that can move through the water without the help of currents or wave action.

Neritic zone: That portion of the ocean that lies over the continental shelves.

Nomads: People or animals who have no permanent home but travel within a well-defined territory determined by the season or food supply.

North Atlantic Drift: A warm ocean current off the coast of northern Scandinavia.

Nutrient cycle: Natural cycle in which mineral nutrients are absorbed from the soil by tree roots and returned to the soil when the tree dies and the roots decay.

Oasis: A fertile area in the desert having a water supply that enables trees and other plants to grow there.

Ocean: The large body (or bodies) of saltwater that covers more than 70 percent of Earth's surface.

Oceanography: The exploration and scientific study of the oceans.

Old stream: A stream with a very wide channel and banks that are nearly flat.

Omnivore: Organism that eats both plants and animals.

Ooze: Sediment formed from the dead tissues and waste products of marine plants and animals.

Oxbow lake: A curved lake formed when a river abandons one of its bends.

Oxygen cycle: Natural cycle in which the oxygen taken from the air by plants and animals is returned to the air by plants during photosynthesis.

Pack ice: A mass of large pieces of floating ice that have come together on an open ocean.

Pamir: A high altitude grassland in Central Asia.

Pampa: A tropical grassland found in South America.

Pampero: A strong, cold wind that blows down from the Andes Mountains and across the South American pampa.

Pantanal: A wet savanna that runs along the Upper Paraguay River in Brazil.

Parasite: An organism that depends upon another organism for its food or other needs.

Passive margin: A continental margin free of earthquake or volcanic action, and in which few changes take place.

Peat: A type of soil formed from slightly decomposed plants and animals.

Peatland: Wetlands characterized by a type of soil called peat.

Pelagic zone: The water column of the ocean.

Perennials: Plants that live at least two years or seasons, often appearing to die but returning to "life" when conditions improve.

Permafrost: Permanently frozen topsoil found in northern regions.

Permanent stream: A stream that flows continually, even during a long, dry season.

Pesticides: Poisons used to kill anything that is unwanted and is considered a pest.

Phosphate: An organic compound used in making fertilizers, chemicals, and other commercial products.

Photosynthesis: The process by which plants use the energy from sunlight to change water (from the soil) and carbon dioxide (from the air) into the sugars and starches they use for food.

Phytoplankton: Tiny, one-celled algae that float on ocean currents.

Pingos: Small hills formed when groundwater freezes.

Pioneer trees: The first trees to appear during primary succession; they include birch, pine, poplar, and aspen.

Plankton: Plants or animals that float freely in ocean water; from the Greek word meaning "wanderer."

Plunge pool: Pool created where a waterfall has gouged out a deep basin.

Pocosin: An upland swamp whose only source of water is rain.

Polar climate: A climate with an average temperature of not more than 50°F (10°C) in July.

Polar easterlies: Winds occurring near Earth's poles that blow in an easterly direction.

Pollination: The carrying of pollen from the male reproductive part of a plant to the female reproductive part of a plant so that reproduction may occur.

Polygons: Cracks formed when the ground freezes and contracts.

Pond: A body of inland water that is usually small and shallow and has a uniform temperature throughout.

Pool: A deep, still section in a river or stream.

Prairie: A North American grassland that is defined by the stature of grass groups contained within (tall, medium, and short).

Prairie potholes: Small marshes no more than a few feet deep.

Precipitation: Rain, sleet, or snow.

Predator: An animal that kills and eat other animals.

Primary succession: Period of plant growth that begins when nothing covers the land except bare sand or soil.

Producers: Plants and other organisms in the food web of a biome that are able to make food from nonliving materials, such as the energy from sunlight.

Profundal zone: The zone in a lake where no more than 1 percent of sunlight can penetrate.

Puna: A high-altitude grassland in the Andes Mountains of South America.

Rain forest: A tropical forest, or jungle, with a warm, wet climate that supports year-round tree growth.

Raised bogs: Bogs that grow upward and are higher than the surrounding area.

Rapids: Fast-moving water created when softer rock has been eroded to create many short drops in the channel; also called white water.

Reef: A ridge or wall of rock or coral lying close to the surface of the ocean just off shore.

Rhizomes: Plant stems that spread out underground and grow into a new plant that breaks above the surface of the soil or water.

Rice paddy: A flooded field in which rice is grown.

Riffle: A stretch of rapid, shallow, or choppy water usually caused by an obstruction, such as a large rock.

Rill: Tiny gully caused by flowing water.

Riparian marsh: Marsh usually found along rivers and streams.

Rip currents: Strong, dangerous currents caused when normal currents moving toward shore are deflected away from it through a narrow channel; also called riptides.

River: A natural flow of running water that follows a well-defined, permanent path, usually within a valley.

River system: A river and all its tributaries.

Salinity: The measure of salts in ocean water.

Salt lake: A lake that contains more than 0.1 ounce of salt per quart (3 grams per liter) of water.

Salt pan: The crust of salt left behind when a salt or soda lake or pond dries up.

Saltwater marsh: A wetland fed by saltwater and characterized by poorly drained soil and plant life dominated by nonwoody plants.

Saltwater swamp: A wetland fed by saltwater and characterized by poorly drained soil and plant life dominated by trees.

Saturated: Soaked with water.

Savanna: A grassland found in tropical or subtropical areas, having scattered trees and seasonal rains.

Scavenger: An animal that eats decaying matter.

School: Large gathering of fish.

Sea: A body of saltwater smaller and shallower than an ocean but connected to it by means of a channel; sea is often used interchangeably with ocean.

Seafloor: The ocean basins; the area covered by ocean water.

Sea level: The height of the surface of the sea. It is used as a standard in measuring the heights and depths of other locations such as mountains and oceans.

Seamounts: Isolated volcanoes on the ocean floor that do not break the surface of the ocean.

Seashore: The strip of land along the edge of an ocean.

Secondary succession: Period of plant growth occurring after the land has been stripped of trees.

Sediments: Small, solid particles of rock, minerals, or decaying matter carried by wind or water.

Seiche: A wave that forms during an earthquake or when a persistent wind pushes the water toward the downwind end of a lake.

Seif dunes: Sand dunes that form ridges lying parallel to the wind; also called longitudinal dunes.

Shelf reef: A type of coral reef that forms on a continental shelf having a hard, rocky bottom. A shallow body of water called a lagoon may be located between the reef and the shore.

Shoals: Areas where enough sediments have accumulated in the river channel that the water is very shallow and dangerous for navigation.

Shortgrass prairie: North American grassland on which short grasses grow.

Smokers: Jets of hot water expelled from clefts in volcanic rock in the deep-seafloor.

Soda lake: A lake that contains more than 0.1 ounce of soda per quart (3 grams per liter) of water.

Softwoods: Woods usually produced by coniferous trees.

Sonar: The use of sound waves to detect objects.

Soredia: Algae cells with a few strands of fungus around them.

Source: The origin of a stream or river.

Spit: A long narrow point of deposited sand, mud, or gravel that extends into the water.

Spores: Single plant cells that have the ability to grow into a new organism.

Sport fishing: Fishing done for recreation.

Spring tides: High tides that are higher and low tides that are lower than normal because the Earth, sun, and moon are in line with one another.

Stagnant: Term used to describe water that is unmoving and contains little oxygen.

Star-shaped dunes: Dunes created when the wind comes from many directions; also called stellar dunes.

Steppe: A temperate grassland found mostly in southeast Europe and Asia.

Stone circles: Piles of rocks moved into a circular pattern by the expansion of freezing water.

Straight stream: A stream that flows in a straight line.

Strait: The shallow, narrow channel that connects a smaller body of water to an ocean.

Stream: A natural flow of running water that follows a temporary path that is not necessarily within a valley; also called brook or creek. Scientists often use the term to mean any natural flow of water, including rivers.

Subalpine forest: Mountain forest that begins below the snow line.

Subduction zone: Area where pressure forces the seafloor down and under the continental margin, often causing the formation of a deep ocean trench.

Sublittoral zone: The seashore's lower zone, which is underwater at all times, even during low tide.

Submergent plant: A plant that grows entirely beneath the water.

Subpolar gyre: The system of currents resulting from winds occurring near the poles of Earth.

Subsistence fishing: Fishing done to obtain food for a family or a community.

Subtropical: Term used to describe areas bordering the equator in which the weather is usually warm.

Subtropical gyre: The system of currents resulting from winds occurring in subtropical areas.

Succession: The process by which one type of plant or tree is gradually replaced by others.

Succulents: Plants that appear thick and fleshy because of stored water.

Sunlit zone: The uppermost part of the ocean that is exposed to light; it reaches down to about 650 feet (200 meters) deep.

Supralittoral zone: The seashore's upper zone, which is never underwater, although it may be frequently sprayed by breaking waves; also called the splash zone.

Swamp: A wetland characterized by poorly drained soil, stagnant water, and plant life dominated by trees.

Sward: Fine grasses that cover the soil.

Swell: Surface waves that have traveled for long distances and become more regular in appearance and direction.

Taiga: Coniferous forest found in areas bordering the Arctic tundra; also called boreal forest.

Tallgrass prairie: North American grassland on which only tall grass species grow.

Tannins: Chemical substances found in the bark, roots, seeds, and leaves of many plants and used to soften leather.

Tectonic action: Movement of Earth's crust, as during an earthquake.

Temperate bog: Peatland found in temperate climates.

Temperate climate: Climate in which summers are hot and winters are cold, but temperatures are seldom extreme.

Temperate zone: Areas in which summers are hot and winters are cold but temperatures are seldom extreme.

Thermal pollution: Pollution created when heated water is dumped into the ocean. As a result, animals and plants that require cool water are killed.

Thermocline: Area of the ocean's water column, beginning at about 1,000 feet (300 meters), in which the temperature changes very slowly.

Thermokarst: Shallow lakes in the Arctic tundra formed by melting permafrost; also called thaw lakes.

Tidal bore: A surge of ocean water caused when ridges of sand direct the ocean's flow into a narrow river channel, sometimes as a single wave.

Tidepools: Pools of water that form on a rocky shoreline during high tide and that remain after the tide has receded.

Tides: Rhythmic movements, caused by Earth's rotation and the gravitational pull of the sun and moon, that raise or lower the surface level of the oceans.

Tombolo: A bar of sand that has formed between the beach and an island, linking them together.

Trade winds: Winds occurring both north and south of the equator to about 30 degrees latitude; they blow primarily east.

Transverse dunes: Sand dunes lying at right angles to the direction of the wind.

Tree: A large woody perennial plant with a single stem, or trunk, and many branches.

Tree line: The elevation above which trees cannot grow.

Tributary: A river or stream that flows into another river or stream.

Tropical: Term used to describe areas close to the equator in which the weather is always warm.

Tropical tree bog: Bog found in tropical climates in which peat is formed from decaying trees.

Tropic of Cancer: A line of latitude about 25 degrees north of the equator.

Tropic of Capricorn: A line of latitude about 25 degrees south of the equator.

Tsunami: A huge wave or upwelling of water caused by undersea earthquakes that grows to great heights as it approaches shore.

Tundra: A cold, dry, windy region where trees cannot grow.

Turbidity current: A strong downward-moving current along the continental margin caused by earthquakes or the settling of sediments.

Turbine: An energy-producing engine.

Tussocks: Small clumps of vegetation found in marshy tundra areas.

Typhoon: A violent tropical storm that begins over the ocean.

Understory: A layer of shorter, shade-tolerant trees that grow under the forest canopy.

Upstream: The direction from which a river or stream is flowing.

Upwelling: The rising of water or molten rock from one level to another.

Veld: Temperate grassland in South Africa.

Venom: Poison produced by animals such as certain snakes and spiders.

Vertebrates: Animals with a backbone.

Wadi: The dry bed of a stream that flows only after rain; also called a wash or an *arroyo*.

Warm-bodied fish: Fish that can maintain a certain body temperature by means of a special circulatory system.

Wash: The dry bed of stream that flows only after rain; also called an *arroyo* or a *wadi*.

Water column: All of the waters of the ocean, exclusive of the sea bed or other landforms.

Water cycle: Natural cycle in which trees help prevent water runoff, absorb water through their roots, and release moisture into the atmosphere through their leaves.

Waterfall: A cascade of water created when a river or stream falls over a cliff or erodes its channel to such an extent that a steep drop occurs.

Water table: The level of groundwater.

Waves: Rhythmic rising and falling movements in the water.

Westerlies: Winds occurring between 30 degrees and 60 degrees latitude; they blow in a westerly direction.

Wet/dry cycle: A period during which wetland soil is wet or flooded followed by a period during which the soil is dry.

Wetlands: Areas that are covered or soaked by ground or surface water often enough and long enough to support plants adapted for life under those conditions.

Wet meadows: Freshwater marshes that frequently dry up.

Xeriscaping: Landscaping method that uses drought tolerant plants and efficient watering techniques.

Xerophytes: Plants adapted to life in dry habitats or in areas like salt marshes or bogs.

Young stream: A stream close to its headwaters that has a narrow channel with steep banks.

Zooplankton: Animals, such as jellyfish, corals, and sea anemones, that float freely in ocean water.

Coniferous Forest

A tree is a large woody plant with one main stem, or trunk, and many branches that lives year after year. A forest is a large number of trees covering at least 25 percent of an area where the tops of the trees, called crowns, interlock to form an enclosure or canopy at maturity. Coniferous (koh-NIH-fuhr-uhs) forests primarily contain conifer trees including spruces, pines, firs, larches, cedars, and junipers. Almost all coniferous trees, such as pines and firs, bear their seeds inside cones. Most also have stiff, flattened or needlelike leaves that usually remain green all winter.

Coniferous forests are found in Asia, primarily in Siberia, China, Korea, and Japan, and on the slopes of the Himalaya and Hindu Kush Mountains. In Europe, they cover much of Scandinavia and the coast of the Baltic Sea and are found on the primary mountain ranges—the Alps, the Vosges, and the Carpathians. In North America, coniferous forests stretch across the northern part of the continent from Alaska to Newfoundland; down into Washington, Oregon, and California; and along the Cascades, the Sierra Nevadas, and the Rocky Mountains. In the Southern Hemisphere, they are found in Mexico, along the western coast of South America, in parts of Argentina and Brazil, in parts of the Australasia region, and in portions of Africa.

How Coniferous Forests Develop

The first forests evolved during Earth's prehistoric past. Since then, all forests have developed by means of a process called succession.

The first forests   The first forests evolved from clubmosses, ferns, and other prehistoric plants, which, over time, adapted to the surrounding environment, and grew more treelike. Trees that preferred a warm, humid, tropical climate developed first, followed by those that gradually adapted to drier, cooler weather. Coniferous forests flourished during the Jurassic Period, about 160 million years ago.

1

WORDS TO KNOW

Boreal forest: A type of coniferous forest found in areas bordering the Arctic tundra. Also called taiga.

Clear-cutting: The cutting down of every tree in a selected area.

Deciduous: Term used to describe trees, such as oaks and elms, that lose their leaves during cold or very dry seasons.

Epiphytes: Plants that grow on other plants or hang on them for physical support.

Montane forest: The moist and cool sloped areas near mountains.

Muskeg: A type of wetland containing thick layers of decaying plant matter.

Pioneer trees: The first trees to appear during primary succession; they include birch, pine, poplar, and aspen.

Predator: An animal that kills and eat other animals.

Succession: The process by which one type of plant or tree is gradually replaced by another.

Taiga: Coniferous forest found in areas bordering the Arctic tundra; also called boreal forest.

About one million years ago, during the Ice Ages, glaciers (slow-moving masses of ice) covered about one-third of the land surface of the Earth. Eventually, the glaciers retreated, but not before they had destroyed many of the world's forests and scoured the land of plants. Roughly twelve thousand years ago, trees began to repopulate the land that had been covered by ice. Spruce, larch, ash and birch trees were among the first species to make a comeback, preparing the way for other trees.

Succession Trees compete with one another for sunlight, water, and nutrients, thus a forest is constantly changing. The process by which one type of plant or tree is gradually replaced by others is called succession. During succession, different species of trees become dominant as time progresses and the environment changes. Succession began following the last Ice Age and continues today. It can occur naturally, when different species of trees become dominant as time progresses and the environment changes. It can also occur from natural disasters, such as forest fires.

Primary succession Primary succession usually begins on bare soil or sand where no plants grew before. When the right amount of sunlight, moisture, and air temperatures are present, seeds begin to germinate (grow). These first plants are usually made up of the grasses and forbs (a non-woody broad-leaved plant) type. They continue to grow and eventually form meadows. Over time, and as conditions change, other plants

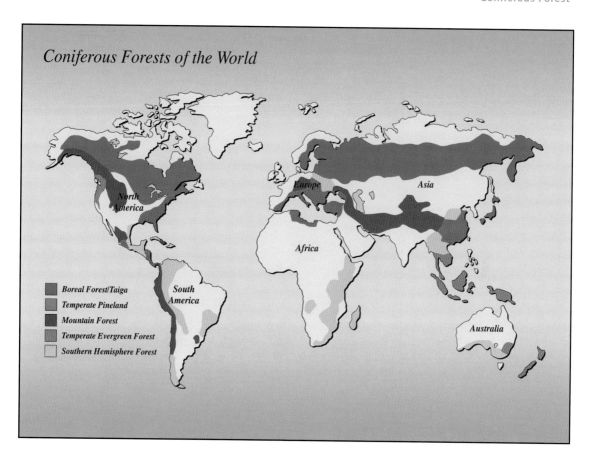

Coniferous Forests of the World

- Boreal Forest/Taiga
- Temperate Pineland
- Mountain Forest
- Temperate Evergreen Forest
- Southern Hemisphere Forest

begin to grow such as shrubs and trees. These plants become dominant and replace or take over where the grasses and forbs originally grew.

As primary succession continues, "pioneer" trees begin to thrive. In North America, examples of pioneer trees include birch, pine, poplar, and aspen. They are all tall, sun-loving trees, and they quickly take over the meadow. However, they also change the environment by making shade. If conditions are right, a mixed forest of sun-loving and shade-loving trees may continue for many years. Eventually, more changes occur.

The climax forest   Seedlings from pioneer trees do not grow well in shade; therefore, new pioneer trees do not grow. As the mature trees begin to die from old age, disease, and other causes, the broad-leaf, shade-loving trees become dominant. The shade from these trees can be too dense for their own seedlings as well. As a result, seedlings from the trees that prefer heavy shade, such as beech and sugar maple, begin to thrive and dominate

Stages in Forest Succession

FIRST STAGE:
Bare rocks with
lichens

SECOND STAGE:
Ferns, mosses
and grasses

THIRD STAGE:
Pioneer trees
dominate

FOURTH STAGE:
Deciduous trees
become dominant

CLIMAX STAGE:
All one Species

the forest. These trees produce such deep shade that only trees or plants that can survive in complete shade succeed there. When this happens, the result is a climax forest characteristic of a certain region, for example an oak-hickory forest in the eastern United States.

Few true climax forests actually exist because forests are dynamic and changes take place that interfere with stability. Fires, floods, high winds,

Fire in the forest

About 12,000,000 acres (4,800,000 hectares) of forest in the United States are damaged or destroyed by fire every year. Forest fires can spread as fast as 10 miles (15 kilometers) per hour downwind. Most forest fires are caused by humans and occur in coniferous forests, where both the air and the wood tend to be dry. Also, pine needles contain resin (sap), which burns easily.

Fires not only burn trees, but they also destroy other plant and animal life. Ground fires burn up organic material beneath the vegetation on the forest floor. Although ground fires move slowly, they do much damage. Fires that burn small vegetation and loose material are called surface fires. A crown fire is one that moves quickly through the tops of trees or shrubs.

Forests can actually benefit from fire. The huge fire in Yellowstone National Park in 1988 is an example. In the beginning, it was a controlled fire. The park's managers allowed it to burn naturally in order to restore the natural balance of the forest. The fire eventually got out of control and destroyed about 20 percent of the park. It left ashes rich in minerals such as calcium and phosphorous. These minerals promoted the growth of new plants, such as pine grass, that grows beneath Douglas firs and flowers only after a fire. The standing dead trees now attract certain types of birds, like the woodpecker and tree swallow. Smoke and heat killed harmful insects and parasitic fungi that endangered trees. The comparatively few animals that died provided food for other species. Many of the burned areas now support tree seedlings, as well as many other plants.

and people can all destroy a single tree or several acres of trees. Glaciers can mow them down; volcanoes can smother them with ash or molten rock or knock them over with explosive force. When this happens, the process of succession starts over.

Secondary succession   When the land has been stripped of trees, it will eventually be covered with them again if left alone. This is called secondary succession and can take place more quickly than primary succession. Seeds from other forests in neighboring regions are blown by the wind or carried by animals to the site. The seeds take root and seedlings sprout restarting the process.

Kinds of Coniferous Forests

Forests can be classified in many ways. In general, coniferous forests are categorized as boreal/taiga, mountain, temperate evergreen, temperate pine, or Southern Hemisphere forests.

Boreal forest/taiga   The word boreal (BOHR-ee-yuhl) means "northern," and taiga (TAY-guh) is a Russian word for "little sticks." Boreal forests, or

A conifer for St. Nick

The most popular tree used as a Christmas tree is the coniferous fir. Fir trees are cone-shaped and can grow between 30 and 150 feet (9 and 46 meters) tall. Their needles are very fragrant and remain on the tree for a long time after it has been cut. Most of the trees used for Christmas trees are not wild but are grown on tree plantations.

taiga, are found in regions bordering the Arctic tundra (a region so dry and cold that no trees can grow). These are the great northern forests of Canada, Alaska, Russia, and Scandinavia. They form some of the largest forest biomes in the world. About 11 percent of the Earth's land surface is considered to be taiga.

Trees in the boreal forest grow at higher latitudes (a distance north or south of the equator measured in degrees), usually between 45° and 70° North, than trees in any other type of forest. The most common are spruce, pine, and fir.

The boreal forest may be divided into three zones. The northernmost zone is the forest-tundra, where trees meet treeless land. Few species are able to survive here. The second zone is the lichen (LY-ken; an algae and fungi combination) woodland, or sparse taiga. Here, trees grow far apart and a lichen mat covers the forest floor. The southernmost region is the closed-canopy forest where many species of conifers grow close together and the forest floor is covered with mosses that grow well in shade.

Mountain coniferous forest   Mountain coniferous forests are found on mountains below the permanent snowfields. They are located in the Rockies, Cascades, and Sierra Nevadas of North America; the Alps and Carpathians in Europe; and the Hindu Kush and Himalayas in Asia.

COMMON SOFTWOOD TREES		
Europe	**North America**	**South America**
Austrian pine	Balasam fir	Alerce
Cedar	Cedar	Manio
European larch	Douglas fir	Monkey-puzzle tree (Chile pine)
Maritime pine	Larch	
Norway spruce	Norway spruce	Parana pine
Siberian yellow pine	Pine	
Silver fir	Sequoia	
Southern cypress		

Forests on the upper slopes just below the snowfields are called subalpine forests. At these higher elevations, where the weather is harshest, trees such as the bristlecone pine are long-lived but often stunted in growth. Lodgepole pines grow erect, but alpine firs grow close to the ground, as if shrinking from the harsh climate. Forests on the lower and middle slopes are called montane forests. In this more moderate climate conifers grow taller.

Trees common in mountain forests vary from region to region. In North America, Douglas fir, sierra redwood, and ponderosa pine predominate. Silver fir and larch are found in Europe, and chir pines, Himalayan firs, and morinda spruces grow in Asian forests.

Temperate evergreen forest Temperate evergreen forests grow in regions with moderate, humid climates. Summers are warm and winters may be cool, but temperatures are seldom extreme. In North America, these forests range along the Pacific coast from Alaska and British Columbia to west central California, where they are sometimes called temperate rain forests. Common tree species include western hemlock, western red cedar, Douglas fir, and coast redwood.

The giant redwoods of California and southern Oregon are the tallest trees in America, many exceeding 300 feet (91 meters) in height and measuring up to 22 feet (7 meters) in circumference. The tallest individual tree, Hyperion, measures 379.1 feet (115.5 meters). A species of redwoods found on the western slopes of the Sierra Nevada Mountains, giant Sequoias, are among the world's oldest trees. One Sequoia, named

COMMON SOFTWOOD TREES

Africa	Asia	Australia	Central America
Pencil cedar	Benguet pine	Celery-top pine	Caribbean pitch pine
Podo	Chir	Kauri	Yellowwood
Radiata pine	Hemlock	Radiata pine	
Thuya	Himalayan silver fir	Rimu	
Yellowwood	I-Ching pine		
	Indian juniper		
	Japanese fir		
	Pencil cedar		
	Sugi		

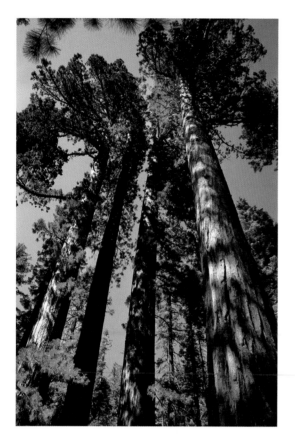

The Bachelor and the Three Graces are redwoods in Yosemite National Park.

"General Sherman", stands 275 feet (84 meters) tall, has a diameter of 36.5 feet (11 meters), and may be as many as 2,000-2,300 years old. It is also the largest tree by volume in the world, measuring 52,500 cubic feet (1,515 cubic meters).

Where winters are mildest, temperate evergreen forests often contain broad-leaved evergreen trees. The humid conditions help the growth of moss and other moisture-loving plants on the forest floor.

Temperate pine forest Temperate pinelands grow in hilly or upland regions with warm, dry climates. In the United States, they are found in southern California and in the region stretching from New Jersey to southern Florida and west to Texas. They also occur in Mexico, China, and throughout the regions bordering the Mediterranean Sea.

Southern hemisphere coniferous forest Coniferous forests located primarily in the Southern Hemisphere, including those of Africa, Southeast Asia, Australia, and New Zealand, are not the same as forests in the Northern Hemisphere. In general, the native coniferous trees are smaller and their leaves have different forms. Members of the monkey-puzzle family are common. Most are found in the mountains or high plateaus.

In South America, native conifers include the Parana pine, monkey-puzzle, Patagonian cedar, and Chilean cedar. In Australia, bunya pine, white cypress pine, and hoop pine grow. Forests of kauri pine grow in New Zealand, and the South African yellowwood is found in southern Africa. The Norfolk Island pine, native to the island of that name, is a popular ornamental tree worldwide.

Climate

The climate of a coniferous forest depends upon where it is located. In general, the farther north the latitude, the cooler the climate. The presence of mountain ranges and oceans also affects the climate of

Cedar

Different conifer genera have species called cedar. They are durable and fragrant woods that have been used by humans since at least 2000 BC. True cedars (*Cedrus*) are in the pine family. They do not easily rot and are resistant to fire and high winds. Great cedar forests were once found in Algeria, Morocco, the Himalayas, the Pacific Northwest in the United States, and Lebanon in the Middle East. The Phoenicians, who lived in Lebanon, were excellent carpenters and sold much of their wood.

Some of the Phoenicians' best customers were ancient Egyptians who lived in the Nile Valley where few trees grow. Because cedar is so strong, the Egyptians used it to construct homes and other buildings and for wooden rollers that moved huge stones into place for the construction of the pyramids. Cedar sawdust was used in the process of mummifying the dead, and the resin was used for embalming and coating coffins.

Cedar was also used in the construction of King Solomon's temple in Jerusalem between 965 to 926 BC. The Romans used it to build ships, and the Roman emperor Hadrian brought about legislation to conserve the cedars of Lebanon between 117 and 138 AD.

The North American western red cedar (*Thuja plicata*) is a member of the cypress family (Cupressaceae). Native Americans on the Pacific coast made clothing and baskets from the bark, rope from the branches, and canoes and lodges from the trunks. Various types of Cupressaceae have also long been valued in Japan, where conservation was first practiced during the sixteenth century. These trees form stands more than 1,000 years old.

Although most of the once mighty cedar forests are gone, the western red cedar and the Atlantic white cedar (*Chamaecyparis thyoides*, also a member of the cypress family) is still used for building boats and homes. The cedar used in clothes closets and chests, where the aroma of cedar is said to repel cloth-eating moths, comes from junipers (*Juniperus*) and eastern red cedar (*J. virginiana*).

---

an area. In Japan, for example, Siberian air masses bring severe winters to some forests, while other forests are influenced by warm ocean currents, and have a more tropical climate.

Boreal forest/taiga The most severe climate is found in the boreal forest, or taiga, where temperatures are below freezing for more than half of the year. Winter temperatures range from -65° to 30°F (-54° to -1°C), and summer temperatures from 20° to 70°F (-7° to 21°C). However, because the taiga is a land of extremes, temperatures can drop as low as -76°F (-60°C) in winter or climb as high as 104°F (40°C) in summer.

Record holding trees!

Not to be outdone by the redwoods with their reputation as the world's tallest trees, the Mexican cypress has its own world record. An outstanding individual cypress in Tule, Mexico, known as "El Gigante," is the world's fattest tree. Although El Gigante is only 140 feet (43 meters) tall, the circumference of its trunk measures 115 feet (35 meters).

Most of the precipitation (rain, snow, or sleet) in the boreal forest comes from summer rain, which averages 12 to 33 inches (30 to 85 centimeters) per year.

Mountain coniferous forest Mountain forests face cold, dry climates and high winds. The higher the elevation, the harsher the conditions. Scientists estimate that for every 300 feet (91 meters) in elevation, the temperature drops more than 1°F. On Alaskan mountains, temperatures in January average about 8°F (-13°C) and in July only 47°F (8°C).

In general, northern hemisphere forests found on the northern side of mountains are shaded from the sun and the air is cooler. The forests receive more rainfall and have denser stands (groups) of trees and other plants. Forests on the southern side of mountains are drier, warmer and have less vegetation.

Temperate evergreen forest The redwood and Pacific Northwestern forests have a climate that is moderated by the Pacific Ocean and the coastal mountain ranges. In the Olympic Rain Forest in Washington, for example, the temperature is always above freezing in winter and is seldom higher than 85°F (29°C) in summer. Up to 145 inches (368 centimeters) of rain fall annually.

Temperate pine forest In the Mediterranean and parts of California, winters are warm and wet, while summers are hot and dry. Droughts (extremely dry periods) may be common. In the Mediterranean region, for example, winter temperatures usually do not fall below freezing.

Southern hemisphere coniferous forest The climate in Southern Hemisphere forests varies, depending upon where they are located. In the tropics (the regions around the equator), where the forests are at higher elevations, clouds of mist may blanket them creating cool and damp conditions. In more temperate regions, such as in the mountains of Chile, conditions are drier and colder.

Geography of Coniferous Forests

The geography of coniferous forests includes landforms, elevation, soil, mineral resources, and water resources.

Landforms   Coniferous forest landforms vary, depending upon the location, and may include mountains, valleys, rolling hills, or flat plateaus. The boreal forest landscape is dotted with wetlands, lakes, and ponds. Unique to the Canadian and Alaskan forest is the muskeg, a type of bog or marsh with thick layers of decaying plant matter. The muskeg looks like moss-covered ground, but is actually so wet and spongy that hikers may sink while passing through. When the muskeg freezes in winter, irregularly shaped ridges, called hummocks, may form.

Treeless hollows are often found in coniferous forests in the Northern Hemisphere. These hollows are usually created when glaciers move over the area and destroy the trees. The glaciers also leave behind basins that eventually fill with water and become lakes. Streams and rivers are common in these forests as well.

Elevation   Coniferous forests grow at different elevations throughout the world, from sea level (the average height of the surface of the sea) to more than 15,000 feet (4,600 meters) above sea level. Temperate rain forests along the northern Pacific coast are usually found below 2,700 feet (820 meters). The mountain forests in the Pacific Northwest range between 3,000 and 7,000 feet (910 and 2,100 meters), and those in the Rocky Mountains between 4,000 and 7,500 feet (1,200 and 2,300 meters). The giant Sequoias in the Sierra Nevada Mountains grow between 4,500 and 8,000 feet (1,400 and 2,400 meters). Subalpine forests in the Sierra Nevadas are found between 6,500 and 11,000 feet (2,000 and 3,400 meters) and in the Rockies between 7,500 and 11,500 feet (2,300 and 3,500 meters).

In Peru, mountain forests begin around 9,800 feet (3,000 meters) and subalpine forests grow to an altitude of 15,000 feet (4,500 meters). In central Japan, mountain forests are common above 6,560 feet (2,000 meters), however, on the island of Hokkaido, coniferous forests are

The oldest of all living things?

High in the Rocky Mountains of southwest California, Nevada, Utah, Arizona, New Mexico, and Colorado live the bristlecone pines, the oldest trees in the world. A tree cut down on Wheeler Ridge contained 4,900 rings of growth, and the oldest living specimen, the Methuselah Tree of California, is estimated at 4,800 years old. These twisted, ancient trees exist only at high altitudes—between 8,000 and 10,000 feet (2,432 and 3,040 meters)—and seldom grow more than 30 feet (9 meters) tall.

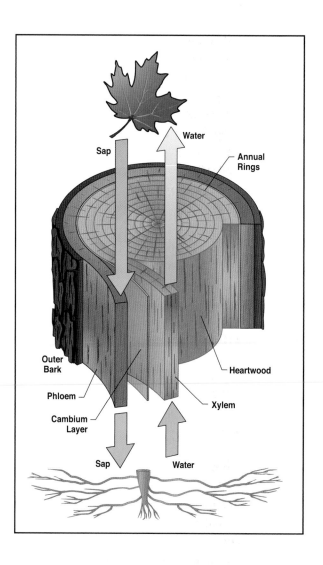

Sap

Water

Annual Rings

Outer Bark

Heartwood

Phloem

Cambium Layer

Xylem

Sap

Water

The parts of a tree, including the annual rings and the direction of water and sap.

found at sea level. Himalayan conifers dominate below 10,000 feet (3,000 meters) and Himalayan firs above that point.

Soil   The presence of trees protect soil from erosion by holding it in place with their roots. Even fallen trees are important in conserving and cycling nutrients back into the soil and in reducing erosion. Trees also create windbreaks that help prevent topsoil from being blown away. A coniferous forest's soil is acidic because the needles of coniferous trees have high acid content. The soil is also affected by both climate and location.

In the boreal forest, for example, soil is poorly developed because of the cold temperatures. In areas adjacent to tundra, a layer of permafrost (permanently frozen soil) prevents rain and melting snow from being absorbed deep into the ground. The topsoil is soggy because the moisture stays close to the surface. Cold temperatures are also responsible for the slow rate of decomposition of dead plants and animals, which means that soil forms slowly and there are not a lot of soil-mixing creatures.

Mountain soil is usually dry because the sloping terrain allows rain and melting snow to run off. This runoff washes away nutrients. The soil often makes up only a thin layer over a rocky foundation. As a result, tree roots do not penetrate deeply.

In the temperate evergreen forests of North America, the soil is often reddish in color and high in aluminum and iron. Decomposition takes place rapidly because of the high moisture content. This richer soil supports more plant growth on the forest floor.

Mineral resources   Mineral resources found deep in the ground below coniferous forests began developing millions of years ago. As ancient trees died and soil gradually built up over them, their remains were compressed and evolved into coal, oil, and natural gas in a process that takes millions of years.

In northern Russian forests, coal, oil, and gas are found beneath the forest floor. In other parts of the taiga, aluminum is mined. In the province of Cita in far eastern Russia, mining and primary-ore processing dominate the economy. Gold, tin, tungsten, molybdenum, and lead are among the many minerals found there.

Gold was often mined from the rivers and streams that run through the forests of the Pacific northwest in the United States and Canada, and nickel was occasionally found in the northern forest of Manitoba, Canada.

Broad-leaved evergreens—the trees-in-between

In northern climates, most broad-leaved trees lose their leaves in the autumn. However, some that live in climates where winters are mild but wet and summers are hot and dry remain green all year long. They are not conifers, because they are flowering plants that produce seeds enclosed in fruits, but they have learned to conserve moisture as conifers do by producing small leaves that they retain for several years. In effect, they are somewhere in-between conifers and deciduous trees, having characteristics of both. Common species include the olive tree of the Mediterranean region, the eucalyptus of Australia and South America, the cork oak of Spain and Portugal, and the canyon live oak of California.

Certain broad-leaved evergreens have other unusual characteristics. For example, the cork oak produces bark as thick as 1 foot (30 centimeters), which can be harvested and used for corks. Another example is the eucalyptus, the giant tree of the southern hemisphere. Called the "giant gum" in Australia, some trees attain heights of 300 feet (91 meters), rivaling the giant Sequoias of the Northern Hemisphere.

A job in the woods

Forestry is the profession that deals with development and management of forests. The main objective is to ensure that there will always be trees and a supply of timber. Foresters are also involved with the conservation of soil, water, and wildlife resources, and with preserving land for recreation. By the mid-1990s, there were more than 20,000 foresters and conservation scientists in the United States, and about 50 colleges and universities offered degrees in the field.

Silviculture is a branch of forestry focused on forest growth. Foresters in this branch cultivate different types of forests and encourage them to grow as quickly as possible using such methods as fertilizers. Some forests are developed for lumber, paper, or pulp. Researchers use scientific breeding methods to raise the type of tree best fit for each purpose.

With a need for superior quality trees grown for specific uses, cloning may become a tool of the forester. A clone is the genetically identical copy of an organism. An entire forest could be cloned from one ideal parent tree.

Water resources In temperate regions, water resources include rivers, streams, springs, lakes, and ponds. Permafrost prevents water from sinking very deeply into the soil, so wetlands, lakes, and ponds form in the boreal forests. Mountain forests are often dotted with lakes and ponds that were carved out by glaciers. Mountains formed by volcanic action usually have craters that filled with water and became lakes. Crater Lake in Oregon is an example of such a lake.

Plant Life

Most forests contain a mixture of trees, and coniferous forests are no different. Stands of deciduous (dee-SID-joo-uhs) trees, such as larches (a type of conifer), birches, and poplars, may exist within their boundaries. (Deciduous trees lose their leaves at the end of each growing season.)

These mixed trees and smaller plants grow to different heights forming "layers" in the forest. The tallest trees create a canopy, or roof, over the rest. In the coniferous forest, these trees are often spruces and firs. Beneath the canopy grows the understory, a layer of shorter, shade-tolerant trees, such as the Pacific dogwoods of California. The next layer, only a few feet off the ground, is composed of small shrubs, such as junipers, blueberry, witch-hobble, and mountain laurel. Growing close to the ground are wild flowers, grasses, ferns, mosses, and mushrooms. In a coniferous forest, the canopy is so dense that little light is able to penetrate down to the forest floor. As a result of this limited light and high humidity, organisms such as algae, fungi, and lichens tend to flourish.

Algae, fungi, and lichens It is generally recognized that algae (AL-jee), fungi (FUHN-ji), and lichens do not fit neatly into the plant category. In this chapter, however, they will be discussed as if they were plants.

Algae Many algae are single-celled organisms, although quite a few are multicellular. Most algal species have the ability to make their own food by means of photosynthesis (foh-toh-SIHN-thuh-sihs), the process by which plants use the energy from sunlight to change water and carbon dioxide into the sugars and starches they use for food. Others absorb nutrients from their surroundings.

Algae may reproduce in one of three ways. Some algae split into two or more parts, each part becoming a new, separate plant. Other algae form spores (single cells that have the ability to grow into a new organism). A few algae can reproduce sexually, during which cells from two different plants unite to create a new plant.

Fungi Unlike algae, fungi cannot make their own food by means of photosynthesis. Some fungi, like mold and mushrooms, obtain nutrients from dead or decaying organic matter (derived from living organisms). They assist in the decomposition (breaking down) of this matter and in releasing into the soil the nutrients needed by other plants. Parasitic fungi attach themselves to other living things. Fungi reproduce by means of spores.

One type of fungi, called mycorrhizae, surround the roots of conifers, helping them absorb nutrients from the soil. Slippery jack, a toadstool fungus that grows in coniferous forests, gets its name from the slimy material on its cap.

Lichens Lichens are combinations of algae and fungi that live in cooperation. The fungi surround the algal cells, and the algae produce food for themselves and the fungi by means of photosynthesis. The fungi may help keep the algae moist. In harsher climates, such as that of the forest-tundra, lichens are often the only vegetation to survive. They have no root system and they can grow on bare rock. While their growth is slow, lichens often live for hundreds of years. Hemlock forests may contain as many as 150 species of lichens. Reindeer moss, a common type of lichen, is found in many coniferous forests.

Like algae, lichens can reproduce in several ways. If a spore from the fungus lands next to an algea, they can join together to form new lichen. Lichens can also reproduce by means of soredia. Soredia are algal cells with a few strands of fungus around them. When soredia break off, they may form new lichens wherever they land.

Green plants other than trees Most green plants need several basic things to grow: light, air, water, warmth, and nutrients. In the coniferous woodland, light, water, and warmth are not always abundant. Nutrients, such as nitrogen, phosphorus, and potassium, are obtained from the soil, which may not always have a large supply. For this reason, plants beneath many coniferous trees can be sparse and must often make special adaptations in order to survive. The pitcher plant, for example, catches insects for food, while others compete with trees for space and nutrients by emitting chemicals into the soil that prevent the germination of trees.

Coniferous woodlands are home to both annual and perennial plants. Annuals live only one year or one growing season. Perennials live at least two years or two growing seasons, often appearing to die when the climate becomes too cold or dry, but returning to life when conditions improve.

Common coniferous forest green plants other than trees Typical green plants found in coniferous forests include mosses, forbs, and ferns.

Mosses Mosses are plentiful in forests; as many as 25,000 species exist. They grow on the ground, tree trunks, decaying logs, and rocks. Mosses range in size from a few millimeters to rare varieties that reach 6.5 feet (2 meters) long. Each moss plant is formed like a tiny tree, with a single straight trunk and leaflike structures growing from it. Mosses grow close together and can store large quantities of water.

Plume moss, also called feather moss or boreal forest moss, resembles an ostrich plume. It forms dense, light-green mats on rocks, rotten wood, or peaty (highly rich, organic) soil, especially in mountain forests of the Northern Hemisphere.

Some mosses are epiphytes, plants that grow on other plants for physical support. Epiphytes are found in warmer climates, such as that of the Pacific Northwest. They absorb water and nutrients from rain and debris that collects on the supporting plants rather than from their own roots.

Forbs   Forbs are non-grass, non-woody, flowering plants. They have extensive root systems, and some can live as long as 50 years. Yellow trout lilies, large-flowered trilliums, and lupines are most common in non-conifer forests. Because little sunlight may reach the forest floor, some forbs store food in bulbs and rootstocks beneath the ground. Their small flowers grow low to the ground, and bloom before taller plants block all sunlight.

Ferns   Many species of ferns grow in coniferous forests. Ferns are nonflowering perennial plants, which reproduce by means of spores. Sword ferns are long and wispy, with toothed leaflets. Licorice ferns grow on tree trunks and stumps and are often seen draped over branches. Deer ferns prefer the moist forest floor.

Growing season   Location, soil, and moisture all help to determine the number and types of green plants that grow in the forest. Many different plants are found in the temperate evergreen forests, where the rich soil, warm climate, and moisture promote growth year-round. Fewer plants are found in the colder, drier, boreal forests where the growing season may last only about twelve weeks. In the hot, dry climate of the Mediterranean forests, plant growth prospers during the rainy, winter season.

Reproduction   Most green plants, such as wildflowers, reproduce by means of pollination (the process during which pollen is carried by visiting animals or the wind from the male reproductive flower part to the female reproductive part). As the growing season comes to an end, seeds are usually produced. The seed's hard outer covering protects it during cold winters, or long dry seasons until it sprouts.

A few woodland plants, such as ferns, reproduce by means of spores. Perennial grasses produce rhizomes—long, rootlike stems that spread out below ground. These stems develop their own root systems and send up sprouts that grow into new plants.

Coniferous trees   Most coniferous trees have a single strong stem, or trunk, and live 100 to 250 years. Some of the oldest living things on Earth are the bristlecone pines of the western United States, which may be as old as 5,000 years. Most of the tree's growth is directed upward. Redwoods

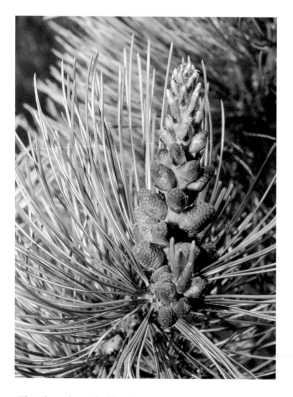

This photo shows the blooming stage of the pine cone. IMAGE COPYRIGHT MAXIM TUPIKOV, 2007. USED UNDER LICENSE FROM SHUTTERSTOCK.COM.

can reach nearly 400 feet (122 meters) in height and their trunks may weigh over 1,000 tons (907 metric tons). While broad-leaved trees spread their limbs and branches out from the trunk to create a crown of leaves, conifers devote their energy to growing taller. Without interference from diseases, natural disasters, and human interference, these trees can attain huge proportions.

Each year a tree grows, its trunk is thickened with a new layer, or ring, of cells. When the tree is cut down, its age can be determined by how many of these rings are present, although those in conifers are not as pronounced. As the tree ages, the cells from the center outward become hardened to produce a sturdy core. Like all green plants, trees grow by means of photosynthesis, during which they release the oxygen essential to animals and humans back into the air.

In general, trees are divided into two groups according to how they bear their seeds. Angiosperms have flowers and produce their seeds inside fruits, and many shed their leaves during cold or very dry periods. Broad-leaved trees, such as oaks and elms, are often angiosperms. Conifers are gymnosperms that produce seeds on scales that are usually clustered to form a cone, which may be woody or berrylike. Gymnosperm seeds are "naked," not enclosed in fruits.

Conifers are well adapted to cool or cold temperatures and long dry periods. Their stiff, narrow needles prevent loss of moisture and offer less resistance to strong winter winds, which results in less wind damage. They stay green all year and are often called "evergreens." They remain ready for sudden warm weather and can take advantage of a short growing season. Coniferous trees do not shed their needles every autumn. However, evergreens do shed the inner growth of needles approximately every two to three years. Since these needles were formed during past growth, their loss does not hinder new growth of the tree.

Fir trees are cone-shaped and can grow between 30 and 150 feet (9 and 46 meters) tall. Their needles are very fragrant and remain on the tree long after it has been cut. These characteristics make them a popular choice as a Christmas tree.

Common coniferous trees   Common coniferous trees include parana pine, bunya pine, lodgepole pine, white pine, yew, Norway spruce, and yellowwood.

Parana pine   In South America, the parana pine, or candelabra tree, is a conifer found in the hilly countries of Brazil and Argentina. It is a slow-growing tree with a very straight trunk that can reach a height of 150 feet (46 meters) with a diameter of 12-70 inches (30-180 centimeters). It is an important source of timber because its trunk has no branches up to 100 feet (30 meters)—it can produce up to six, 16 foot (5 meter) logs. The parana pine is being overharvested because it grows very slowly, so it is being replaced by other types of faster-growing pines. It is commonly found on high mountain ranges at elevations 1,800-3,500 feet (550-1,100 meters) above sea level.

Bunya pine   The fast-growing bunya pine is a large Australian conifer native to the ranges and rain forests of Brisbane. Reaching 147 feet (45 meters) or more in height, it is known for its large leafy crown and symmetrical branches. The wood is used for boxes, plywood, and veneers. The bunya produces both male and female cones. The female cones contain edible seeds and can weigh as much as 22 pounds (10 kilograms). Even though the trees can only be harvested every three years, the food is plentiful enough to be useful.

Lodgepole pine   The lodgepole pine is common in British Columbia, the Pacific Northwest, the Rocky Mountains, and along the Alaskan coast. Its needles are about 2 inches (5 centimeters) long and very sharp. Cones are yellowish brown, often grow in clusters of six or more, and are 0.8 to 1.6 inches (2 to 4 centimeters) long. Because the tree is so straight, Native Americans used the trunk as the main support in their lodges, giving the tree its name. Today it is also commonly used as plywood and paneling.

White pine   The white pine is a valuable North American timber tree for its large trunk and soft, even wood. Capable of reaching 200 years of age, it ranges between 50 and 100 feet (15 and 30 meters) in height, has a trunk more than 3 feet (1 meter) in diameter, and needles 3 to 5 inches (8 to 13 centimeters) long. Eastern white pines once grew in large stands in Maine and Minnesota, as well as Manitoba, Canada. Western white pines once flourished in British Columbia and the northwestern United States. However, because of overharvesting, very few of either species remain.

Yews   Once widespread in Europe, the Yew is now rare and protected. Native to Scandinavia and North Africa, it can also be found from Great Britain to the Asia minor, as well as in Syria, Iran and the Himalayas. This small tree, not usually taller than 82 feet (25 meters), is quite poisonous, though it has been historically used in medicinal remedies, and is currently used to treat some cancers. The Fortingall Yew tree in Glen Lyon, Perthshire, Scotland is estimated to be 3,000 to 5,000 years old. This tree does not form the rings traditionally used to calculate age, so its age can not be determined accurately.

Norway spruce   Norway spruces have thick crowns and grow symmetrically, sometimes to heights of 150 feet (46 meters). Cones are long and tapered, and male cones produce so much pollen that the forest floor is often yellow from it. Norway spruces are common in Europe and Asia.

Growing season   In general, forests need at least 10 to 15 inches (25 to 38 centimeters) of annual precipitation and at least 14 weeks of weather warm enough to promote growth. However, these conditions vary depending upon the location of the forest.

The growing season in the taiga, for example, is short, lasting only about 12 weeks. With little precipitation and cold temperatures, trees do not develop well. Even the oldest of trees is short and stunted. Sub-alpine forests also experience harsh climates, but their growing season is longer, enabling trees to grow taller.

Forests in more temperate climates have more moisture, warmer weather, and a longer growing season. Growing conditions are so favorable in the Pacific Northwest, trees like the redwoods grow to gigantic proportions. Warm pineland climates also produce rapid growth, as long as the rainy season is consistent.

Reproduction Coniferous plants have female and male cones, many of which grow on the same tree. Male cones are small and soft. They produce pollen that fertilizes the eggs in the female cone. These eggs become seeds, which eventually fall from the cones and produce new trees.

Conifers also reproduce by layering. Layering occurs when a branch that is low to the ground is covered by soil. Roots form from the buried portion of the branch and grow into a new tree.

We're back!

Lodgepole pines and jack pines are among the first trees to grow after a fire. Their seeds are sealed in cones by resins (sap) and may remain inactive for a long time on the forest floor. Some lodgepole pine seeds, for example, have been known to survive this way for more than 80 years. Only the heat from a fire can melt the resin, thus releasing the seeds. The seeds quickly germinate in the ash-enriched soil, and a new forest begins to grow.

Endangered species   Trees can be threatened by natural dangers, such as forest fires, animals, and diseases, as well as by humans. Fires are more of a threat in dry climates, while animals and diseases seem prevalent in all climates. For example, when deer populations get too large, they can destroy forests by eating wildflowers and tree seedlings. Also, if enough insects attack a stand of trees, all the leaves are eaten and the trees die. Pollution is a serious threat because it appears to weaken trees, allowing pests and diseases to overtake them more easily.

In New Zealand, the kauri pine, once threatened by overharvesting, is now protected. At 200 feet (61 meters) tall, it is one of the largest commercial trees in the world. Similarly, forests in the Himalayan Mountains in Asia are currently being overharvested. In the European Alps, people have interfered with forest growth to such an extent that the trees now grow 500 feet (152 meters) lower on the mountain slopes than they did 1,000 years ago. According to the World Conservation Union (IUCN), 25 percent of all conifers in the world are endangered.

Animal Life

Coniferous forests support a wide range of animals, and different regions are home to different species. These animals can be classified as microorganisms, invertebrates, amphibians, reptiles, birds, and mammals.

Microorganisms   A microorganism is an animal, such as a protozoan, that cannot be seen without the aid of a microscope. Every forest is host to millions of these tiny creatures. Microscopic roundworms, or nematodes, for example, live by the thousands in small areas of soil in coniferous forests and aid the process of decomposition.

Bacteria   Bacteria are microorganisms that are always present in woodland soil where they help decompose dead plant and animal matter. In temperate climates, bacteria help create nutrient-rich humus (broken down organic matter). Fewer bacteria are at work in dry climates or in moist climates with long dry seasons.

Invertebrates   Animals without backbones are called invertebrates. They include simple animals such as worms, and more complex animals such as the wasp and the snail. Certain groups of invertebrates must spend part of their lives in water. These types are not usually found in the trees, but in ponds, lakes, and streams, or in pools of rainwater.

The mantid is one of many insects that live in the coniferous forest. IMAGE COPYRIGHT AITOR BOUZO ATECA, 2007. USED UNDER LICENSE FROM SHUTTERSTOCK.COM.

Insects are found in abundance in coniferous forests and they multiply very quickly when the weather warms up. Mosquitoes and midges swarm in clouds in boreal forests.

Common coniferous forest invertebrates The pine panthea moth caterpillar and white pine weevil live on white pine trees. The caterpillar eats the needles and the weevil's larva eats the new shoots at the tips of stems. Because the weevil kills the shoots at the top, new shoots grow out of the sides of the stem instead, and the tree grows crookedly.

Engelmann spruce bark beetles, which bore under tree bark, live in the high spruce forests in Colorado. At one time the beetle population became so numerous that millions of spruce trees were killed.

The caterpillar of the pine hawk moth does serious damage to European pine trees. However, the adult moth, which lives only long enough to mate and lay eggs, eats very little.

Food The green plants in the forest provide food for some insects, such as caterpillars and moths. Other insects, like wood ants and pine-bark beetles, eat dying or dead trees. Certain insects have very specific food requirements. Caterpillars of the Pandora moth feed on healthy pine trees, often killing them. White pine butterfly larvae feed only on the needles of the Douglas fir. Some insect larvae store fat in their bodies and do not have to look for food.

Snails prefer to eat plants, while bees, butterflies, and moths gather pollen and nectar (sweet liquid) from flowers. Arachnids (spiders), which are carnivores, prey on insects. If they are big enough, certain spiders can eat small lizards, mice, and birds.

Reproduction The first part of an insect (the most common invertebrates) life cycle is spent as an egg. The second stage is the larva (such as a caterpillar), which may actually be divided into several stages between which the outer casing is shed as the animal increases in size. During the third, or pupal, stage, the animal's casing offers as much protection as an egg. An example of this stage is seen when a caterpillar spins a cocoon to live in while it develops into a moth. Finally, the adult emerges, usually by chewing its way out of its casing.

In coniferous forests, insect eggs and pupae are found on twigs, under the snow, or in tree cracks. Caterpillars often emerge from eggs laid in the bark of trees. Some insects are picky about the trees they use. The white pine butterfly, for example, deposits its eggs only in Douglas firs. Pools of water on the damp forest floor provide a good location for the breeding of insects that require water, especially mosquitoes and midges.

Amphibians Amphibians are vertebrates (animals with backbones) that usually spend part, if not most, of their lives in water. Most amphibians are found in warm, moist, freshwater environments and in temperate zones (areas where temperatures are seldom extreme). Amphibians found in coniferous forests include salamanders, newts, toads, and frogs. They generally live in moist areas like the underside of a log or beneath a mass of leaves. Only a few amphibians are found in the colder boreal forests.

Amphibians breathe through their skin, and only moist skin can absorb oxygen. Therefore, they usually remain close to a water source, although mature animals leave the pools for dry land where they feed on both plants and insects. In warm climates, amphibians must find shade during the day or risk dying in the heat of the sun.

Amphibians are cold-blooded animals, which means their bodies are about the same temperature as their environment. As temperatures get cooler, they slow down, seeking a warm environment in order to remain active. During the winter season in temperate climates, they hibernate (remain inactive). In hot, dry climates, amphibians go through estivation, an inactive period similar to hibernation. While the soil is still moist from the rain, they dig themselves a foot or more into the ground, where they remain until the rain returns. Only their nostrils remain exposed to the surface.

Salamanders generally live in the moist areas of the forest floor. IMAGE COPYRIGHT ANITA HUSZTI, 2007. USED UNDER LICENSE FROM SHUTTERSTOCK.COM.

Common coniferous forest amphibians   The black salamander is commonly found in the high mountain forests in Europe, especially where Norway spruces grow. The black coat of the salamander absorbs heat and helps maintain a higher body temperature. The salamander is viviparous (vy-VIP-ah-ruhs), meaning that the young are kept inside the mother's body until they are fully developed.

The Pacific tree frog, which lives in the Pacific coast coniferous forests, is small and slender with long legs and suction cups on the bottom of its toes that aid in climbing.

Food   Amphibians often use their tongues to capture their prey. Even though some have teeth, they swallow their food whole without chewing. Their larvae are mostly herbivorous, feeding on vegetation. Adult frogs and toads feed not only on algae and other plants, but also on insects, such as mosquitoes.

Reproduction   Mating and egg-laying for most amphibians must take place in water. Usually, male sperm are deposited in the water and swim to and penetrate the jellylike eggs laid by the female. As the offspring develop into larvae and young adults, they often have gills for breathing that require a watery habitat. Once they mature, they develop lungs and can live on land. Male salamanders deposit sperm directly into the female for internal fertilization of the eggs.

Some amphibian females carry their eggs inside their bodies until they hatch. Certain species protect the eggs until the young are born, while others lay the eggs and abandon them.

Most amphibians reach maturity at three or four years. They breed for the first time about one year after they become adults.

Reptiles   Reptiles are cold-blooded vertebrates, such as lizards, turtles, and snakes, that depend on their environment for warmth. They are usually most active when the weather is warm. Reptiles do not do well in extreme temperatures, whether hot or cold. During hot, dry periods, they find shade or a hole in which to wait for cooler weather. During chilly nights, they become slow and sluggish. In temperate climates, snakes may hibernate in burrows during the long winter.

Common coniferous forest reptiles   Garter snakes, rattlesnakes, western pond turtles, and skinks are all found in the California redwood forests. Skinks are lizards, some of which climb trees. Some species are herbivorous, while others eat mostly insects.

The web of life: Predator and prey

Some people shudder at the thought of predators killing deer. After all, deer are so cute and those mountain lions and wolves so bloodthirsty! But a balance is needed between predators and prey or other problems arise. For example, in 1905, the Kaibab Forest in Arizona supported about 4,000 deer. Because the forest had the potential of supporting up to 30,000, people who wanted to enlarge the deer herd destroyed the predators that fed on the deer. They killed 7,000 coyotes, 716 mountain lions, and a number of wolves.

By 1918, the deer herds had increased to more than 40,000, and the plants the deer used for food began to diminish. By 1923, the herd had increased to 100,000, and many food plants had been completely wiped out. During the winter of 1924–25, 60,000 deer, many of which were fawns, died of starvation. The only solution was to restore the balance and return the predators to the forest.

African pine forests are home to the agama lizard. Other reptiles found in dry regions include many species of snakes such as the night, the puff, and the Gabonan adders.

Food   Most reptiles are carnivorous. Snakes consume their prey whole—and often alive—without chewing. Their teeth can curve backward, which keeps their prey from escaping. It can take an hour or more to swallow a large prey.

A lizard's diet varies, depending upon the species. Some have long tongues with sticky tips and specialize in insects. Many are carnivores that eat small mammals and birds. The water they need is usually obtained from the food they eat. Turtles, for example, feed on soft plant material, small animals, or both.

Reproduction   Most reptiles reproduce sexually, and their young come from eggs. The eggs are leathery and tough, and the offspring are seldom coddled. Some females remain with the eggs, but most reptiles bury the eggs in a hole and abandon them. The young are left to hatch by themselves. Once free of the eggs, the babies dig themselves out of the hole and begin life on their own.

Birds   Coniferous forests are home to hundreds of bird species. Some, such as insect-eating wood warblers, Canada geese, and northern goshawks, are migratory, which means they travel from one seasonal breeding place to another. Canada geese and northern goshawks return to northern forests by the thousands each spring and summer from areas with warmer winter climates.

During excessively cold or dry periods, birds can fly to more comfortable regions. Some birds, such as the blue jay, live in a particular forest year-round. If food is plentiful, the evening grosbeak, pine siskin, and red crossbill also choose to not migrate during the winter weather.

Feathers protect birds not only from cold winters but also from tropical heat. Air trapped between the layers of feathers acts as insulation.

Common coniferous forest birds   In temperate forests, common birds include screech owls, great horned owls, hummingbirds, woodpeckers, nuthatches, wood thrushes, American redstarts, hawks, blue jays, cardinals, scarlet tanagers, chickadees, and turkey vultures. Wrens, falcons, weaverbirds, thrushes, and chats are found in dry regions. Other common forest birds include the American dipper and the crossbill.

American Dipper   The American dipper lives year-round in the mountain forests along the Pacific coast, from Alaska to Mexico. These birds stay near swift streams in which they wade and swim in search of insects, freshwater shrimp, snails, and fish. Since the dipper must dive into the water to catch its food, it maintains a waterproof covering. The dipper spreads oil over its feathers from oil glands and a special flap keeps water out of its nostrils. Its long toes help it grasp underwater surfaces. Dippers can stay submerged for about 30 seconds and dive as deep as 30 feet (9 meters).

A male ground agama in bright breeding colors is seen here in Kalahari, South Africa. IMAGE COPYRIGHT ECOPRINT, 2007. USED UNDER LICENSE FROM SHUTTERSTOCK.COM.

Dippers breed in February or March and lay their eggs in nests out of materials found along the streams in which they hunt for food. Baby birds hatch after about two weeks and learn to dive very quickly.

Crossbill   The crossbill lives year-round in coniferous forests and has a beak specially designed for digging the seeds out of pine cones. Only 5.5 to 6 inches (14 to 15 centimeters) in length, crossbills eat about 1,000 seeds each day. Different species of crossbills vary in color, like red or yellow, and their beaks are shaped differently depending upon where they live and what kind of cones they must open. The birds summer in the more northern forests in Alaska and Canada and winter in the warmer mountain forests of North Carolina and Oregon.

Food   Millions of insects attract summer birds, such as kinglets, woodpeckers, and flycatchers, to coniferous forests. Birds that stay in the forest all year must work hard for their food during the winter. For example, the nutcracker uses its powerful jaws to rip open cones for seeds. Blue grouse and the capercaillies, the largest species of European

Rare bird in a rare forest

Kirtland's warblers are rare songbirds that breed only in young jack pine forests in north-central Michigan. They usually build their nests on the ground under the small, growing trees. After jack pines reach more than 20 feet (6 meters) in height and no longer provide enough shelter, the birds abandon them. However, new jack pines will sprout and grow only after a forest fire, many of which are put out by humans. As a result, few new trees grow and, therefore, few warblers can raise families.

grouse, have an easier time, preferring to eat the conifer needles. Small birds and rodents are food for predators like eagles, owls, and hawks.

Reproduction   All birds reproduce by laying eggs. One parent sits on the eggs to protect them from heat or cold until they hatch.

Mammals   Mammals are warm-blooded vertebrates having some hair. They bear their live young and produce their own milk. A few large mammals, such as mountain lions, bears, and deer, live in northern coniferous forests. Most coniferous forests are home to many small mammals, including mice, squirrels, woodchucks, and foxes.

During cold winters, mammals may burrow underground or find shelter among thick evergreens or under the snow. Snow dens are used by shrews and voles that remain active all winter. Some mammals, such as black bears, hibernate. In a study completed by the University of Iowa, the bear's heart rate dropped from 40–50 beats per minute to only 8 beats per minute while in hibernation. This is the bear's method of conserving body energy. Chipmunks accumulate deposits of fat below their skin that help insulate them and provide nourishment while they hibernate. In dry, warm climates, small mammals may remain inactive during hot weather.

Common coniferous forest mammals   Common mammals found in the boreal forest are wolverines, grizzly bears, lynxes, pine martins, minks, ermines, and sables. These animals are all predators and feed on other common boreal mammals like voles, snowshoe hares, marmots, and tiny tree mice. Chamois, red deer, moose, and elks live in the European mountain forests, while the mountain forests in Canada are home to moose, beavers, Canadian lynxes, black bears, and wolves.

Tree Vole   The tree vole spends most of its life at the top of fir trees in the Pacific Northwest and almost never walks on the ground. This small mammal is a type of rodent with a stout body and short tail. Voles construct treetop nests and tunnels from twigs and eat parts of pine needles.

Wolverine   The wolverine is the largest member of the weasel family and grows to be about 4 feet (1.2 meters) long from the tip of its nose to the end of its tail. This stocky carnivore can weigh up between 24 and 40 pounds (10.9 and 18.1 kilograms). Thick fur protects them from the snow and cold. Wolverines live in North America and Eurasia and are famous as savage hunters and ravenous eaters, capable of killing and eating an entire deer. They may wander up to 15 miles (24 kilometers) at a time to locate food, and can live up to twelve years in the wild.

Female wolverines give birth in early spring to two to four pups. The nest is usually in a crevice or other protected spot.

Chamois   The chamois (SHAM-ee) is a small goatlike, antelope found in European mountain forests in the Alps, Pyrenees, and Dolomites. The males range from 65-110 pounds (29-59 kilograms) in size, and measures from 3 to 4 feet (1 to 1.2 meters) in length. The females are typically slightly smaller. Both males and females grow straight horns with backward-bending tips. In the summer, the chamois is reddish-brown in color with a black stripe on the rump. In the winter, its coat turns black or brown to help absorb heat.

The chamois has adapted to the mountains by developing rubbery hoof pads that help the animal keep its footing on slippery rocks. It eats mountain vegetation, especially clover, and some fir needles. If winter is especially harsh, the chamois moves to deciduous forests at lower elevations to find food. The chamois can live up to seventeen years in captivity.

Grizzly Bear   The grizzly bear is one of the fiercest animals in North America. They are strong enough to carry full-grown cattle. Most have broad heads, extended jaws, big paws, and powerful claws. Grizzlies eat insects, like ants and bees, as well as seeds, roots, nuts, and berries. They also eat salmon, and are famous for their fishing skills.

Food   Mammals may be herbivores (plant eaters), carnivores (meat eaters), or omnivores (plant and meat eaters). Moss and lichens provide food for caribou, while downed trees and brush feed beaver and elk. Green plants, such as rushes, feed marmots and voles. Shrews eat insects that they dig out of the ground. Some carnivores, like the wolf, hunt in packs for deer and other animals. Bears are omnivores.

Reproduction   Mammals give birth to live young that have developed inside the mother's body. Some mammals, like the hare, are helpless at birth, while others, such as deer, are able to walk and even run almost immediately.

Endangered species   In the United States, acid rain (a mixture of water vapor and polluting compounds in the atmosphere that falls to Earth as rain or snow) has endangered the peregrine falcon. The grizzly bear,

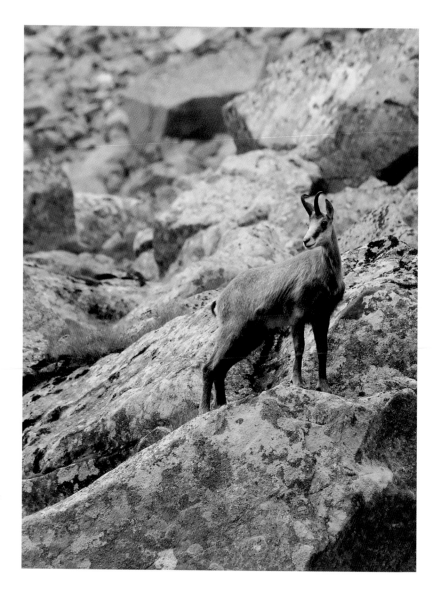

The chamois is well adapted to its rocky, rugged terrain because it is very surefooted and nimble. IMAGE COPYRIGHT RADOVAN SPURNY, 2007. USED UNDER LICENSE FROM SHUTTERSTOCK.COM.

beaver, and timber wolf are threatened in the United States and Canada. In Australia some species of kangaroos are threatened.

Kirtland's warblers   Kirtland's warblers are endangered songbirds that conceal their nests in shrubs below five- to twenty-year-old jack pines in north-central Michigan. New jack pines sprout and grow only after a forest fire, many of which are put out by humans. As a result, few new trees grow and few warblers can raise families, making it a rare bird.

Grizzly bears fish for salmon in Alaska. Besides being one of the fiercest animals in North America, the grizzly bear is also quite large, weighing up to 1,000 lbs (454 Kg). IMAGE COPYRIGHT OKSANAPERKINS, 2007. USED UNDER LICENSE FROM SHUTTERSTOCK.COM.

Grizzly bear   Before the great expansion of the population westward, it is estimated that 100,000 grizzly bears lived in North America. By the 1990s, fewer than 1,000 existed, with most of them living in preserves such as Yellowstone National Park, though some can be found in British Columbia, Alberta, the Yukon, and the Northwest Territories. Even though grizzly bears are occasionally shot, the greatest threat to the bear's survival is destruction of its habitat. Since bears are huge animals, weighing as much as 1,000 pounds (454 kilograms), they require large spaces to roam and huge quantities of food. In 2006, the World Conservation Union (IUCN) listed the grizzly bear as low risk and conservation dependent.

Beaver   The beaver once ranged over North America from Mexico to the Arctic regions. It was widely hunted for its fur and for a liquid called castorium, produced in the beaver's musk glands and used in perfume. The beaver is now confined largely to northern wooded regions. Beavers were also common throughout northern Europe, where they are now almost extinct, except in some parts of Scandinavia, Germany, and Siberia.

Human Life

Many animals, including humans, are creatures of the forest. In early North America, native tribes, such as the Nootka and Haida, lived in the forests, hunting, trapping, and gathering for their survival.

Impact of the coniferous forest on human life   Forests have an important impact on the environment as a whole by contributing to the environmental cycles. From the earliest times, forests have offered food and shelter, a place to hide from predators, and many useful products. Forests are an integral part of life on Earth.

Environmental cycles   Trees, soil, animals, and other plants all interact to create a balance in the environment from which humans benefit. This balance is often maintained in cycles.

The oxygen cycle   Plants and animals take in oxygen from the air and use it for their life processes. When animals and humans breathe, the oxygen they inhale is used and carbon dioxide is given off as a byproduct. This oxygen must be replaced, or life could not continue. Trees help replace oxygen during photosynthesis when they release oxygen into the atmosphere through their leaves.

The carbon cycle   Carbon dioxide is also necessary to life, but too much is harmful. During photosynthesis, trees and other plants pull carbon dioxide from the air. This helps maintain the oxygen/carbon dioxide balance in the atmosphere.

When trees die, the carbon in their tissues is returned to the soil. Decaying trees become part of Earth's crust, and after millions of years, this carbon is converted into oil and natural gas.

The water cycle   Coniferous forests shade the snow, allowing it to remain in deep drifts. The trees' root systems and fallen needles help build an absorbent covering on the forest floor, letting water from rain and melting snow trickle down into the Earth to feed underground streams and groundwater.

Not only do forests help preserve water in this way, but they also protect the land from erosion during heavy rain by acting as a wall or barrier. When forests are cut down, there are no trees to act as barriers, and no tree roots to hold the soil in place, so it washes away. As a result, flooding is more common. For example, by 2007, 19 million residents of India and Bangladesh had been evacuated from their homes due to severe flooding, caused in part by cutting of forests in the nearby Himalaya Mountains.

Trees take up water through their roots and use it for their own life processes. Extra moisture is then released through their leaves back into the atmosphere, helping to form clouds and continue the water cycle.

The nutrient cycle   Trees get the mineral nutrients they need from the soil. Dissolved minerals are absorbed from the soil by the tree's roots and are sent upward throughout the tree. These mineral nutrients are used by the tree much like humans take vitamins. When the tree dies, these nutrients, which are still contained within parts of the tree, decompose and are returned back into the soil making them available for other plants and animals to use.

Food Since the earliest times, forests have been home to game animals, such as rabbits, which have supplied meat for hunters and their families. Forests also supply fruits, seeds, berries, and nuts. Several species of pines, for example, produce edible seeds (pine nuts) that are still collected by hand.

Shelter During prehistoric times, humans lived in the forest because it offered protection from predators and the weather. Today, people who choose to live in forested areas usually do so because they enjoy their beauty.

Economic values Forests are important to the world economy, since many commercially used products, such as wood, medicine, resins and oils, are obtained from forests.

Wood Trees produce one of two general types of wood, hardwood or softwood, based on the trees' cell wall structure. Hardwoods are usually produced by deciduous trees, such as oaks and elms, while most coniferous trees produce softwoods. These names can be confusing because some softwood trees, such as the yew, produce woods that are harder than many hardwoods and some hardwoods, such as balsa, are softer than most softwoods.

Wood is used not only for fuel, but also for building structures and manufacturing other products, such as furniture and paper. Hardwood from deciduous trees is more expensive because the trees grow more slowly. As a result, it is used primarily for fine furniture and paneling. Wood used for general construction is usually softwood, such as white pine, Douglas fir, and spruce. Araucaria and kauri are commercially important conifers of the Southern Hemisphere. In order to conserve trees and reduce costs, some manufacturers have created engineered wood, which is composed of particles of several types of wood, combined with strong glues and preservatives. Engineered woods are very strong and can be used for many construction needs.

Medicines   Since the earliest times, plants have been used for their healing properties. For example, the yew was once considered a worthless "weed" tree and was burned by loggers after clearing a section of forest. Then taxol, an anti-cancer drug, was discovered in the bark of the yew. It takes the bark of six trees to make enough medicine for one cancer patient. In 1994, a synthetic form of taxol was created in the laboratory (though difficult to make) reducing the need for yew trees.

Resins and oils   Tree resins (REH-zihns; sap) and oils are also valuable. Conifer resins are used to make turpentine, paints, and varnish, while their oils are used as the fragrance in air fresheners, disinfectants, and cosmetics.

Recreation   More people live in cities today than ever before, and many feel the need to occasionally escape to more natural surroundings. The beauty and quiet of coniferous forests draw many visitors for hiking, horseback riding, skiing, fishing, hunting, bird watching, or just sitting and listening to the sounds of nature.

Other resources   Forest rivers are often dammed to provide a source of water for hydroelectric power. Norway, Sweden, Canada, and Switzerland rely heavily on hydroelectricity. The United States, Russia, China, India, and Brazil also use hydroelectric power, but on a smaller scale.

Impact of human life on the coniferous forest   Forests originally covered 48 percent of the Earth's surface. Half of this quantity is now gone, and about one-fifth of the remainder are, as of yet, undisturbed. In North America, more than 430,000 miles (692,000 kilometers) of road cut through U.S. National Forests. Although it was once thought that forests of the far north were so inhospitable they were safe from human interference, the building of railroads made the area accessible. As a result, each year more land is being cleared for logging and mining operations.

Use of plants and animals   As more and more forest land is being developed, native vegetation and wildlife habitats are destroyed. Trees are cut down and used for lumber and other products. In Canada, for example, much of the timber in the southern forests is gone, and northern forests are now being invaded by logging companies.

Trees are not the only forest plants in danger from overharvesting. In northern forests, mosses from the forest floor are used as fuel by construction workers and are being removed in large quantities. Without the insulation provided by the moss, permafrost is melting and causing floods.

Timber!

Logging is the harvesting of trees, sawing them into logs, and transporting them to a sawmill. About one percent of the world's timber is cut down each year. Half of it is used for fuel, and the rest for wood products, paper, and packaging materials. Most trees used for paper products are raised on tree farms and do not come from wild forests.

In the nineteenth century, logging was done by men using hand axes and saws. This method took a lot of people and time. In the 1950s, power chainsaws were used, and, by the 1970s, a variety of machines had revolutionized the logging industry.

Because logging machines can cut trees no bigger than about 2 feet (0.6 meter) in diameter, large trees are still cut by hand. A wedge is chopped from the trunk on one side of the tree and a cut is made with a saw on the other side. This causes the tree to fall in the direction of the wedge. After the tree is down, the limbs are removed and it is cut into lengths that can be easily moved.

In general, trees are removed either selectively or by clear-cutting. With selective methods, only certain trees are cut from a stand (group of trees). With clear-cutting, all the trees from several acres (hectares) of land are removed. Ideally, trees of the same species are then replanted, but many times this is not the case.

In India, some logging is done by "girdling." In girdling, a circular cut made around the tree trunk prevents water or nutrients from being carried to the branches. Several years later, when the tree is dead, it is harvested.

As too much logging destroys mountain forests, villages are at risk from landslides and avalanches that were once held in check by the dense trees.

Clear-cutting disrupts wildlife habitats, and new roads give hunters better access to wildlife, which sometimes results in overhunting. In some Canadian areas, for example, grizzly bears and bighorn sheep are now easy targets. Despite conservation efforts, parks and other protected areas are not necessarily safe from development. In British Columbia, mining interests have gained access to once-protected areas in parks.

Quality of the environment   The quality of the forest environment is threatened not only by the direct effects of logging, mining, and hydroelectric development, but also by pollution and visitors. Roads, drilling rigs, and pipelines, all a necessary part of mining, destroy wilderness and disrupt habitats. Mercury, a poisonous liquid metal used in gold mining operations, and waste from chemical and petrochemical plants contaminate forest water sources. In Lake Baikal in the Siberian taiga, for example, mining activities have destroyed life on the lake bottom.

Millions of acres (hectares) of forests in industrialized Europe, North America, and China are dead or dying from pollution and acid rain. Acid rain is a type of air pollution that forms when pollutants such as sulfur or nitrogen combine with moisture in the atmosphere to produce sulfuric or nitric acids. These acids can be carried long distances by the wind before they fall, either as dry deposits, or in the form of rain or snow. When acid rain is absorbed into the soil, it can destroy nutrients and make the soil too acidic to support some species of trees. In coniferous forests, acid rain causes needles to drop and their color to fade and turn brown. Forests in northern Europe, southern Canada, and the eastern United States have been damaged by acid rain.

A large increase in the number of tourists all over the world has also put a tremendous stress on the forest environment. Many "wilderness" areas are being developed, and fragile forests are endangered as tourists hike, bike, ski, and snowmobile over the vegetation and disturb wild animals with their noise.

Forest management   The National Forest Service was established in the United States in 1905 to protect forest resources. More than 193,000,000 acres (78,000,000 hectares) of land are now publicly owned. Most of this acreage is west of the Mississippi. Forests in the eastern half of the United States are usually managed by state programs.

Forest fires consume trees, vegetation, animals, and insects, but are also an important part of the ecosystem, promoting wilderness diversity. IMAGE COPYRIGHT ARNOLD JOHN LABRENTZ, 2007. USED UNDER LICENSE FROM SHUTTERSTOCK.COM.

Most of these forests consist of areas that can be used for logging and other commercial purposes. However, the rest of the land is kept for recreation and conservation.

Several other nations, including Great Britain, Japan, China, and India, have also established programs to conserve and replant forests.

Native people By 1950, native people in industrialized parts of the world had abandoned most of their tribal lands and customs. Many went to live in cities. In remote regions, some people still live a traditional lifestyle. For example, some taiga peoples are found in small Siberian towns that are accessible via the Trans-Siberian Railway. Other people live in mountain forests, especially in the Alps and Himalayas.

The Evenki In the northern Asian taiga of Siberia, Mongolia, and China live the Evenki (which means *he who runs swifter than a tiger*). Traditionally, the Evenki were nomads, surviving by means of hunting or reindeer herding. Although small groups still live this way, their traditional way of life is being threatened as oil, coal, and gas are mined and their homelands are taken over.

Many Evenki were removed from their lands by the government and settled onto collective farms after the Russian Revolution in 1917, and only 30,000 remain. In 1930, the Evenki national district was created, providing a permanent home for the people. This district contains some tundra vegetation and is covered by larch forest, but the climate is severe, with long, cold winters. The livelihood of the Evenki is supplemented by fur farming, farming, and jobs in industry or government.

Along with other native groups in Russia and China, like the Oroqen, the Evenki are working to preserve their culture.

The Cree   The Ouje-Bougoumou Cree are a native people from the James and Hudson Bay area of Quebec in Canada. Some Cree tribes, collectively known as the Cree nation, lived on the plains and cultivated corn. Others lived in the forests and fished and hunted caribou, moose, bear, beaver, and hare.

The Cree believe they have a special relationship with nature—nature provides them with food and they take care of the land and hunt only what is necessary for life. Beginning in 1920 when the first non-native miners came onto their land searching for gold and copper, the Cree were forced to relocate their villages. About 14,500 Cree remain, primarily in the James and Hudson Bay regions. Clear-cutting of the boreal forests and hydroelectric development in the James Bay area continues to threaten their lifestyle. The Cree nation has been fighting since the 1970s to disband the James Bay hydroelectric project. They continue to negotiate treaties with the Canadian government involving the destruction in their homeland.

The Pehuenche   The Pehuenche live in the forests of southeastern Chile. To them, the coniferous monkey-puzzle tree is sacred, and they refuse to cut it down. Its seeds are ground and turned into flour. Even though the Chilean government outlawed cutting the trees, logging continues and endangers the existence of both the people and the tree.

The Food Web

The transfer of energy from organism to organism forms a series called a food chain or food web. All the possible feeding relationships that exist in a biome make up its food web. In the forest, as elsewhere, the food web

A young Cree Indian with his face painted, and dressed in traditional costume.
AP IMAGES.

consists of producers, consumers, and decomposers. An analysis of the food web shows how energy is transferred within a biome.

Green plants are the primary producers in the forest. They produce organic materials from inorganic chemicals and outside sources of energy, primarily the sun. Trees and other plants turn energy into plant matter, such as pine cones, needles, and seeds.

Animals are consumers. Primary consumers are plant-eating animals like squirrels, voles, mice, and beetles. Secondary consumers eat the plant-eaters. Tertiary consumers are the predators, like owls, wolves, and humans that eat other animals. Bears and humans are also omnivores, eating both plants and animals.

Decomposers eat the decaying matter from dead plants and animals and help return nutrients to the environment. Small underground insects called springtails and mollusks, such as the banana slug, help the decomposition process by breaking down dead plants. This allows other organisms, like bacteria and fungi, to reach the decaying matter and decompose it further.

Spotlight on Coniferous Forests

Bonanza Creek Experimental Forest   Bonanza Creek Experimental Forest was established in 1963 with 8,300 acres (3,359 hectares) and increased to 12,487 acres (5,053 hectare) in 1969. This area is located south of Fairbanks, Alaska, in the Yukon-Tanana uplands in the Tanana Valley State Forest, south of the Brooks Mountain Range and north of the Alaska Range.

Within the Yukon-Tanana uplands are forests, grasslands, wetlands, and alpine tundra (a cold, dry, windy region where no trees grow). The Tanana river crosses the region at 394 feet (120 meters) of elevation.

The climate in the Alaskan taiga is extreme, with temperatures ranging from -58° to 95°F (-50° to +35°C) in January and July, the coldest and warmest months. The average annual temperature is 26°F (-3.3°C). July is the warmest month with an average daily temperature of 61.5°F (16.4°C). For about 233 days each year, freezing temperatures are possible. About 70 percent of the area's precipitation falls as rain in the summer; the other 30 percent is snow, which falls from October to April. The annual average precipitation over the last 50 years is about 11 inches (28 centimeters).

Taiga soils are often poorly developed. In some areas, a layer of permafrost (permanently frozen soil) is on the lowlands and northern slopes of mountains, and prevents rain and melting snow from being absorbed into the ground. Since the moisture stays close to the surface, the soil is soggy.

**Bonanza Creek
Experimental Forest**
Location: Alaska
Area: 12,487 acres (5,053 hectares)
Classification: Boreal forest/taiga

Predominant trees in the area are white spruce, black spruce, paper birch, and aspen.

Numerous insects found on the taiga include budworms, sawflies, midges, and beetles. The northern wood frog is one of the few amphibians that live there.

Woodpeckers, swallows, sparrows, peregrine falcons, great horned owls, snowy owls, and boreal owls are among the birds that make the Bonanza Creek Forest their home.

Mammals include a number of voles and lemmings, muskrats, red squirrels, and meadow jumping mice. Moose and caribou migrate here to breed. Carnivores include coyotes, gray wolves, and wolverines.

Olympic National Park Olympic National Park is a 922,000 acre (373,120 hectare) area located on the Olympic Peninsula in northwestern Washington state. Forests in the park lie between sea level and 2,000 feet (609 meters) above sea level. Just 90 miles (145 kilometers) from the thriving city of Seattle, 95 percent of this park has been declared as wilderness.

Among the coniferous forests in the park is a temperate rain forest found in its lower western and southern regions. Temperate rain forests grow at higher latitudes than tropical rain forests. Forests on the western side of the park experience heavy precipitation, 12-14 feet (3.6-4.3 meters) annually. Forests in the eastern portion of the park are the driest areas of the Pacific coast, north of Los Angeles. The nearness of the ocean keeps the temperatures somewhat moderate with very few days of below-freezing weather in winter. In summer, temperatures rarely exceed 85°F (29°C).

The forest floor supports toadstools, creepers, and ferns, such as sword, bracken, and licorice ferns. Club moss and algae hang from the trees. Shrubs found in the park include red huckleberry and salmonberry. The western thimbleberry can be recognized by its large, hairy, maplelike leaves. Wildflowers include western starflower, western trillium, and foamflower. The deerfoot vanillaleaf lives deep in the woods.

Douglas fir and Pacific silver fir are common trees. The species of the Sitka spruce found there rarely grows far from salt water. The grand fir also grows only in this region.

Invertebrates include the unusual banana slug, a scavenger and decomposer that helps to keep the forest floor and soil healthy.

Olympic National Park
Location: Washington
Area: 908,447 acres
(363,379 hectares)
Classification: Temperate
evergreen forest

Springtails, golden buprested beetles, and questing spiders can also be found here.

The Pacific tree frog and the bullfrog live in the park, as do several species of snakes.

More than 200 species of birds are common to the Olympic Peninsula including flicker, crow, cliff swallow, winter wren, water ouzel, pileated woodpecker, northern spotted owl, winter wren, raven, and jay. Both golden and bald eagles also frequent the area. Ruffled grouse stay all winter and grow long, feathery "snowshoes" on their toes.

The park is home to one of the largest herds of Roosevelt elk, and was nearly named Elk National Park. An adult male can weigh an average of 875 pounds (397 kilograms), and the elk are a major hunting and tourist attraction. Other mammals found on the peninsula are the coyote, mountain beaver, Olympic marmot, raccoon, skunk, Columbian black-tailed deer, Rocky Mountain goat, black bear, mountain cottontail rabbit, and snowshoe hare. Cougars may be found in remote areas.

Yellowstone National Park   The first national park in the United States, Yellowstone is located primarily in the state of Wyoming, with small portions in southern Montana and eastern Idaho, and was established in 1872. It covers an area of 2,219,789 acres (898,317 hectares). Mountains, lakes, rivers, and waterfalls cross the terrain. Most of the park is coniferous forest, but Yellowstone is also famous for the geyser (GY-zuhr) called Old Faithful, and its hot springs, steam vents, and mud caldrons.

Located on a high plateau, Yellowstone is 11,358 feet (3,462 meters) above sea level at its highest point, Eagle Peak. Its lowest elevation is 5,282 feet (1,610 meters), Reese Creek. Eighty percent of the park is forested, while the other 20 percent is grassland and water.

Annual precipitation varies from one end of the park to the other. In the north the average is 10 inches (26 centimeters). In the south, it is 80 inches (205 centimeters). Average annual snowfall is about 150 inches (380 centimeters). The average temperature is 10°F (-12°C) in January and 80°F (27°C) in July.

Eight species of conifers grow in the park, with lodgepole pine being the most common. Smaller stands of Douglas fir are found at both lower and higher elevations. Engelmann spruce and alpine fir abound. The park also has more than 170 species of colorful flowering plants, 80 percent of which are exotic.

Yellowstone National Park
Location: Wyoming
Area: 2,219,791 acres (898,318 hectares)
Classification: Mountain coniferous forest

The park supports about ten species of reptiles and amphibians. Its lakes are stocked with fish, including some non-native species.

Hundreds of species of birds live in the park, including the western tanager, goshawk, bald eagle, and dipper.

Large mammals include buffalo, elk, bighorn sheep, moose, and grizzly bear. Wolves, which had been eliminated by ranchers who feared they would prey on cattle, were reintroduced to the park in 1995. The park also supports a large herd of wapiti deer, or American elk. This once common animal is now found only in the Rocky Mountains and southern Canada. The wapiti is hunted for its hide, flesh, and head, which is usually displayed as a trophy. The park also protects five threatened and endangered species; the bald eagle, the grizzly bear, the lynx, the whooping crane and the gray wolf.

Coniferous forests of Japan   Japan is a 4,400 square mile (11,500 square kilometer) chain of four islands in the Pacific Ocean—Hokkaido, Honshu, Shikoku, and Kyushu. The coniferous forests in Japan are found primarily in northeastern Honshu and Hokkaido.

Japan's climate is influenced by the presence of mountain ranges, the Sea of Japan, and the range of latitudes it crosses. In general, Japan receives more than 40 inches (102 centimeters) of precipitation annually, mostly as rain during June and July. Typhoons (ocean storms) are not uncommon during this time. The southern islands are generally warmer. In Hokkaido, the average temperature in January, the coldest month, is 16°F (-9°C), and in August, the hottest month, it is 70°F (21°C).

Coniferous trees are found from sea level up to 5,900-9,800 feet (1,800-3,000 meters) in the mountains. Common conifers in the forests of Hokkaido are Hondo and Sakhalin spruce and Maries and Veitch firs. Mosses and lichens are found on the forest floor and hanging from tree branches.

Many native forests have been destroyed and replanted with coniferous forests that are managed as commercial plantations. Two of the most important timber trees are the hiba and the Japanese cedar. The cedars, often exceeding 150 feet (46 meters), have long trunks, reddish bark and spread 15-25 feet (4.6-7.6 meters).

Natural stands of Japanese cedars, with trees more than 2,000 years old, cover about 4,133 square miles (10,747 square kilometers) on Yaku Island south of Kyushu. These trees grow in rocky areas with little soil and light, and as a result, their growth is stunted. Because the grain of their

Coniferous forests of Japan
Location: Japan
Classification: Mountain coniferous forest and temperate evergreen forest

wood is tightly compacted and contains large quantities of resin, they do not easily decay. Many cedars on the island exceed the average life span of 500 years. The Yaku sugi tree, which also grows here, is a decay-resistant conifer related to the redwood. Also on Yaku are mixed forests containing broad-leaved trees. In 1993, the Yaku forests were declared a World Heritage Property by the World Heritage Convention.

Japan's forests are home to about 150 species of songbirds, as well as birds of prey such as eagles, hawks, and falcons. Bramblings and Eurasian nutcrackers are also common.

Brown bears, wild boars, Siberian chipmunks, Asiatic pika, and Hokkaido squirrels live in the forests. An unusual inhabitant is the raccoon dog, or tanuki, a native of eastern Asia that some scientists place in the dog family and others in the raccoon family. The tanuki looks like a raccoon, with dark face markings that stand out against a yellow-brown coat. Its long fur is sold commercially.

Lapland National Parks   Much of Scandinavia (Norway, Sweden, and Finland) is covered in coniferous forest. The Lapland National Parks are comprised of three parks, Sarek National Park, Padjelanta National Park, and Stora Sjofallet National Park. Both Sarek and Stora were established in 1909; Padjelanta was established in 1962. All three parks are boreal forests and are interspersed with wetlands, lakes, and mountains. Of the three, Padjelanta is the most accessible park.

Many people visit Padjelanta, which has marked trails and cross-country ski paths. Scientists visit to conduct research on plants, animals, geology, glaciers, and water resources. The flora and fauna are impressive, with over 400 species spread across 490,257 acres (198,400 hectares) of land. The wildlife is also unique, and visitors may catch a glimpse of snowy owls, arctic foxes, and wolverines. The open mountain landscape and the large lakes make it a very scenic location.

To the left of the Padjelanta park lies the Sarek National Park. Sarek, with the most wilderness, is mostly alpine landscape with glaciers, tall mountain peaks, and alpine tundra (a cold, treeless region). Its 486,798 acres (197,000 hectares) is home to over 200 mountains and 100 glaciers that are mostly unspoiled. Though plants are more scarce than at Padjalenta, the animal population is rich in bears, wolverines, lynxes and elk. Of the three parks, Sarek is the least accessible and not recommended for beginners.

Lapland National Parks
Location: Scandinavia
Area: 1,292,300 acres (523,200 hectares)
Classification: Boreal forest/taiga

North of Sarek Park lies the Stora Sjofallet National Park. At 315,800 acres (127,800 hectares), it is the smallest of the three parks. The forest is nearly bisected by a hydroelectric power facility, which destroyed much of the original landscape.

Coniferous forests of New Zealand New Zealand is an island nation in the South Pacific, about 1,000 miles (1,600 kilometers) southeast of Australia. A temperate evergreen forest with mixed deciduous and coniferous trees grows in the north.

New Zealand's climate has no real extremes. In general, summer temperatures are above 70°F (21°C), and winter temperatures are rarely below 50°F (10°C). Annual rainfall ranges from 29 to 59 inches (64 to 150 centimeters).

Conifers make up most of the canopy in the forests and include the huge kauri tree, as well as trees in the plum pine family. The rimu, or New Zealand red pine, grows as tall as 150 feet (45 meters) and its wood is reddish-to-yellowish brown. Rimu is used in construction and furniture making, and its bark contains a tanning agent that colors leather red. The radiata pine, a native of California, was transplanted in New Zealand and has become a key species there. Only a few flowers, like yellow kowhai and pohutakawa (New Zealand's Christmas tree), grow in the New Zealand forests. The pohutakawa reaches averages of 100 feet (30 meters) high, and 3 feet (1 meter) wide. It can live anywhere between 700 and 800 years. Approximately 80 percent of the flora in the park is native to New Zealand.

Very few animals are native to New Zealand. They include several species of frogs and bats, as well as the gecko lizard and the tuatara. Europeans introduced deer, opossums, and goats.

Coniferous forests of Russia and Siberia At 2.5 billion acres (1 billion hectares), Russia and Siberia are home to 22 percent of the all the world's forests combined. The most popular trees are larch, spruce and pine.

The climate in the forests varies. In the more northern section, the weather is harsh and summers are short. In the Yakut taiga, located in eastern Siberia, for example, winter temperatures may reach -85°F (-65°C). The average annual temperature is only around 10°F (-12°C). Temperatures in the middle taiga, such as that near Lake Baikal, are less severe, and conditions for tree growth are better. There, the average annual temperature is about 19°F (-7°C), and the growing season lasts from twelve to seventeen

Coniferous forests of New Zealand
Location: New Zealand
Classification: Southern Hemisphere forest

Coniferous forests of Russia and Siberia
Location: Russia and Siberia
Classification: Boreal forest/taiga

weeks. An even milder climate is characteristic in the southernmost region of the taiga where the growing season may last more than twenty weeks.

Conifers found here include pine, spruce, fir, larch, cedar, Japanese stone pine, Jeddo spruce, and dwarf mountain pine. Many trees are stunted by the cold wind; reaching only about 19 feet (6 meters) in height. Where trees are protected from the wind, they grow about 50 feet (15 meters) tall. Shrubs like crowberry and bilberry grow in the understory. Mosses and lichens grow on the forest floor.

Some areas of the taiga are richer in wildlife than others. The more southern regions support hundreds of species of birds and about 50 species of mammals. The hazel hen and Siberian jay are unique to the taiga. Mammals include the moose, lynx, brown bear, Siberian red deer, wolverine, Asiatic chipmunk, northern pika, and sable. The sable is hunted for its highly prized fur, known as "soft gold." Once endangered, it is now being protected in nature reserves such as the Barguzin Nature Reserve near Lake Baikal.

Coniferous forests of the Southeastern United States Temperate pinelands in the United States are found primarily in New Jersey, Virginia, North Carolina, South Carolina, Georgia, Alabama, Mississippi, Louisiana, Arkansas, Florida, and Tennessee. The pines that grow here are called southern pines, and loblolly, slush, longleaf, and shortleaf pines predominate. Many of these trees took over farms and plantations abandoned after the Civil War (1861–65).

The temperate climate with its mild winters favors tree growth. In Georgia, for example, average annual temperatures are about 40°F (4.4°C) in the mountains and 54°F (12°C) on the southern coast. Average annual rainfall is about 50 inches (127 centimeters).

The soil of these forests tends to be rich and supports much tree growth, including oak and hickory, in addition to the many pines.

Wildlife includes many species of snakes and birds, as well as rabbits, squirrels, opossums, badgers, moles, deer, and wildcats.

Coniferous forests of the Southeastern United States
Location: Southeastern states
Classification: Temperate pineland

For More Information

BOOKS

Allaby, Michael. *Biomes of the Earth: Temperate Forests.* New York: Chelsea House, 2006.

Allaby, Michael. *Biomes of the Earth: Tropical Forests.* New York: Chelsea House, 2006.

Brockman, C. Frank. *Trees of North America: A Guide to Field Identification,* Revised and Updated. New York: St. Martin's Press, 2001.

Burie, David, and Don E. Wilson, eds. *Animal.* New York: Smithsonian Institute, 2001.

Day, Trevor. *Biomes of the Earth: Taiga.* New York: Chelsea House, 2006.

Jacke, Dave. *Edible Forest Gardens.* White River Junction, VT: Chelsea Green Publishing Co., 2005.

Jose, Shibu, Eric J. Jokela, and Deborah L. Miller *The Longleaf Pine Ecosystem: Ecology, Silviculture, and Restoration.* New York: Springer, 2006.

Miller, James H., and Karl V. Miller. *Forest Plants Of The Southeast And Their Wildlife Uses.* Athens: University of Georgia Press, 2005.

O'Shea, Mark, and Tim Halliday. *Smithsonian Handbooks: Reptiles and Amphibians.* New York: Dorling Kindersley, 2001.

Zabel, Cynthia, and Robert G. Anthony. *Mammal Community Dynamics: Management and Conservation in the Coniferous Forests of Western North America.* New York: Cambridge University Press, 2003.

PERIODICALS

Morris, John. "Will the Forest Survive?" *Wide World.* 13. 1 September 2001: 15.

"Siberia Sees the Wood from the Trees." *Geographical.* 73. 1 January 2001: 10.

ORGANIZATIONS

Environmental Defense Fund, 257 Park Ave. South, New York, NY 10010; Telephone: 212-505-2100. Fax: 212-505-2375; Internet: http://www.edf.org

Environmental Protection Agency, 401 M Street, SW, Washington DC 20460; Telephone:202-260-2090; Internet: http://www.epa.gov

Friends of the Earth, 1717 Massachusetts Ave. NW 300, Washington, DC 20036; Telephone:877-843-8687; Fax:202-783-0444; Internet: http://www.foe.org

Global ReLeaf, American Forests, PO Box 2000, Washington, DC 20013; Telephone:202-737-1944; Internet: http://www.amfor.org

Greenpeace USA, 702 H Street NW, Washington, DC 20001; Telephone: 202-462-1177; Internet: http://www.greenpeace.org

Izaak Walton League of America, 707 Conservation Lane, Gaithersburg, MD 20878; Telephone:301-548-0150; Internet: http://www.iwla.org

Sierra Club, 85 Street, 2nd fl., San Francisco, CA 94105; Telephone:415-977-5500; Fax:415-977-5799; Internet: http://www.sierraclub.org

The Wilderness Society, 1615 M St. NW, Washington, DC 20036; Telephone: 800-the-wild; Internet: http://www.wilderness.org

World Wildlife Fund, 1250 24th Street NW, Washington, DC 20090; Internet: http://www.wwf.org

WEB SITES

National Geographic Magazine. http://www.nationalgeographic.com (accessed August 25, 2007).

National Park Service. http://www.nps.gov (accessed August 25, 2007).

Ouje-Bougoumou Cree Nation. http://www.ouje.ca (accessed August 25, 2007).

Scientific American Magazine. http://www.sciam.com (accessed August 25, 2007).

Swedish Environmental Protection Agency. http://www.internat.naturvardsverket.se (accessed August 25, 2007).

Continental Margin

The continental margin is that part of the ocean floor at the edges of the continents and major islands where, just beyond the shoreline, it tapers gently into the deep sea. The continental margin is made up of the continental shelf, the continental slope, and the continental rise.

The continental shelf begins at the shoreline. It is flat and its width varies. For example, off the Arctic coast of Siberia it is 800 miles (1,280 kilometers) wide. Rich sediment (particles of soil and decaying matter) from rivers that flow to the sea filters down to the shelf. Over time, deposits of these sediments may become many thousands of feet (meters) thick. At its deepest points, the continental shelf is usually less than 660 feet (200 meters) below sea level (the level surface of the sea). Although the continental shelf is easier to explore than deeper areas of the ocean, there is still much to learn.

At the end of the continental shelf is a steep dip that marks the edge of the continent. This is called the continental slope, which descends to depths of 10,000 to 13,000 feet (3,048 to 3,962 meters) and ranges in width from 12 to 60 miles (20 to 100 kilometers). The continental slope usually resembles the edge of a mountain range, and in some places the drop is spectacular. Along the coast of Chile in South America, where the Andes Mountains meet the sea, the drop from the highest mountain peak on land—Aconcagua—to the bottom of the continental slope is more than 9 miles (14 kilometers).

Beyond the continental slope is the continental rise, where sediments drifting down from the continental shelf have collected. These deposits may extend as far as 600 miles (1,000 kilometers) out into the ocean floor, where the deep-sea basin begins.

Formation of the Continental Margins

The World Ocean, which is all the oceans taken together, covers a total of 139,782,000 square miles (363,433,200 square kilometers)—about 71 percent of Earth's surface. Over 200 million years ago, the World Ocean

WORDS TO KNOW

Abyssal plain: The flat midportion of the ocean floor that begins beyond the continental rise.

Canyon: A long, narrow valley between high cliffs that has been formed by the eroding force of a river.

Continental shelf: A flat extension of a continent that tapers gently into the sea.

Estuary: The place where a river traveling through lowlands meets the ocean in a semi-enclosed area.

Kelp: A type of brown algae that usually grows on rocks in temperate water.

Lagoon: A large pool of seawater cut off from the ocean by a bar or other landmass.

Salinity: The level of salt.

Subduction zone: Area where pressure forces the seafloor down and under the continental margin, often causing the formation of a deep ocean trench.

Tsunami: A huge wave or upwelling of water caused by undersea earthquakes that grows to great heights as it approaches shore.

Water column: All the waters of the ocean, exclusive of the sea bed or other landforms.

was one body of water that surrounded one large continent. As time passed, this land mass began to pull apart. As a result, the continents and islands were formed.

The breakup of that one large continent was caused by heat forces welling up deep within Earth. As earthquakes split the ocean floor, molten rock from below Earth's crust flowed into the fracture and became solid. For millions of years this process was repeated until the upper parts of Earth's crust, on which the continents sit, were pushed even farther apart. About 50 million years ago, the continents took their present shapes and positions.

About 20 million years ago, when the sea level was at its lowest, the area that now makes up the continental shelves was above water. Forests may have grown there and it may have been home to many animals. Over millions of years, rain, wind, and wave action eroded (wore away) the shelf surface, and rivers and glaciers flowed across it. Gradually, sediments from the shelves were washed into the water. Later, as the glaciers melted, the sea level rose and covered the shelves so that the entire continental margin was under water.

The Water Column

All of the waters of the ocean, exclusive of the sea bed or other landforms, is referred to as the water column.

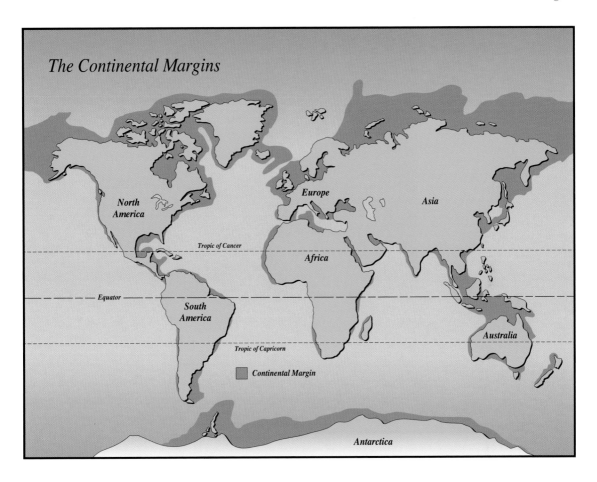

The Continental Margins

■ Continental Margin

Every element known on Earth can be found in ocean water. It is 3.5 percent dissolved salts by weight. The percentage of these salts determines the ocean's salinity (level of salts). These salts also make seawater heavier than fresh water. The ocean water closest to the surface is usually less salty because of rainfall and fresh water flowing in from rivers.

The temperature of the oceans varies. Temperature changes are greatest near the surface where the heat of the sun can be absorbed. In the warmest regions of the world, this heat absorption occurs to depths of 330 to 1,650 feet (100 to 500 meters).

Zones in the ocean   Different parts of the ocean have different features and different kinds of creatures live in them. These different parts are called zones. Some zones are determined by the amount of light that reaches them.

Crashing waves wear at the shoreline, changing its shape over time. COPYRIGHT © 2005 KELLY A. QUIN.

Over the continental shelves and in the open ocean there is enough light to support photosynthesis, the process by which plants use the energy from sunlight to change water and carbon dioxide into the sugars and starches they use for food. These surface waters, called the sunlit zone, reach down as far as 660 feet (200 meters) below the surface. The sunlit zone supports more plant and animal life than any other zone.

Below the sunlit zone and extending about halfway down the continental slope is the twilight zone, which ranges from 650 to 3,300 feet (198 to 1,006 meters) in depth. Only blue light can filter down to this level. It is too dark for plant life here, but animals can live at this depth.

Beginning about halfway down the continental slope and extending into the deepest region of the oceans is the dark zone. Like the twilight zone, the dark zone is unable to support plant life, but a variety of animals are able to live in its depths.

Circulation   The oceans are constantly, restlessly moving. This movement takes the form of tides, waves, and currents, all of which affect the continental margins.

Tides   Tides are rhythmic movements of the oceans that cause a change in the surface level of the water. They are created by a combination of the gravitational pull of the sun and moon and Earth's rotation.

Low tide in the Bay of Fundy, Nova Scotia, leaving boats such as these scallop draggers completely exposed. IMAGE COPYRIGHT V. J. MATTHEW, 2007. USED UNDER LICENSE FROM SHUTTERSTOCK.COM.

High tide occurs when the water level rises. When the level lowers, it is called low tide.

Sea level refers to the average height of the ocean when it is halfway between high and low tides and all wave motion is smoothed out. Sea level changes over time.

Waves Waves are rhythmic rising and falling movements on the surface of the water. Most surface waves are caused by wind. Their size is due to the speed of the wind, the length of time it has been blowing, and the distance over which it has traveled. Breakers are waves that collapse on a shoreline because the water at the bottom of the wave is slowed by friction as it rolls along the shore. The top of the wave then outruns the bottom and topples over in a heap of bubbling foam.

One type of wave called a tsunami (soo-NAH-mee) is mainly caused by undersea earthquakes. When the ocean floor moves during the quake its vibrations create a powerful wave that travels to the surface. Tsunamis that strike inhabited coastal areas can destroy entire towns and kill many people.

Currents Currents are flows of water in a certain direction. They can be both large and strong. Most currents are caused by the wind, the rotation of Earth, and the position of continental landmasses. In the North Pacific, for example, currents moving west are pushed northward by Asia and southward by Australia. The same currents then move east until they reach North and South America, which send them

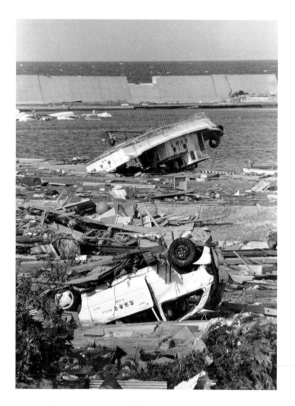

Tsunamis are caused by undersea earthquakes and are capable of causing massive destruction. AP IMAGES.

back toward the equator. Longshore currents are those that move along a shoreline.

Upward and downward movement of water also occurs in the ocean. Vertical currents are mainly caused by differences in water temperature and salinity. In some coastal areas strong wind-driven currents carry warm surface water away. An upwelling (rising) of cold water from the deep ocean occurs to fill the space. This is more common along the western sides of the continents. These upwellings bring many nutrients from the ocean floor to the surface waters.

At the continental margins, large quantities of sediments enter the ocean and move out along the sea floor. The sediments are often sped along by turbidity (tur-BID-ih-tee) currents, which may be caused by earthquakes or sudden slumping of loose sediments. The thick mixture of sediment and water rushes down the continental slope and through any submarine canyons at considerable speeds for long distances, much like an avalanche of snow. They are so strong they have been known to break underwater cables that lay in their path hundreds of miles away. Turbidity currents can cause many changes to the margin floor.

Geography of Continental Margins

The general shape of the continental margin is usually determined by the shape of the coastline from which it extends. If it extends from a plain, then the margin will be broad and level. If it extends from a mountainous coast, then it will be steep and rocky. Steep cliffs that may have been formed by wave action when the level of the sea was lower may now be submerged and form part of the margin.

The present shape of a continental margin may be due to several influences. Movement of Earth's crust may have given it a folded appearance where the sea floor cracked and was pushed underneath the margin. Huge boulders and rocks may indicate that a glacier once moved across the region. The presence of a river may mean a larger quantity of sediment

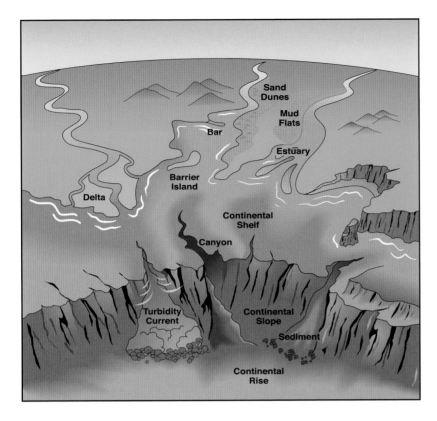

Sand
Dunes

Mud
Flats

Bar

Estuary

Barrier
Island

Delta

Continental
Shelf

Canyon

Turbidity
Current

Continental
Slope

Sediment

Continental
Rise

A cross-section of the continental margin, including the continental shelf and continental slope.

where it enters the ocean, and the weight of tons of this sediment may have forced the underlying rock to sink.

A continental margin located in an area prone to many earthquakes or volcanoes is considered an active margin. It is constantly changing due to the continuous earthquake and volcanic activity. Active margins are often found in the Pacific Ocean, such as those along the west coast of South America. They are narrow and often drop sharply into a deep trench (steep valley).

Passive margins are less active and usually free of earthquakes and volcanoes. They are found where the ocean floor is still gradually spreading. In most cases there is a wide rise. Continental margins along the Atlantic and Indian Oceans are passive margins.

Dams   Volcanic action, earthquakes, or a reef (a ridge of rock or other material) may create a dam at the end of the slope or rise. This dam causes sediments to build up and become an extension of the shelf. A new slope

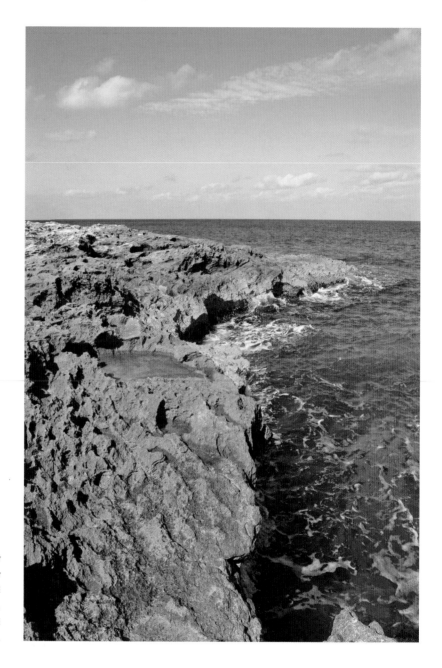

Volcanic rock forms the coastline of a small cay in the Caribbean Sea. IMAGE COPYRIGHT LORI FROEB, 2007. USED UNDER LICENSE FROM SHUTTERSTOCK.COM.

and rise form at its end. Salt domes, huge mounds of salt that have moved upward from beds buried deep in the ocean floor, can form dams and trap sediment. A salt dam has helped form the shelf in the Gulf of Mexico off the U.S. coast.

Subduction zones and trenches   The sea floor is continuously spreading. When it presses against the edges of the continents, they resist its movement. This results in an area of extreme pressure called a subduction zone. The enormous pressure forces the sea floor to crack, pushing it down and causing it to slide under the continental margin, often causing a deep, V-shaped trench to form. The greatest depths in the oceans are found in these trenches, and the deepest trenches are located in the Pacific Ocean. The Mariana Trench is the deepest at 36,201 feet (11,033 meters). Many earthquakes occur in subduction zones.

Underwater canyons   The continental slope is often cut by deep, V-shaped, underwater canyons (deep, narrow depressions in Earth's crust). These canyons vary in size but are not as deep as trenches. A canyon off the coast of Africa extends 15 miles (25 kilometers) across, but its depth is only 1,480 feet (450 meters).

The origin of canyons is different from that of trenches. Some canyons appear to be related to rivers on land that during prehistoric times may have extended into the area now covered by ocean. The huge Monterey Canyon off the coast of California is an example. The Salinas River once flowed into its bed during the Ice Ages.

The method of formation for some canyons is a mystery. The Bering Canyon north of the Aleutian Islands in the North Pacific Ocean is an example. It cuts through the continental margin for more than 255 miles (410 kilometers) and is the longest canyon in the world. However, there is no evidence it was ever associated with a river and it is unknown why or how it was formed.

Reefs   A reef is a ridge or wall of material lying close to the surface of the water just offshore. Reefs are made of rock or coral. A coral reef is a wall formed in shallow ocean areas by small, soft, jellylike animals called corals and marine algae that store calcium deposits. Corals attach themselves to hard surfaces and build a shell-like external skeleton. Many corals live together in colonies. Young coral builds its skeleton next to or on top of older skeletons. Gradually, over hundreds, thousands, or millions of years a wall, or reef, of these skeletons is formed. Reef corals cannot live in cold waters. They are found only in warm waters north and south of the equator. The water must be clear and free of sediment. Coral reefs do not form where rivers flow into the sea.

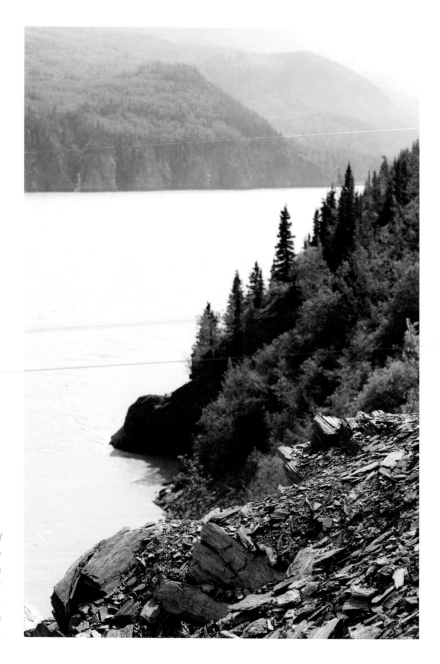

The rockslide in the foreground shows one of the ways the continental margin continues to change. IMAGE COPYRIGHT ROMAN KROCHUK, 2007. USED UNDER LICENSE FROM SHUTTERSTOCK.COM.

When a coral reef grows tall enough to break the surface of the water, it may begin to collect sand, gravel, weeds, and other matter. Gradually, an island, called a cay (KEE) or key, begins to form. The wind or visiting animals bring seeds, and plants begin to grow, especially small trees called mangroves. As the plants die and decay, soil forms. After a time, the island may be able to support certain larger species of trees.

Three main types of coral reefs are found on the continental margins: shelf reefs, fringing reefs, and barrier reefs. Shelf reefs form on a continental shelf having a hard, rocky bottom. A shallow body of water called a lagoon may be located between the shelf reef and the shore. Fringing reefs develop close to the land and no lagoon separates them from the shore. The longest is found in the Red Sea, where it stretches for 2,000 miles (3,200 kilometers). Barrier reefs line the edge of the continental shelf and separate it from deep ocean water. A barrier reef may enclose a lagoon and even small islands.

Estuaries and deltas When a river traveling through lowlands meets the ocean in a semi-enclosed channel (stream bed) or bay, the area is called an estuary. The water in an estuary is brackish—a mixture of fresh and salt water. In these gently sloping areas, river sediments collect, creating muddy shores. When the muddy sediments form a triangular shape over the continental shelf, the area is called a delta. The Mississippi Delta is one of the largest, spanning 60 miles (100 kilometers) across.

Glacial moraines A glacial moraine is a pile of rocks, gravel, and sand created when a glacier moves across the surface of the land. Glacial moraines are found on some continental shelves that were crossed by glaciers during the Ice Ages more than 10,000 years ago. When the glaciers shrank, the level of the sea rose and covered the area with water. The tops of some glacial moraines remain above the water and form islands. The Aland Islands in the Baltic Sea are an example.

Bars and shoals Bars and shoals can form where tides and currents move large quantities of sediment, such as sand or gravel. A bar is a ridge of sand that accumulates across a channel. Shoals are areas where enough sediment has accumulated that the water is very shallow and dangerous for

World's Biggest Ice Cubes

Thousands of icebergs form each year and float freely in the ocean. Those in the Arctic are usually produced by large glaciers moving across Greenland. As the glacier reaches the ocean, huge portions break off. Arctic icebergs often contain soil and other evidence of their origin on land. Antarctic icebergs are gigantic chunks of pack ice that form on open water. Unlike glacier ice, they do not originate on land, and therefore, contain no sediments.

The exposed portion of an iceberg may be more than 200 feet (61 meters) high, but this is only a hint of its actual size. About 90 percent of an iceberg remains underwater. That means its submerged portion could be 1,800 feet (549 meters) deep!

Tiny, But Deadly

Pfiesteria piscidia, a species of tiny, one-celled dinoflagellate algae, has suddenly become more dangerous than its size would indicate. In the late 1980s this normally nontoxic organism turned poisonous and began killing fish in North Carolina waters. Over a billion fish have been destroyed since 1991.

Pfiesteria release strong poisons into the water. The poisons cause fish to gasp for oxygen and develop bleeding sores on their bodies. *Pfiesteria* then feed on the dying tissues. The poisons are harmful to shellfish and even mammals, including humans, who develop impaired memory and learning abilities.

Most dinoflagellates obtain food by means of photosynthesis, but *Pfiesteria* passes through many different life stages, and in some stages, it appears to dine on other organisms. Experts suspect that the changes in *Pfiesteria* may have been caused by fertilizer and sewage runoff from hog and chicken farms in the area.

navigation. The shoals around Nantucket Island, off Massachusetts, for example, have sunk at least 2,100 ships.

Plant Life

Most ocean plants live in waters above the continental shelf. They include tiny, one-celled organisms and many kinds of seaweed and seagrasses. Some scientists estimate that plants over the continental shelf produce more oxygen for Earth than all the forests on land.

Ocean plants are surrounded by salt water at all times. For this reason most have not developed the special tissues and organs needed by land plants for conserving water. Seaweeds, for example, use their "roots" only to anchor them in one spot, not to draw water from the soil.

Water also offers support to ocean plants. Trees on land require a tough, woody stem to hold it erect, but giant underwater plants do not require woody portions because the water helps hold them upright. Their stems are soft and flexible, allowing them to move with the current without breaking.

Marine plants can be classified as either plankton or benthos. Plankton (a Greek word meaning "wanderers") are plants that float freely on the water's surface. Benthic (a Greek word meaning "depth") plants anchor themselves in the sea floor.

Ocean plants can be divided into two main groups: algae (AL-jee) and green plants.

Algae   Algae are single- or multi-celled organisms that do not fit neatly into the plant category. They can range from microscopic blue-green algae, which are really bacteria, to giant brown algae kelp nearly 200 feet (61 meters) long. Other algae are green or red. Green algae are the ancestors of land plants. Like plants, nearly all algae have the ability to make their own food by means of photosynthesis (foh-toh-SIHN-thuh-sihs). They use energy from sunlight to change water and carbon dioxide into the sugars and starches they need for food. Other algae absorb nutrients from their surroundings.

Phytoplankton are a form of algae so tiny they cannot be seen with the naked eye. They float freely in the water, allowing it to carry them from place to place. Other species of algae are massive and live in vast underwater forests anchored to the seafloor. These are the benthic species.

Common algae Two types of algae commonly found along the continental margins include phytoplankton and kelp.

Phytoplankton Phytoplankton are microscopic single-celled algae that float on the surface of waters within the sunlit zone. They are responsible for about 90 percent of the photosynthesis carried out in the oceans. During photosynthesis, phytoplankton release oxygen into the atmosphere. Two forms of phytoplankton, diatoms and dinoflagellates (dee-noh-FLAJ-uh-lates), are the most common.

Diatoms have simple, geometric shapes and hard, glasslike cell walls. They live in colder regions and even within arctic ice. Dinoflagellates have two whiplike attachments that make a swirling motion. They live in tropical regions around the equator.

Kelp Kelps are usually brown benthic algae that grow on rocks in temperate waters (41° to 72°F [5°C to 22°C]). In northern regions, benthic plants grow below 200 feet (61 meters). In tropical regions, where the sun's rays are more vertical and can penetrate farther into the water, kelps grow as deep as 400 feet (122 meters). There is evidence that some can grow as deep as 1,000 feet (305 meters), where no light penetrates, because they may obtain food from decomposing matter that filters down from above instead of by means of photosynthesis.

There are several different species of kelp but only two basic forms. One type has a simple trunk between 20 inches and 8 feet (50 centimeters and 2.5 meters) long and a leaflike frond (branches) on top. The second type may grow to more than 250 feet (76 meters) in length and has fronds all along its trunk. Some kelp have gas-filled chambers at the bases of their fronds that help them remain upright. Kelp resemble green plants, but they have no true leaves, stems, or roots. Instead they have a rootlike structure called a holdfast that anchors them to the ocean floor.

Kelp reproduce sexually; cells from a male and female plant unite to form another plant.

Kelp grow in huge, floating groups, or forests, that cover hundreds of square miles (square kilometers) and provide shelter and food for animals such as fish, crabs, and sea otters. On the water's surface, kelp can be so thick that sea otters can lie down on them as if in a hammock. Sea urchins, which also feed on kelp, can grow so numerous they eventually destroy the kelp beds unless checked by natural predators.

Growing season   Algae contain chlorophyll, a green pigment used to turn energy from the sun into food. As long as light is available, algae can grow. In some species, the green chlorophyll is masked by orange-colored pigments, giving the algae a red or brown color.

Growth of ocean plants is often seasonal. In some areas, such as the Arctic, most growth occurs during the summer when the sun is more nearly overhead. In temperate (moderate) zones, growth peaks in the spring but continues throughout the summer. In regions near the equator, no growth peaks occur since growth is steady throughout the year.

Food   Most algae grow in the sunlit zone where light is available for photosynthesis. Algae require other nutrients found in the water, such as nitrogen, phosphorus, and silicon. In certain regions, upwelling of deep ocean waters during different seasons brings more of these nutrients to the surface. This results in algal blooms, sudden increases in the number of algae. Algal blooms also occur when nitrogen and phosphorus are added to a body of water by sewage or by runoffs from farmland.

Reproduction   Algae reproduce in one of three ways. Some split into two or more parts, with each part becoming a new, separate plant. Others form spores (single cells that have the ability to grow into a new organism). A few reproduce sexually, during which cells from two different plants unite to create a new plant.

Green plants   The true green plants found in the ocean are seagrasses, such as turtle grass, and are similar to land plants. Green algae are often considered green plants. Unlike algae, green plants have roots and bloom underwater. Beds of seagrass occur in sandy bottoms in areas protected from currents, such as in lagoons or behind reefs. Large beds slow the movement of water and help prevent erosion of the shelf. Some marine animals use seagrasses for food and for hiding places.

Animal Life

The oceans are the largest animal habitat on Earth, and most species are found along the continental margins. The continental shelves underlie only about 8 percent of the total area of the oceans, but their shallow waters support more forms of life than any other area in the ocean—perhaps any other place on Earth. Scientists estimate as many as 30 million species of sea life may still be undiscovered. The types of animals found along the upper continental slope depend on whether the floor is sandy, muddy, or rocky. The lower slope and rise are home to fewer animals.

Animals that live in the sea have developed ways to cope with its high salinity. Naked (covered with thin "skins" or shells) animals maintain high levels of salt in their blood normally and do not need to expel any excess. Others, such as most fish, have special organs that remove extra salt from their system and release it into the water.

Water offers support to marine (ocean) animals as it does to plants. Many marine animals have special chambers in their bodies that allow them to adjust their buoyancy (BOY-un-see; ability to float) so they can float in either shallow or deep water. Some, such as seals, have flippers to make swimming easier. Others, such as octopi, forcefully eject water in a kind of jet stream to help them move.

Marine animals are classified as microorganisms, invertebrates, or vertebrates. Like plants, they can be classified according to their range and style of movement. Plankton drift in currents and include such animals as jellyfish. Many plankton move up and down the water column by regulating the amount of gas, oil, or salt within their bodies. (Production of gas or oil and removal of salt causes the organism to rise; the reverse causes them to sink.) Many larger animals spend part of their young lives as plankton. Crabs, which move about on legs as adults, but float with the current in their larval form, are an example. Larger animals that swim on their own, such as fish and dolphins, are called nekton. Benthos are the animals that live on the seafloor. These include snails and clams.

Microorganisms Most microorganisms are zooplankton (tiny animals that drift with the current). They include foraminiferans, radiolarians, acantharians, and ciliates, as well as the larvae or hatchlings of animals that will grow much larger in their adult form. Some zooplankton eat phytoplankton and are preyed upon by other carnivorous (meat-eating) zooplankton, such as arrow worms.

Bacteria Bacteria are another type of microorganism found throughout the ocean. They make up much of the dissolved matter in the water column and provide food for microscopic animals. Their numbers increase

Sea-Going Dinosaurs

About 63,000,000 years ago, a number of dinosaur species lived in the oceans. The Tylosaurus was 25 feet (7.6 meters) long and resembled a chubby crocodile with flippers rather than feet. Plesiosaurs, which could have been as long as 50 feet (15 meters), had flippers and long, giraffelike necks. Flying reptiles, called pteranodons, glided through the air over the ocean on leathery wings looking for fish. They returned to land only to lay their eggs.

The hairy clinging crab is found among the rocks and sand of the continental margin.
COPYRIGHT © 2005 KELLY A. QUIN.

along the continental shelf where most animal life is found because they help decompose the dead bodies of larger organisms.

Invertebrates   Animals without backbones are called invertebrates. They compose 95 percent of marine animals. Many invertebrate species, such as worms and squids, are found in the ocean. Perhaps the most numerous and diverse group of invertebrates are crustaceans, which have hard outer shells for protection from potential predators. Crustaceans include animals such as lobsters and crabs.

Common invertebrates   Invertebrates found along the continental margins range from planktonic jellyfish to nektonic octopi to benthic starfish and corals.

Jellyfish are commonly found close to shore where they float on the surface. All jellyfish move by squeezing their bodies to push out water that forms a kind of jet stream behind them. Most of the time they live as plankton and simply float with the current. Jellyfish eat small prey, such as shrimp, tiny fish, and other plankton, which they catch by stinging them with their tentacles.

Another common invertebrate that lives along the continental margins is the octopus. Octopi may crawl around the ocean bottom using their tentacles, or move through the water by means of jet propulsion. Different species are found throughout the ocean, and they vary in size. Those found in shallow water are generally the smallest. Giant octopi with a tentacle spread of 32 feet (9.7 meters) have been found off the coast of Alaska.

Food   Invertebrates may eat phytoplankton, zooplankton, or both. Some also eat plants or larger animals. The cone shell uses a harpoonlike tooth to spear its prey and inject it with poison. Others, including lobster, roam along the bottom to feed on dead organisms by grasping them with their large pincher front claws.

Reproduction   Marine invertebrates reproduce in one of three ways. Two ways use external fertilization (outside the female's body) of eggs. The first way involves a parent watching over the young in the early stages and offspring number in the hundreds. The second way does not require parental care and offspring number in the millions. Survival depends upon the absence of predators and the direction of currents. The third method of reproduction is internal fertilization (inside the female's body). A parent cares for the young in the early stages and offspring number in the thousands.

Reptiles   Reptiles are cold-blooded vertebrates, which means their body temperature changes with the temperature of their surroundings. In cold temperatures they become sluggish but can still function. This means they do not have to use energy keeping their body temperatures up as most do mammals and birds.

Only one species of lizard has adapted to life at sea, the marine iguana. There are only two species of crocodile, the Pacific saltwater crocodile and the American saltwater crocodile, that spend a large amount of time off shore. The reptiles most commonly found in the oceans are the sea turtle and the sea snake.

Common marine reptiles   Sea turtles can be distinguished from land turtles by their paddlelike limbs called flippers, which enable them to swim. Sea turtles have glands around their eyes that remove excess salt from their bodies, a process that makes them appear to cry. At least one species of turtle hibernates on the seabed during winter. Green turtles are

The Clockwork Worm

Some animals seem to have built-in "clocks," like one species of marine worm called the palolo worm. This little creature, which lives in the waters of the central Pacific, develops eggs and sperm in the rear half of its body. This rear section detaches from the rest of its body and swims to the surface like clockwork on the day of the last quarter of the October-November moon. On this day, the surface waters grow thick with the rising egg sections from millions of worms.

Although sea turtles live in the water, they lay their eggs on shore. This is an endangered Kemp's Ridley sea turtle.
AP IMAGES.

migratory and travel as far as 1,250 miles (2,000 kilometers) to return to a particular breeding area where they lay their eggs.

At least fifteen species of sea snakes live in tropical oceans (those around the equator). Half of these are found in regions around Australia and New Guinea. They have long bodies like land snakes, some of which attain 9 feet (2.7 meters) in length. Special salt glands help them maintain a body fluid balance. Their tails are paddle shaped to move them through the water. All sea snakes are venomous. The yellow-bellied sea snake may be the most abundant reptile on Earth.

Food Sea turtles eat soft plant foods as well as small invertebrates, such as snails and worms. Turtles have no teeth. Instead, the sharp, horny edges of their jaws are used to shred the food so they can swallow it. All seven species of sea turtle are either threatened or endangered.

Sea snakes are carnivorous, feeding primarily on fish and eels they find along the ocean bottom in rocky crevices. They first bite their prey, injecting it with venom so that it cannot escape.

Reproduction Both snakes and turtles lay eggs. Turtles dig a hole with their flippers on a sandy shore and lay their eggs. They cover the eggs with sand and abandon them, taking no interest in the offspring. Six weeks later the eggs hatch and the young turtles make a run for the water and immediately begin swimming. Sea snakes either come to shore to breed and lay their eggs on land or bear live young at sea, depending upon the species.

Fish Fish are primarily cold-blooded verte-brates that have gills and fins. Gills are used to draw in water from which oxygen is extracted, and fins help propel the fish through the water. Most fish are long and sleek in design, but shapes vary greatly. Manta rays, for example, are flat and round, while seahorses are narrow and swim in a vertical position.

Most fish species live over the continental shelf in the sunlit zone. In the twilight and dark zones species such as the hatchetfish, the swallower, and the black dragon-fish can be found.

Common fish Mackerels and rays are commonly found over the continental margins. Mackerels live over the continental shelves in temper-ate and tropical oceans. They gather in schools (groups) in the upper waters during the warm months and descend to deeper waters in the winter. Their primary food is zoo-plankton, such as fish eggs. Mackerels lay their eggs in mid-water where they drift with the cur-rents. Some species are popular as game fish, and many species are important commercially in the fishing industry.

Rays are relatives of the shark, but they have flat, broad bodies. Their eyes are on top and their mouths are on the underside. They feed by flapping and gliding over the seabed in search of clams and similar prey. Some species have the ability to give an electric shock for defense or to kill prey. The largest species, the devil or manta ray, can grow as much as 20 feet (6 meters) in diameter. Most species bear live young.

Food Plant-eating fish, such as anchovies, have a diet primarily of phytoplankton, benthic algae, or sea grasses. Fish that must swim in search of prey, such as swordfish, have more streamlined bodies than those, like the sea robin, that glide close to the bottom sediments in search of a meal. Many dark zone species eat carrion (decaying flesh).

A Dentist's Dream

Sharks may have as many as 3,000 teeth in their mouths at one time. These teeth are arranged in rows, and only the first few rows are used. If a tooth is lost during feeding, the next tooth in line moves up to take its place.

The largest species of ray, the manta ray, can grow to as much as 20 feet (6 meters) in diameter. IMAGE COPYRIGHT SPECTA, 2007. USED UNDER LICENSE FROM SHUTTERSTOCK.COM.

Sea gulls often eat fish and other small creatures found in the ocean's continental margin. IMAGE COPYRIGHT STEPHEN ORSILLO, 2007. USED UNDER LICENSE FROM SHUTTERSTOCK.COM.

Reproduction Most fish lay eggs. Some fish, like the Atlantic herring, abandon eggs once they are laid. Other fish build nests and care for the new offspring. Still others carry the eggs with them, usually in a special body cavity or in their mouths, until the eggs hatch. A few fish, such as certain species of sharks, bear live young.

Sturgeons are one type of fish that travel thousands of miles to return to a particular breeding area where they lay their eggs and then die. By some inherited means of guidance, their young will make the same journey when their turn comes to breed, and the cycle is repeated.

Seabirds Only 4 percent of bird species have adapted to sea life. Most seabirds remain near land where they can nest during breeding season. Many have adapted to marine environments by means of webbed feet and special glands for removing excess salt from their blood.

Common seabirds Birds living along the ocean's margins are divided into four groups. The first group includes pelicans and their relatives, such as frigate and cormorants. This is a varied group, but all members share the common trait of webbing on all four toes. The second group is called tubenoses and is known to be a group of superb flyers. Petrels, shearwaters, and albatrosses belong to this group. Another group contains a mix of gulls, terns, puffins, and auks. Finally, penguins, which do not fly but can swim in the water, are the last group. There are seventeen species of penguin and all of them live in the Southern Hemisphere (below the Equator).

Food Seabirds are carnivorous. They eat fish, squid, or zooplankton and live where food is plentiful. Several species, such as sea ducks, dive underwater to feed on shrimps, worms, or crabs. Other species, such as cormorants, spot their prey from high above in the sky and then plunge in just deep enough to catch it. Some, like terns, swoop down on fish swimming close to the surface.

Reproduction All seabirds nest on land. Some nest in huge colonies on the ground, others dig burrows, and still others prefer ledges on cliffs. Like land birds, seabirds lay eggs and remain on the nest until the young can leave on their own. Some birds live and feed in one area and migrate to another for breeding. Birds that nest on sandy shores tend to lay speckled or blotchy eggs in beige and brown colors that blend in with the sand and pebbles.

Marine mammals Mammals (warm-blooded vertebrates that bear live young nursed with milk) must come to the surface to breathe, and many, such as seals and polar bears, live part of the time on land. Whales, porpoises, sea cows, and their relatives remain in the water at all times.

Mammals must maintain a high body temperature. Most marine mammals have a special layer of fat below their skin to protect them from the cold water. Some, such as walruses, have very thick skins that make it difficult to keep cool in the sun. Others, such as seals, are covered with fur that helps insulate them against the cold.

Common marine mammals Whales, dolphins, and porpoises are mammals that resemble fish. The killer whale, a relative of the dolphin, hunts in large groups and feeds on other mammals as well as fish and birds. Another fishlike mammal, the narwhal, or sea unicorn, has a tooth that grows into a spiral as much as 10 feet (3 meters) in length.

Seals are common along the continental shelves where they may plunge as deep as 3,300 feet (1,000 meters) in search of fish. Some species can stay underwater for as long as 30 minutes. Seals usually gather in huge on-shore colonies to breed.

Although polar bears are usually thought of as land animals, they spend much of their time in the water and may swim 20 miles (32 kilometers) or more in search of food. Their primary prey is seal. They may wait for hours along a shore for a seal to surface. If they catch it, they drag it ashore to eat it.

Food Sea cows, such as the dugong, are the only plant-eating mammals that truly live in the sea. Marine mammals are typically carnivorous. Seals and walruses, for example, feed on fish and squid

The Web of Life: Animal Partners

Many animals of different species form partnerships that help them survive. Certain fish, such as the moray eel, attract parasites that irritate their skin, gills, and mouth. That is when a cleaner fish comes in handy. The cleaner fish swims into the mouth of the eel, picks off the parasites, and eats them. Sometimes the customer forgets why the cleaner fish is there and has it for a snack.

Another partnership is formed between the clownfish and the sea anemone. Sea anemones (ah-NEH-moh-nees) are soft-bodied animals that attach themselves to rocks and reefs. These colorful creatures look like underwater flowers. However, they have long, poisonous tentacles they use to kill their prey. The clownfish cautiously approaches and rubs itself against the anemone. For some reason, this prevents the anemone from stinging the clownfish, which settles in among the tentacles and waits for dinner to swim by. The clownfish feeds on prey that escape the anemone and draws other fish into the anemone's grasp so it, too, can eat.

The Brainiest Mammal

The mammal with the largest brain is the sperm whale, a species found in all oceans. The whale's head makes up one-third of its body. Since an average-sized male whale is about 63 feet (19 meters) long, its head would be about 20 feet (6 meters) long.

that live on the continental shelf. Other mammals, like killer whales, hunt for seals and other mammals.

Reproduction   Marine mammals usually have only one offspring at a time. The young are nursed on the mother's milk until they are able to find food on their own. This is true whether the mammal spends all its time in the water or part of the time on shore.

Endangered species   Sea turtles lay their eggs on beaches, which makes the eggs easy to hunt and/or destroy. Turtle eggs are a popular food among humans in many parts of the world, as are the turtles themselves. Turtles must come to the surface to breathe air where many get caught in fishing nets that pull them below the water, and they drown. Over 70 conservation laws have been passed to protect the sea turtles.

Many fish used as food have been caught in such large numbers that they are disappearing. Since the 1970s, the number of bluefin tuna has decreased 90 percent and Atlantic swordfish have decreased by 30 percent.

In certain areas, other animals are threatened. They include the starlet sea anemone, the giant clam, the Olive Ridley turtle, the loggerhead turtle, the coelacanth, the Dalmatian pelican, the West Indian manatee, the marine otter, the monk seal, and the polar bear.

About 11 percent of coral reefs were destroyed by human actions before 1998. Another 16 percent were lost during the El Niño event in 1997–98. El Niños are extreme weather conditions caused by the slackening of the southeast Pacific trade winds. Due to a resulting shift in temperature, the corals eject their color, which is created by the colorful dinoflagellate algae that live on them. This is called coral bleaching because the corals become pale. It is estimated that by the year 2020 another 30 percent of coral reefs will be lost. As a result, all of the animals that depend upon the reef for food and shelter will be affected.

Human Life

The waters over the continental shelves have been explored by humans more than any other area of the ocean because the water is fairly shallow

The monk seal is one of several animal residents of the continental margin that is also endangered. IMAGE COPYRIGHT DON LONG, 2007. USED UNDER LICENSE FROM SHUTTERSTOCK.COM.

and reachable by divers. Most commercial fishing areas are located over the shelves, as are those areas from which oil and natural gas are extracted.

The best-known shelves are those off the coasts of the United States, eastern Canada, western Europe, and Japan. In these places, scientific studies are routinely conducted and the information is made available to everyone. Oil companies that work in other areas, such as the Persian Gulf, obtain knowledge about them. Oceanographic organizations have studied the Red Sea, the Yellow Sea, and the shelf off the coasts of Argentina and northwestern Africa. A few developing countries have closed their waters to foreign scientists; as a result, little is known about those shelves.

Impact of the continental margin on human life   The continental margin is the ocean area most easily reached by humans and so it has an important effect on human life.

Food   About 90 percent of the world's marine food resources come from the waters over the continental shelves. Most of those resources consist of fish. Different methods and equipment are used to catch fish, depending upon the type of fish desired and where they are found. Some fish live in the water column and may be caught on the surface or in mid-water, while others live on the ocean floor. These two categories may be divided further into fish caught at the shoreline, above the continental shelf, or in mid-ocean.

Sport fishing is done for recreation. The catch is taken home and may be eaten, but the family does not depend upon it for food. Subsistence fishing is done to obtain food for a family or even an entire community. Extra fish may be sold to neighboring communities. Native peoples who live on islands often do subsistence fishing.

Commercial fishing is done to earn money. When carried out by small owner-operated companies, much of the work is done by hand. The equipment is usually simple and the number of fishing boats small. Industrial, large-scale fishing usually involves modern, high-powered equipment. Huge factory ships may be as long as 330 feet (100 meters) and are equipped with automatic machinery needed to catch, handle, store, and process huge amounts of fish.

Energy Millions of years ago, sediments from dead animal and plant life collected on the ocean bottom. Over time, these sediments fossilized (turned to stone). More time, heat, and pressure from overlying rock worked to liquefy these sediments and turn them into fossil fuels, primarily gas and oil. To obtain fossil fuels, oil companies build large rigs—platforms high above the ocean surface but anchored to the sea bed. From these platforms, drilling is done into the rocky ocean floor, releasing the gas or oil, which is then pumped to shore through pipelines. Most gas and oil deposits have been obtained from offshore rigs. More than $1 billion worth of gas and oil is pumped from the continental shelves of the United States each year.

Ocean surface waters absorb large quantities of solar energy (energy from the sun). A process known as ocean thermal energy conversion is used to capture some of that energy for human use. Conversion plants are located in Hawaii and other tropical islands. Energy from ocean currents and waves is also being explored as a source of power. One day it may be possible to anchor a turbine (energy-producing engine) in a fast-moving current, such as the Gulf Stream, and use it to produce power.

The energy in the tides has already been harnessed in different ways. The tides are channeled into salt ponds, where salt from the water is collected for sale. The tides also lift ships in and out of drydock where repairs are made. The first tidal power station was developed in an estuary in France where turbines were built into a dam that spans the estuary. As the tides flow in and out of the estuary, they turn the turbine blades, which produce electricity.

Minerals and metals   Minerals and metals are other important oceanic resources. Rocks, sand, and gravel dredged from the sea bottom, especially in the North Sea and the Sea of Japan, are used in the construction of roads and buildings. Along the Namibian coast of southwest Africa, diamonds are mined from the sea floor. Some minerals, such as sulfur, are pumped from the ocean beds as liquids.

A fishing ship comes into harbor. About 90 percent of the world's marine food resources come from the waters of the continenal shelves. IMAGE COPYRIGHT ERIC GEVAERT, 2007. USED UNDER LICENSE FROM SHUTTERSTOCK.COM.

Impact of human life on the continental margin   The area of the ocean most affected by human action is over the continental margin.

Use of plants and animals   After World War II (1939–45) the technology of commercial fishing improved, and a growing population increased the demand for fish as a food source. By the 1970s major food species, such as herring and cod, had been greatly reduced. By 1995, 22 percent of marine fishing areas had been overused or depleted, and in 44 percent of fishing areas the maximum numbers of fish allowed by

Wells in the Sea

The first offshore oil well was drilled off the coast of California by 1897. This well, and those that followed, was drilled from a pier extending from shore. The first free-standing drilling structures were not built until the 1940s.

Since that time, the design of drilling rigs has changed. To stand in deep water and withstand storms at sea, they require long legs and a sturdy platform. One of the tallest platforms currently in operation is off the coast of Santa Barbara, California. The distance from its base anchored in the ocean floor to the top of a derrick on its platform high above the water is 1,165 feet (355 meters). This makes the rig only about 100 feet (30 meters) shorter than the Empire State Building in New York.

Exploration for wells is often done by mobile rigs positioned on drilling ships. The ships maintain their positions over the well using special propellers, and drilling in deeper waters is possible. During the 1980s, test wells were drilled from these ships in waters more than 6,500 feet (2,000 meters) deep.

regulations were being taken. Commercial fishing is done primarily with large nets that may also catch other unwanted creatures, many of which die. For every 1 pound (2.2 kilograms) of shrimp caught in the ocean, 5 pounds (11 kilograms) of other species are thrown away.

It has been said that human greed and carelessness have threatened many species of fish. However, not all scientists agree that the problems are serious or that they lack solutions. For example, between 1983 and 1993, the total number of fish available increased slightly. Conservation ideas include monitoring the numbers of fish in certain species to prevent overfishing and extending human consumption to more types of fish.

Fish farms are another means of helping maintain certain species of commercially popular fish. Also called aquaculture, fish farming involves raising fish species under the best growing conditions in farms built along waterways. The fish most commonly farmed are shellfish, such as oysters, mussels, scallops, clams, and shrimp. Crabs, lobsters, salmon, trout, and tilapia are also farm raised, but to a lesser extent. The output of fish farms has tripled since 1984, and it is estimated that more than 30 percent of all the seafood eaten comes from fish farms.

Other sea plants and animals are endangered because they are collected as souvenirs or art objects. Seashells left behind by dead animals can usually be taken with no harm. However, many shells available commercially are taken from living animals and, as a result, the animals are left to die.

In response to these problems, marine parks and reserves have been set up all over the world to protect endangered species. They include the Shiprock Aquatic Reserve in Australia and the Hervey Bay Marine Park in California.

Natural resources   Large quantities of natural resources, such as oil and minerals, can be found in the ocean water or beneath the ocean floor.

These resources have not been used up because they are still too difficult or too expensive to obtain. As methods improve that may change. The first areas likely to be depleted are those around the continental margins. Already, some sections of the sea floor have slumped because underlying oil and gas have been removed.

The Law of the Sea   After World War II, many countries began to expand their use of the oceans. Some countries started using ocean areas other countries had already claimed for themselves, and arguments resulted. In 1994, the United Nations approved a treaty among all nations called the Law of the Sea.

The Sneaky Vegetable

Although seaweed is popular as a food in some countries, particularly Japan, many people in the United States associate it with those slimy green things lying draped over the rocks at the beach. Most people have eaten seaweed and never realized it. As a product called carra-geenan, seaweed is added to toothpaste, ice cream, gelatin, peanut butter, marshmallows, and even some meat products. It acts as a glue to help hold the other ingredients together.

The Law of the Sea Treaty maintains that a country's territory extends about 14 miles (22.2 kilometers) from its coast. That country has a right to defend that territory. The same country also has the right to control the natural resources on its continental shelf, or an area extending about 230 miles (370 kilometers) from its coast. This includes resources obtained from fishing and drilling for oil and natural gas. The rest of the ocean is international territory and all countries can share in its resources.

Quality of the environment   In 1996, 14 billion pounds (31 billion kilograms) of waste were dumped into the oceans. Most oceanic pollution caused by humans is concentrated along the continental margins. Sewage and industrial wastes are contributed from coastal cities, adding dangerous metals and chemicals to the water. Discarded items, such as plastic bags and old fishing nets, pose a hazard for animals that get caught in them. Medical wastes, such as needles and tubing, are also a danger.

Insecticides (insect poisons) and herbicides (weed poisons) reach the oceans when rain washes them from fields into rivers that carry them to the sea. These poisons often enter the food chain, become concentrated in the bodies of some fish and other organisms, and are consumed by humans who eat the fish. Fertilizers and human sewage create another problem. They cause phytoplankton to reproduce rapidly. When the plants die, their decaying bodies feed bacteria. The bacteria rapidly multiply and use up the oxygen in the water, and other organisms, such as fish, soon die.

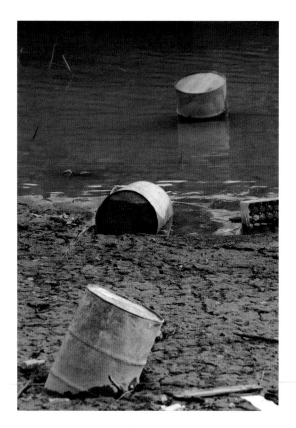

Refuse disposed of in the water can kill organisms, which disrupts the food web. IMAGE COPYRIGHT SASHA RADOSAVLJEVICH, 2007. USED UNDER LICENSE FROM SHUTTERSTOCK.COM.

Oil spills from tanker ships and leaks from pipelines and offshore oil wells are major pollutants to oceans. Power plants and some industries often dump warm water into the oceans, causing thermal (heat) pollution. Organisms that require cooler water are killed by the heat.

Agriculture, construction, and removal of trees on land dig up the soil. Often the rain washes this loose soil into streams and rivers. Eventually, it enters the oceans and collects as sediment in coastal areas. This kills some organisms, such as clams, that cannot survive in heavy sediment.

The Food Web

The transfer of energy from organism to organism forms a series called a food chain. All the possible feeding relationships that exist in a biome make up its food web. In the ocean, as elsewhere, the food web consists of producers, consumers, and decomposers. These types of organisms all transfer energy within the ocean environment.

Phytoplankton are the major primary producers in the oceans. They produce organic materials from inorganic chemicals and outside sources of energy, primarily the sun. Producers are sometimes called autotrophs, meaning "self-feeders." Green plants are an example of producers because they manufacture the compounds they need through photosynthesis.

Zooplankton and other animals are consumers. Zooplankton that eat only plants are primary consumers in the oceanic food web. Secondary consumers eat the plant-eaters and include zooplankton that eat other zooplankton. Tertiary consumers are predators, such as tunas and sharks. Humans fall into this category. Humans are omnivores, which means they eat both plants and animals.

Decomposers feed on dead organic matter. These organisms convert dead organisms to simpler substances. Decomposers include lobsters and large petrels, as well as microscopic bacteria.

Dangerous to the oceanic food web are the concentration of pollutants and harmful organisms that become trapped in sediments where life forms feed. These life forms are fed upon by other life forms, and at each step in the food chain the pollutant becomes more concentrated. Finally, when humans eat these sea animals, they are in danger of serious illness. Diseases such as cholera, hepatitis, and typhoid, can survive and accumulate in certain sea animals. These diseases can be transmitted to humans who eat the infected animals.

Spotlight on Continental Margins

Queensland, Australia and The Great Barrier Reef   The Great Barrier Reef, the longest structure in the world created by living organisms, consists of slightly fewer than 3,000 smaller reefs joined together. It covers approximately 132,974 square miles (344,400 square kilometers), which is almost the size of the state of Kansas. At least 500,000 years old, the reef can be seen from space and was first mapped by the *Apollo 7* astronauts in 1968.

Located at the edge of Australia's continental shelf, the Great Barrier Reef stands in water from 325 to 650 feet (100 to 200 meters) deep. On the landward side is a lagoon. On the seaward side, the continental slope plunges thousands of feet into the deep-ocean basin.

Many of the algae found on the reef live within the bodies of the corals, absorbing sunlight. Red algae, green algae, and kelp grow among the coral skeletons. Grasses and shrubs can be found on many cays, as well as banyan and breadfruit trees. The tree most commonly found is the mangrove.

The reef is home to millions of living creatures, including corals, sea urchins, sea slugs, oysters, and clams. The largest type of clam in the world, the giant clam, is found on the Great Barrier Reef. It weighs up to 1,000 pounds (454 kilograms) and has a diameter of up to 4 feet (1.2 meters). Many species of sea turtles come to the reef to lay their eggs. Parrot fish, squirrelfish, trumpet fish, lionfish, coral trout, and moray eels make the reef their home.

Seabirds nest on the cays and islands. More than 100,000 terns flock together annually on Raine Island. Frigate birds, gannets, and sea eagles can be seen skimming over the waters in search of food.

The sands that line the beaches are valuable to industry, and some people believe that oil lies beneath the shelf. To prevent the reef's

Queensland, Australia and the Great Barrier Reef
Location: The Coral Sea off the northeast coast of Australia
Area: 132,974 square miles (344,400 square kilometers)

destruction, the Australian government established the Great Barrier Reef Marine Park in 1975. The park is the world's largest protected marine area. Visitors are controlled, many areas are reserved only for study, and bird and turtle breeding areas found in the park are closed during breeding season so people do not disturb the animals.

Northwestern Australia and Southeast Asia   On the continental shelf off the coast of northwestern Australia are the islands of Sumatra, Java, Borneo, and the Malaysian Peninsula, the most volcanic islands in the world. Other islands, including New Guinea, New Zealand, and the Philippines, are formed from part of the shelf. South of Java, the slope suddenly plunges into the Indonesian Trench, a deep, steep-sided valley in the ocean floor.

This continental shelf is approximately 140,000 square miles (300,000 square kilometers) and holds the most extensive beds of seagrass in the world, including such species as wireweed and paddleweed. Anchored by the grass, sandbanks over 33 feet (10 meters) thick and many miles (kilometers) long have built up over time.

Blue swimmer-crabs, pen shells, fan mussels, green turtles, and sea snakes are just a few of the marine animals that live over the shelf. Coastal waters yield herring, salmon, sardines, snapper, swordfish, and tuna.

A large colony of dugongs, plant-eating relatives of the manatee, are attracted to the ample supply of seagrass and make this area their home. The dugong population is declining because they are hunted by native peoples for food and are often killed by boat propellers.

In the shallow waters over the shelf, petroleum and natural gas are being extracted. Pearls are harvested here, although in sharply declining volume.

In 1986 the member nations of the South Pacific Forum declared the area a nuclear-free zone in an attempt to halt nuclear testing and prevent the dumping of nuclear waste.

Western United States   The continental margin off the northwestern coast of the United States was partly formed by a dam of rock thrust up by earthquake action about 25 million years ago. Where the dam breaks the surface of the water, it forms the Farallon Islands off San Francisco. The shelf is so narrow here—only about 1 mile (1.6 kilometers) wide—that the heads of many submarine canyons reach almost to the shoreline. Large quantities of sand from the beaches are carried by currents down the canyon walls.

Northwestern Australia and Southeast Asia
Location: Indian and Pacific Oceans
Area: Approximately 140,000 square miles (300,000 square kilometers)

Western United States
Location: Pacific Ocean
Area: Approximately 173,700 square miles (450,000 square kilometers)

Rainfall and runoff from rivers occur only during the winter months. The California Current travels south in the summer, and in winter the Davidson Current appears and moves north.

The North Pacific waters are rich in marine life, including sponges, flying fish, sharks, manta rays, seals, and many species of whales.

Commercial fishing is done all along the coast but primarily in the waters around Alaska. Oil and gas are also obtained from the area.

Northeastern United States   Between 270,000,000 and 60,000,000 years ago, a large dam created by earthquake action was formed off the northeastern coast of the United States. A trench on its landward side was gradually filled in with sediment over time, making it now part of the continental shelf, which measures 71,410 square miles (185,000 square kilometers). Sediment that spilled over the top formed a new continental slope that is unstable and subject to landslides. Few submarine canyons are found here, although the Hudson Canyon, associated with the Hudson River, extends from the river's mouth into the ocean.

Changes in sea level have altered the appearance of the coastline and shelf. Fifteen thousand years ago sea level was much lower and much of the continental shelf in the northeastern United States was exposed. Gradually, as sea levels rose, the shelf was covered by water.

Numerous rivers empty into the Atlantic along this shelf, and the presence of fresh water reduces the ocean's salinity. The warm Gulf Stream current affects water temperature and circulation.

Waters here support a variety of marine life, including sea slugs, starfish, mussels, many species of crabs and lobsters, poisonous toadfish, and sperm whales. Commercially important fish found along this shelf include ocean perch, cod, and haddock. Oil and gas are obtained from the shelf off the coast of Newfoundland and farther north.

The North Sea and Western Europe   The continental shelf off the coast of Europe holds the entire United Kingdom (England and its islands). It measures 212,300 square miles (550,000 square kilometers). Waters over this shelf include the North Sea, the Skagerrak (an arm of the North Sea), and the English Channel. Under the North Sea the shelf slopes gently downward from south to north. Although the southernmost areas are shallow, a deep canyon lies off the mouth of the Humber River, an estuary on the east coast of England. In the northeast is the Norway Deep, or Trough, an underwater canyon running parallel to the Norwegian coast

Northeastern United States
Location: Atlantic Ocean
Area: 71,410 square miles (185,000 square kilometers)

The North Sea and Western Europe
Location: The North Atlantic
Area: 212,300 square miles (550,000 square kilometers)

and into the Skagerrak. Other troughs lie to the west of Ireland. In the north, the coastline is marked by steep cliffs.

Tides are important in the North Sea because they influence ocean traffic. Along the coast of Norway, the tidal range (difference between high tide and low tide) is often less than 3 feet (1 meter). On the French side of the English Channel, tidal ranges of more than 27 feet (8 meters) are common. Tidal currents deposit sand in areas along the coast, causing problems in shipping routes. Several large rivers, such as the Rhine and the Elbe, lower the salinity of the water and create currents where they flow into the sea.

Sediments from the rivers and upwelling from deep, cold waters makes the North Sea rich in nutrients. The rocky shelf supports much algae and plant life, such as kelp, and eel grass. Invertebrates like cockles, mussels, scallops, sponges, and snails thrive in the rocky areas.

More than 170 species of fish live in the North Sea, including sharks, rays, herring, mackerel, haddock, cod, and sole. The fish attract large numbers of sea birds, including puffins, gannets, terns, gulls, and ducks. Among mammals living here are gray seals, harbor seals, dolphins, porpoises, and killer whales.

Fishing has been done in the area since 500 AD. Herring, haddock, plaice, cod, and whiting are commercially important. Atlantic salmon are farmed in some areas.

The North Sea is also the site of offshore oil and gas drilling. By 1989, 149 oil platforms were operated in the North Sea by British, Dutch, Norwegian, Danish, and German companies.

More sand and gravel is removed from the North Sea—24.5 million tons (22 metric tons) annually—than anywhere else in the world. These operations occur close to shore in waters less than 115 feet (35 meters) deep. Lime, another mineral, is mined from the seabed (sea floor). All of these materials are used as construction materials.

The Persian Gulf The Persian Gulf lies between the Arabian Peninsula and Iran. Millions of years ago, it was much larger, but the floor beneath the Persian Gulf is shrinking as the floor beneath its neighbor, the Red Sea, on the opposite side of the peninsula, expands. It is estimated that after another 50,000 years, the Persian Gulf will be completely closed as the peninsula is pushed toward Iran. At one time the floor of the gulf was above sea level. Now it is part of the continental shelf, which measures 92,640 square miles (240,000 square kilometers). No earthquakes or volcanoes are found here, and the seafloor has both muddy and sandy areas.

The Persian Gulf
Location: The Arabian Sea, between Saudi Arabia and Iran
Area: 92,640 square miles (240,000 square kilometers)

Surrounded by desert, the water in the Persian Gulf is warm, salty, and only about 330 feet (100 meters) deep. A small amount of fresh water flows in from the Tigris and Euphrates Rivers, but the climate is so hot that more water is lost from evaporation than is gained.

Large stands of mangrove trees and beds of seagrass are found in the gulf. The mud in which they grow is low in oxygen, so the thickets are not as well developed as those found in other areas.

Few coral reefs are found in the Persian Gulf because the water is too warm. The gulf is home to many kinds of shellfish, such as mussels, shrimp, and oysters. Fish like sardines, anchovies, mackerel, and barracuda are also found here. The largest fish living in the area is the whale shark, which can reach 40 feet (12 meters) in length. Common birds of the gulf include terns, ospreys, and the fish-eating eagle, which travels several thousand miles to Scotland to nest. Porpoises are common, and the narwhal is seen occasionally.

The Persian Gulf has been important for oil production since 1935, and oil platforms dot its surface. Other commercially important minerals and metals found here include salt, copper, and zinc.

Sea cucumbers, shellfish, sardines, and anchovies are all important to the fishing industry. Bahrain, a tiny island in the gulf, has been the source of pearl oysters for 2,000 years. The pearl industry has declined since it became possible to artificially stimulate pearl growth.

Hudson Bay The continental shelf underlying Hudson Bay extends from the Canadian Provinces of Quebec, Manitoba, Ontario, and the Northwest Territories. It measures 480,000 square miles (768,000 square kilometers) and its depth ranges from 120 to 600 feet (36 to 182 meters). A deep canyon cuts through the bay and extends toward Hudson Strait.

The cold waters in Hudson Bay originate in the Arctic. The waters are low in salt because many rivers feed into the bay. From January until May, the bay is covered with floating ice, which in northern regions is slow to melt and makes navigation difficult.

Many fish live in the bay, including cod and salmon. Seabirds found here include ducks, geese, loons, and ptarmigans. Whales frequent the bay, and were at one time hunted. Native peoples still hunt and fish in the area.

During the last half of the twentieth century, the bay and strait became a popular shipping route for goods going to England. Oil and natural gas are being pumped from beneath the shelf in the northern regions, making the shelf important commercially.

Hudson Bay
Location: Northeastern Canada
Area: 480,000 square miles (768,000) square kilometers

For More Information

BOOKS

Carson, Rachel L. *The Sea Around Us,* Rev. ed. New York: Chelsea House, 2006.

Cox, Donald D. *A Naturalist's Guide to Seashore Plants: An Ecology for Eastern North America.* Syracuse, NY: Syracuse University Press, 2003.

Haris, Vernon. *Sessile Animals of the Sea Shore.* New York: Chapman and Hall, 2007.

Peschak, Thomas P. *Wild Seas, Secret Shores of Africa.* Cape Town: Struik Publishers, 2008.

Preston-Mafham, Ken, and Rod Preston-Mafham. *Seashore.* New Edition. New York: HarperCollins Publishers, 2004.

Scientific American, ed. *Oceans: A Scientific American Reader.* Chicago: University Of Chicago Press: 2007.

Worldwatch Institute, ed. *Vital Signs 2003: The Trends That Are Shaping Our Future.* New York: W.W. Norton, 2003.

PERIODICALS

Maynard, Barbara. "Fire in Ice: Natural Gas Locked Up in Methane Hydrates Could Be the World's Next Great Energy Source—If Engineers Can Figure Out How to Extract it Safely." *Popular Mechanics.* 183. 4 April 2006: 40.

ORGANIZATIONS

American Cetacean Society, PO Box 1391, San Pedro, CA 90733, Internet: http://www.acsonline.org.

American Littoral Society, Sandy Hook, Highlands, NJ 07732, Phone: 732-291-0055, Internet: http://www.alsnyc.org.

Center for Marine Conservation, 1725 DeSales Street, NW, Suite 600, Washington, DC 20036, Phone: 202-429-5609; Fax: 202-872-0619, Internet: http://www.cmc-ocean.org.

Environmental Defense Fund, 257 Park Ave. South, New York, NY 10010, Phone: 212-505-2100; Fax: 212-505-2375, Internet: http://www.edf.org.

Environmental Network, 4618 Henry Street, Pittsburgh, PA 15213, Internet: www.environlink.org.

Environmental Protection Agency, 401 M Street, SW, Washington, DC 20460, Phone: 202-260-2090, Internet: http://www.epa.gov.

Friends of the Earth, 1717 Massachusetts Ave. NW, 300, Washington, DC 20036-2002, Phone: 877-843-8687; Fax: 202-783-0444; Internet: http://www.foe.org.

Greenpeace USA, 702 H Street NW, Washington, DC 20001, Phone: 202-462-1177; Fax: Internet: http://www.greenpeace.org.

Sierra Club, 85 2nd Street, 2nd fl., San Francisco, CA 94105, Phone: 415-977-5500; Fax: 415-977-5799 Internet: http://www.sierraclub.org.

World Meteorological Organization, 7bis,avenue de la Paix, Case Postale No. 2300 CH-1211PO Box 2300, Geneva 2, Switzerland, Phone: 41 22 7308111; Fax: 41 22 7308181, Internet: http://www.wmo.ch.

World Wildlife Fund,1250 24th Street NW, Washington, DC 20090-7180, Phone: 202-293-4800; Internet: http://www.wwf.org.

WEB SITES

Discover Magazine. http://www.discovermagazine.com (accessed August 14, 2007).

Journey North Project. http://www.learner.org/jnorth (accessed August 14, 2007).

Monterey Bay Aquarium. http://www.mbayaq.org (accessed August 14, 2007).

National Geographic Society. http://www.nationalgeographic.com (accessed August 14, 2007).

National Oceanic and Atmospheric Administration. http://www.noaa.gov (accessed August 14, 2007).

Oceana. http://www.americanoceans.org (accessed August 14, 2007).

Scientific American Magazine. http://www.sciam.com (accessed August 14, 2007).

Time Magazine. http://time.com (accessed August 14, 2007).

Deciduous Forest

A tree is a large woody plant with one main stem, or trunk, and many branches that lives year after year. A forest is a large number of trees covering at least 25 percent of the area where the tops of the trees, called crowns, interlock forming an enclosure or canopy when the trees mature. Deciduous (dee-SID-joo-uhs) forests primarily consist of deciduous trees, such as oaks, basswoods, and elms. Deciduous trees lose their leaves during cold or very dry seasons, as compared to evergreen trees that keep their leaves year-round, usually for several years at a time.

Temperate deciduous forests grow in areas with cold winters and warm summers. They are generally found in the Northern Hemisphere, the southern most part of South America, and New Zealand. These forests are located primarily in the Great Lakes region and the eastern half of the United States, parts of central and western Europe, parts of Russia, and parts of Japan and China. Tropical deciduous forests grow in areas around the equator where the weather is warm, such as the western coast of Chile and South Island, New Zealand. There are two types of tropical deciduous forests—those that grow in dry climates and those that grow in moist climates. Dry climate forests occur primarily in central India; parts of Brazil; and on the African continent from Angola to Tanzania, northward to the Sudan, and over much of West Africa. Moist climate forests are found primarily in northeastern Australia, eastern India, and parts of Burma, Thailand, and Indonesia.

How Deciduous Forests Develop

Forests evolved during Earth's prehistoric past. Since then, all forests have developed in essentially the same way, by means of a process called succession.

The first forests The first forests evolved from ferns, clubmosses, and other prehistoric plants that, over time, adapted to the surrounding environment and grew more treelike. Trees that preferred a warm, humid, tropical climate developed first, followed by those adapted to drier, cooler weather. The first deciduous trees evolved about 145 million years ago, during the latter part of the Cretaceous period in the Mesozoic Era.

About 1 million years ago during the great Ice Ages, glaciers (slow-moving masses of ice) covered about one-third of the land surface of Earth. Eventually, the glaciers retreated, but not before they had destroyed many of the world's forests and scoured the land of plants. Roughly 12,000 years ago, trees began to repopulate the land that had been covered by ice. In some areas, spruce, larch, ash, and birch trees were among the first species to make a comeback, preparing the way for other trees.

Succession Trees compete with one another for sunlight, water, and nutrients, thus a forest is constantly changing. The process by which one type of plant or tree is gradually replaced by others is called succession. During succession, different species of trees become dominant as time progresses and the environment changes. Succession began following the last Ice Age, and continues today. Succession can occur naturally, when different species of trees become dominant as time progresses and the environment changes. It can also occur from natural disasters, such as forest fires.

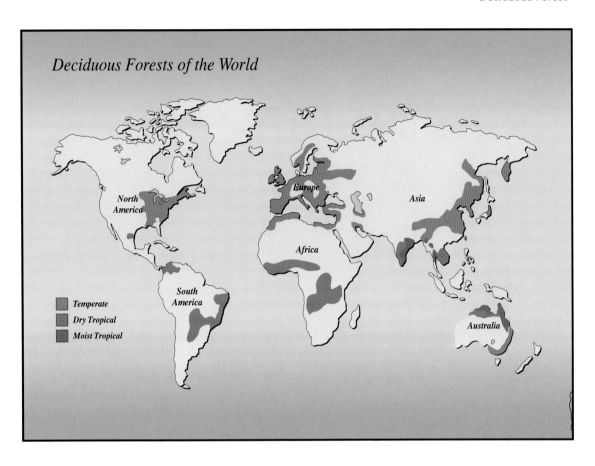

Deciduous Forests of the World

Temperate
Dry Tropical
Moist Tropical

North America
South America
Europe
Africa
Asia
Australia

Primary succession   Primary succession usually begins on bare soil or sand where no plants grew before. When the right amounts of sunlight, moisture, and air temperature are present, seeds begin to germinate (grow). These first plants are often made up of mosses, grasses, and forbs (a nonwoody broad-leaved plant). They continue to grow and eventually form meadows. Over time, and as conditions change, other plants begin to grow such as shrubs and trees. These plants become dominant and replace or take over where grasses and forbs originally grew.

As primary succession continues, pioneer trees (in some cases birch, pine, poplar, and aspen) begin to thrive. These are tall, sun-loving trees, and they quickly take over the meadow. They change the environment by making shade. This allows trees with broader leaves that prefer some protection from the sun, such as red oaks, to take root. If conditions are

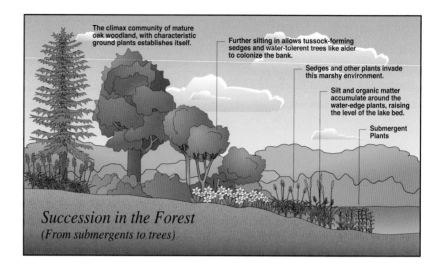

The climax community of mature oak woodland, with characteristic ground plants establishes itself.

Further silting in allows tussock-forming sedges and water-tolerent trees like alder to colonize the bank.

Sedges and other plants invade this marshy environment.

Silt and organic matter accumulate around the water-edge plants, raising the level of the lake bed.

Submergent Plants

Succession in the Forest
(From submergents to trees)

right, a mixed forest of sun-loving and shade-loving trees may continue for many years before more changes occur.

The climax forest   Seedlings from pioneer trees do not grow well in shade; therefore, new pioneer trees do not grow. As the mature trees begin to die from old age, disease, and other causes, the broad-leaved trees become dominant. The shade from these broad-leaved trees can be too dense for their own seedlings too. As a result, seedlings from trees that prefer heavy shade, such as beech and sugar maple, begin to thrive and dominate the forest. These trees produce such deep shade that only those trees or plants that can survive in complete shade will succeed. When this happens, the result is a climax forest—one in which certain species of trees characteristic of the ecological conditions of an area are dominant.

Few true climax forests actually exist because forests are dynamic ecosystems and changes take place that interfere with a forest's stability. Fires, floods, high winds, and people can all destroy a single tree to acres of trees. Glaciers can mow them down; volcanoes can smother them with ash or molten rock or knock them over with explosive force. Then the process of succession starts over.

Secondary succession   Land stripped of trees will eventually be covered with them again if left alone. This is called secondary succession and can take place more quickly than primary succession. Seeds from other forests in neighboring regions are blown by the wind or carried by animals to the site. Soon, the seeds take root and seedlings sprout, and the process begins again.

Kinds of Deciduous Forests

Deciduous forests are broadly classified according to the climate of the region in which they grow—temperate, dry tropical, or moist tropical.

Temperate deciduous forest   Temperate climates are moderate, and temperate deciduous forests can be categorized in terms of the species of trees that are most common. The following three types are common in North America, and similar species predominate in Europe and Asia:

One of the common temperate region deciduous trees is the beech. IMAGE COPYRIGHT SERGE LAMERE, 2007. USED UNDER LICENSE FROM SHUTTERSTOCK.COM.

- Beech-maple: American beech and sugar maple forests mixed with some conifers (trees bearing cones) are found in the southern Great Lakes region, in New England, and in southeastern Canada.
- Oak-hickory: In the southern United States, oaks, such as white oak and chestnut oak, are dominant. Farther west, red oak and black oak are mixed with hickory.
- Mixed mesophytic: Mesophytic means a forest that requires only a moderate amount of water, such as forests in the Appalachian Mountains. Mixed mesophytic forests can be dominated by any of ten or more species of trees, such as buckeye, magnolia, birch, ash, black cherry, sugar maple, and scattered evergreen conifers such as hemlock and white pine.

Dry tropical deciduous forest   Dry tropical deciduous forests occur in regions with long, severe dry seasons, such as the savannas (grasslands) of Africa. The tallest trees are shorter and more twisted than those in a temperate forest, and the bark is thicker. Some trees may store water in their trunks. During the dry season, the trees lose their leaves and many produce flowers. Some, such as wattle trees in Australia, have adapted by producing thorns instead of many leaves.

This Land is My Land

Life in the forest is a constant struggle for food and living space, even among the trees. All around the foot of almost any tree are the seedlings of other trees, ready to take over the space if they can. Some trees have evolved ways to fight back. The black walnut, for instance, has a powerful poison in its leaves, roots, and nutshells. This poison kills the roots of any plants trying to grow in the same soil. Even if the tree is removed, the poison remains in the soil for a long time.

Moist tropical deciduous forest Moist deciduous forests are found in tropical regions where both rainy and dry seasons occur during the year. These forests are different from tropical rain forests in that the trees, including teak and rosewood, are not as tall and have rather thick bark. In the first month of the dry season the leaves fall. New leaves sprout just before the rainy season begins.

Climate

The three types of climates in which deciduous trees grow are temperate, dry tropical, and moist tropical.

Temperate climate Temperate climates, such as in the northeastern United States, are moderate. Winters are cold and summers are warm with few extremely cold and hot days. The average temperature of a temperate deciduous forest is about 50°F (10°C), due to the rare extreme temperatures during the summer and winter.

There is plenty of moisture and few long, dry periods. A temperate forest usually requires at least 20 inches (51 centimeters) of precipitation (rain, snow, or sleet) each year, though most of these forests average between 30 to 60 inches (76 to 152 centimeters). The weather in a temperate climate can be very unpredictable. Precipitation usually occurs throughout the year, but much of it may fall as part of a severe storm system.

Temperate climates have four distinct seasons—spring, summer, fall, and winter. Warm weather begins in spring and temperatures gradually increase through the summer months. In the fall, the cooler weather takes over, and temperatures gradually drop to winter's lows. During these cooler months the leaves of deciduous trees turn colors and then drop off. In winter, the trees are bare.

Dry tropical climate In dry tropical climates, such as that in parts of India and Africa, the drop in precipitation is often accompanied by hotter temperatures. The length of the dry period and the level of heat help determine the type of trees that will grow there. In Tanzania, for example, severe dry periods may last up to seven months. Precipitation is often undependable, and when it does occur it may fall in large amounts. In India, for example, as much as 35 inches (89 centimeters) of rain may fall in a single 24-hour period. Leaves fall from the trees at the start of the dry period and grow again when the rains come.

Moist tropical climate   In tropical regions where moist climates occur, such as Myanmar and parts of India, temperatures remain high, but precipitation is more regular and predictable. In a rain forest, rain falls year-round, but in a moist tropical climate, dry periods occur. The dry periods are not as long or severe as in a dry tropical climate. As in dry climates, the trees shed their leaves when the dry period begins. New growth begins with the rains.

Geography of Deciduous Forests

The geography of deciduous forests includes landforms, elevation, soil, and water resources.

The blanket of snow keeps the soil warm, allowing bacteria and other organisms to continue to break down dead plant matter. IMAGE COPYRIGHT ANDREY STEPANOV, 2007. USED UNDER LICENSE FROM SHUTTERSTOCK.COM.

Surviving the Ice Ages

During prehistoric times, before the great Ice Ages, North America and northern Europe were covered in deciduous trees such as walnut, hickory, sycamore, oak, maple, and chestnut. The climate was warmer than that of present times. As the ice advanced, the more delicate trees were forced to retreat to the south. In North America this was possible because the mountain ranges run north and south, which allowed the trees to spread along the valleys between them. In Europe, however, the mountains tend to run east and west, so the trees were trapped. For this reason, many European species did not survive, and the deciduous forests of Europe have fewer tree species than those of North America.

Landforms   In the Northern Hemisphere, the landscape over which temperate deciduous forests grow includes mountains, valleys, rolling hills, and flat plateaus.

In the Southern Hemisphere, dry deciduous forests tend to occur near grasslands where the land is rolling or more nearly level. Moist deciduous forests are often found on mountainsides or rolling hills.

Elevation   Elevation plays a major role in determining whether forest vegetation will survive because temperature can decrease rapidly with height. In addition, mountains tend to have a wetter climate than flat or low lands. On mountainsides, forests vary, mostly becoming smaller in overall size, and in individual tree size. The moist conditions appeal to lichens, mosses, and ferns, and these plants tend to thrive. Eventually, the elevation reaches a point where no tree can survive—this boundary is called the timberline or treeline. The timberline is contingent on temperature, not height, so it can occur in different places for different areas. For example, in Sierra Nevada, the timberline is located at 11,500 feet (3,500 meters), where as in the central Alps of Europe, the timberline is located at 6,800 feet (2,000 meters).

Soil   The soil in temperate deciduous forests tends to be deep and rich with a wide variety of nutrients because it receives a new blanket of leaves every autumn. The foliage of low-lying plants dies off and adds its own nutrient characteristics to the soil. During the winter, snow blankets the ground. Beneath its protective layer, bacteria, earthworms, and insects continue to break down the dead vegetation, creating dark humus. Humus is the spongy matter produced when the remains of plants and animals are broken down. It contains chemicals, like nitrogen, that are vital to plant growth, and it is able to absorb water. Oak leaves are difficult to break down so the soil beneath oak trees is not as rich.

In tropical climates, the soil differs from region to region. Soils in dry grasslands are sandy and dusty. Long, dry periods between the rainy seasons inhibits decomposition of dead plant matter and the release of nutrients, making the soil less rich. Moist tropical regions may have poor soil because topsoil is often washed away during heavy rains. Also, the shade is so dense that few smaller plants may grow there.

The presence of trees helps protect soil from erosion by holding it in place. Fallen trees are important in conserving and cycling nutrients and in reducing erosion. Trees also create windbreaks, which help prevent topsoil from being blown away.

Water resources   In temperate regions, water resources include rivers, streams, springs, lakes, and ponds. In tropical regions, rivers, seasonal streams, and rain are often the primary sources of water.

Squirrels, as well as chipmunks, are unwitting planters of deciduous trees. They bury nuts in the ground to save them for a later meal, but don't always return to dig them back up. COPYRIGHT © 2007 KELLY A. QUIN.

Plant Life

Most forests contain a mixture of several types of trees and plants, and deciduous forests are no different. Stands (groups) of coniferous and non-coniferous evergreen trees may exist within their boundaries.

The trees and smaller plants in a forest grow to different heights, forming layers. The crowns of the tallest trees create a canopy, or roof. In the deciduous forests of eastern North America, the tallest trees are often oaks and hickories. Beneath their canopy grow shorter, shade-tolerant trees, such as maples. This shorter layer is called the understory. The next layer, only a few feet off the ground, is composed of small shrubs, such as junipers, and some flowering plants. The very lowest layer consists of small plants that live atop the soil.

In addition to trees, plant life within most deciduous forests includes bacteria; algae, fungi, lichens and green plants other than trees.

Algae, fungi, and lichens   Algae (AL-jee), fungi (FUN ji), and lichens (LY-kens) do not fit neatly into either the plant or animal category.

Algae   Most algae are single-celled organisms, although some are multi-cellular, and have the ability to make their own food. During a process called

A Nose for Truffles

In France, pigs, dogs, and even goats are trained to hunt truffles. A truffle is a type of edible fungus that grows under the soil in deciduous woodlands. Pigs are trained to recognize the smell of a truffle and sound an alarm when they find one. The truffles are then dug up and sold to people who consider them a delicacy.

photosynthesis (foh-toh-SIHN-thuh-sihs), they use energy from sunlight to change water and carbon dioxide (from the air) into the sugars and starches they require as food. Other algae may absorb nutrients from their surroundings. Although most algae are water plants, blue-green algae, which are actually bacteria, do appear in woodlands. They survive as spores (single cells that have the ability to grow into a new organism) during dry periods, and return to life as soon as it rains.

Fungi   Fungi cannot make their own food by means of photosynthesis. Some, like molds and mushrooms, obtain nutrients from dead or decaying organic matter (material derived from living organisms). They assist in the decomposition of this matter, thereby releasing the nutrients needed by other plants. Other types of fungi are parasites, attaching themselves to other living things. Fungi reproduce by means of spores.

Fungi prefer moist, dim environments, and they thrive in shadowy forests of temperate regions. Common types of fungi include jack-o-lanterns, pear-shaped puffballs, fawn mushrooms, turkey tails, and destroying angels. Some, like chantarelles, grow directly on the soil, while others grow on the trunks of trees. Many, such as the fly agaric, are mushroomlike. Still others,

Mushrooms help speed forest decay of leaf matter on the forest floor, which enriches the soil and enables new growth.
IMAGE COPYRIGHT FOTOSAV, 2007. USED UNDER LICENSE FROM SHUTTERSTOCK.COM.

such as tree ears, resemble a porch roof as they protrude from tree trunks. Some mycorrhizae, surround the roots of certain trees, such as beeches and oaks, and help the roots absorb nutrients from the soil.

Lichens   Lichens are actually combinations of algae and fungi that live in cooperation. The fungi surround the algae cells. The algae obtain food for themselves and the fungi by means of photosynthesis. It is not known if the fungi aid the algae organisms, although they appear to provide them with protection and moisture.

Lichens often appear on rocks and other woodland surfaces such as tree trunks and limbs. They are common in all types of forests and seem able to survive most climatic conditions. Lichens are a good indicator of air quality because many species will not grow in the presence of air pollution.

Green plants other than trees   Most green plants need several basic things to grow: sunlight, air, water, warmth, and nutrients. In deciduous woodlands, water and warmth are often abundant, at least seasonally. Light may be more scarce, but deciduous trees tend to be well-spaced, allowing sunlight to reach the forest floor. The remaining nutrients, primarily nitrogen, phosphorus, and potassium, are obtained from the soil and may not always be in large supply.

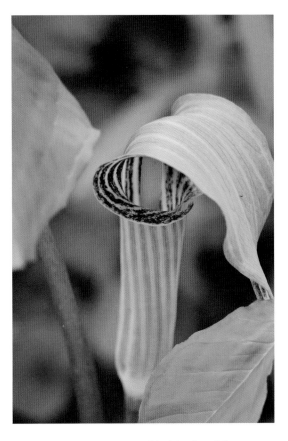

A jack-in-the-pulpit grows comfortably in the shade provided by the shady trees of a deciduous forest. IMAGE COPYRIGHT SHARON D, 2007. USED UNDER LICENSE FROM SHUTTERSTOCK.COM.

Woodlands are home to both annual and perennial plants. Annuals live only one year or one growing season. Perennials live at least two years or two growing seasons, often appearing to die when the climate becomes too cold or too dry, but returning to life when conditions improve.

Common deciduous forest green plants   In temperate climates, many species of small shrubs, mosses, ferns, herbs, and brambles thrive beneath the trees, along the edges of the forest, and in clearings. They include wildflowers such as lady's slipper and columbines, and shrubs such as witch hazel, sumac, and spicebush. Shade-loving plants also grow beneath the trees. These include mayapple, jack-in-the-pulpit, poison ivy, and many species of ferns.

Immortal Trees?

Trees have the ability to continue growing all their lives. This means that, in theory, they could live forever. When a tree dies, its death is usually caused by something in its environment, such as fire, wind, lightning, extremely dry periods, disease, insects, or being cut by humans. As a tree ages, it becomes more susceptible to disease and pests, and most trees die of several causes.

Growing season   Green plants that grow close to the forest floor in temperate climates, such as the anemone, skunk cabbage, and trillium, appear in early spring when full sun can reach them. The primrose and the bluebell quickly bloom as the trees' leafy canopy begins to form overhead. Later, when the trees are in full leaf, only the shade-loving plants, such as fern, moss, and ivy, will thrive. Growth continues throughout the summer then stops in autumn. Annuals die, leaving their seeds to carry through the winter. Although the foliage (above ground growth such as leaves and stems) of perennials die, their roots remain alive to send up shoots again the following spring.

In tropical climates, both dry and moist, the growing season begins just before the onset of the rainy season. It ends as the dry season begins. As in temperate climates, annuals die. Perennials usually have some method of storing water, such as a large taproot (a large center root that grows downward), that enables them to survive long periods without rain.

Reproduction   Most green plants reproduce by means of pollination (the transfer of pollen from the male reproductive flower part to the female). Pollen is carried by visiting animals, such as birds or insects, or by the wind, which blows it from one flower to another. As the growing season comes to an end, most green plants produce seeds. The seed's hard outer covering protects it during cold winters or long dry seasons.

A few woodland plants, such as ferns, reproduce by means of rhizomes, long, rootlike stems that spread out below ground. These stems develop their own root systems and send up sprouts that develop into new plants. They also reproduce by spores that develop on the undersides of the leaf. When these spores mature, they are released from the plant and fall to settle on the soil where they begin to grow into a new fern plant.

In moist tropical regions, a layer of smaller evergreen trees often grows beneath the deciduous canopy. Both high- and low-climbing vines, and most smaller plants may in some cases be almost completely absent. In dry tropical regions, the lower layers may consist of thorny shrubs, cacti, grasses, and small palms.

Deciduous trees   Deciduous trees lose their leaves, which tend to be broad and flat, during cold or very dry periods. When temperatures are warm year-round and rainfall is constant, such as in a rain forest, these same trees may become evergreen and keep their leaves year-round. Trees are hardy perennials, but a number of factors can affect their life spans. Some of these are due to the environment, such as lack of sunlight or water, severe climate changes, disease, and fires. Many trees have short lives due to human consumption for land and timber.

The fact that most trees have a single strong stem, or trunk, gives them an advantage over smaller woody plants in that most of their growth is directed upward. Conifers often devote their energy to growing ever taller, while deciduous trees spread out their limbs and branches from their trunks to create a crown of leaves.

During autumn, trees in temperate regions lose the green color in their leaves because chlorophyll, a green substance in the leaves, breaks down. As a result, other colors present in the leaves are then visible, creating the brilliant hues of the autumn forest. This color change is brought on by shorter days, where hours of sunlight are decreased, and cooler temperatures.

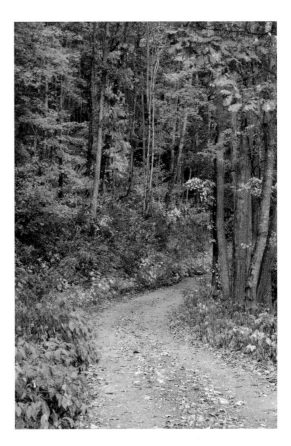

In autumn, tree leaves in deciduous forests provide a scene of brilliant colors. IMAGE COPYRIGHT JILL LANG, 2007. USED UNDER LICENSE FROM SHUTTERSTOCK.COM.

Each year a deciduous tree grows, its trunk is thickened with a new layer, or ring, of vessels and other conduction cells that carry water and nutrients from the roots to the branches. When a tree is cut down, its age can be determined by how many of these rings are present. As a tree ages, the rings from the center outward become hardened to produce a sturdy core. In temperate climates, deciduous trees may grow from 2 to 5 feet (0.6 to 1.5 meters) in diameter and 60 to 100 feet (18 to 30 meters) in height during their life span.

Common deciduous trees Typical deciduous trees in temperate regions include the ash, oak, maple, elm, poplar, birch, ginkgo, and magnolia. Tropical deciduous trees include the acacia, southern beech, baobab, teak, casuarina, cannonball, ebony, peepul, sycamore, and rosewood.

Oak Oaks are perhaps the best-known deciduous trees in temperate regions. Oaks are very adaptable to different environmental conditions. They are found in dry sandy plains to coastal swamps. All species of

Cloning Trees

A clone is an exact genetic copy of its "parent," because it is grown from one of the parent's cells. Cloning may someday become an important part of the forest industry. Cells from a superior adult tree could be cloned in a laboratory and the resulting seedlings planted on tree farms. As the trees grew, they would resemble the parent tree and be more uniform than a natural forest. Cloned trees have been grown from cells of redwood, Douglas fir, apple, citrus, and poplar trees.

oak have at least one thing in common—the acorn, or nut, that bears a scaly cap. The leaves of some oaks, such as the red oak, turn a brilliant color in autumn, while others are less colorful. Oaks are the dominant trees of central and western Europe. They are known for their excellent timber, which is valued for furniture and hardwood floors.

Acacia Acacia (uh-KAY-shuh) trees are called thorn trees in Africa, wattles in Australia, and mimosas in North America and Europe. They are found in dry tropical climates as they can tolerate long, dry periods but they do not grow very tall. Acacias usually have an umbrella shape, yellow flowers, and sharp spines. Their seeds are used by both humans and animals for food.

Baobab Found in dry tropical regions, the baobab (BA-oh-bab) has a soft, spongy trunk and lower branches for storing large quantities of water. The trees lose their leaves during the dry seasons, which reduces water loss.

Baobabs do not grow very tall—about 16 to 82 feet (5 to 25 meters) in height. The trunk is often wide and may reach 23 feet (7 meters) in diameter. Giant baobabs are several thousand years old. Many animals

The baobab is known for its ability to store gallons of water inside its trunk, which it does to survive long, dry spells frequent to its habitat. IMAGE COPYRIGHT ROBERT HARDHOLT, 2007. USED UNDER LICENSE FROM SHUTTERSTOCK.COM.

use the baobab for food and shelter, and pollination of its flowers is done by bats.

Teak   The teak is native to India, Myanmar, and Thailand, where it prefers well-drained soils. It is a large tree with a spreading crown and small white flowers. Mature trees may reach 98 to 131 feet (30 to 40 meters) in height. Teak timber is known for being indestructible, and is commonly used in furniture, flooring, and other woodworking projects.

Growing season   Moisture and temperature conditions are two important environmental factors affecting the growing season of deciduous trees. In temperate climates, the growing season takes place during the spring and summer and may last five to seven months. Some trees, such as beech and maple, produce their leaves earlier in the season, while oaks produce leaves later. In the autumn, cooler temperatures make it harder to absorb the water needed to maintain broad leaves. Broad leaves tend to lose a lot of water into the atmosphere. For these reasons and other factors including temperature and day length, the leaves die and fall off.

In tropical climates, growth slows or stops during hot, dry periods and the trees drop their leaves. Growth begins again when the rain comes. When dry periods are very long, trees in these areas may be stunted and develop very thick bark to protect against moisture loss.

Reproduction   Trees are divided into two groups according to how they bear their seeds. Gymnosperms produce seeds that are often collected together into cones. Most gymnosperms are conifers. In contrast, angiosperms have flowers and produce their seeds inside a fruit. Deciduous trees are usually angiosperms.

In temperate regions, many deciduous trees drop their seeds in the autumn. Some seeds may be contained in fruits in nut form, like acorns and beechnuts, or they may have papery wings, like the fruits of sycamores. In tropical regions, seeds fall just before or during the dry periods.

Endangered species   Trees can be threatened by natural dangers, such as forest fires, animals, and diseases, as well as by humans. Fires are more of a threat in dry climates, while animals and diseases are prevalent in all climates. For example, when deer populations get too large, they can destroy forests by eating wildflowers and tree seedlings. The caterpillar of the gypsy moth eats the leaves from a variety of tree species. If enough of these insects attack a stand of trees, all the leaves are eaten and the trees die. Dutch elm disease, a fungus transmitted by the elm bark beetle first seen in Holland in 1921, destroyed millions of elm trees in the United States in 1930. It was then

Chestnut Blight in the United States

Until 1940 the United States was home to the American chestnut tree, a graceful species with creamy white blossoms that often grew more than 100 feet (30 meters) tall. In 1904 foreign chestnut trees were imported into New York. These trees carried a fungus, called chestnut blight, which soon spread to American chestnuts. Over the next 40 years the fungus destroyed almost all the American chestnuts in the eastern half of the country.

Fortunately, the blight did not travel to the far west, and scattered, healthy American chestnuts are still found there. The roots of stricken chestnuts survived because the blight could not reach them underground. They continue to send up shoots but the shoots soon die because the fungus is still in the soil. Researchers are attempting to cross the American chestnut with other species resistant to the fungus in hopes of reestablishing the trees.

introduced to England in logs exported from the United States. It killed many elms there as well.

Pollution is a threat to birch, beech, ash, and sugar maple trees in the northeastern United States. Pollution appears to weaken the trees so that pests and diseases overtake them more easily. In western Europe, the beech is in decline.

Animal Life

From their roots to their tips, deciduous trees support a wide range of plant-eating animals and wildlife, while many other types of animals live among or beneath the trees. The animals can be classified as microorganisms, invertebrates, amphibians, reptiles, birds, and mammals.

Microorganisms   A microorganism is an animal, such as a protozoan, that cannot be seen without the aid of a microscope. Every forest is host to millions of these tiny creatures. Microscopic roundworms, or nematodes, for example, live by the thousands in small areas of soil in deciduous forests and aid the process of decomposition.

Bacteria   Bacteria are always present in woodland soil where they help decompose dead plant and animal matter. In temperate climates, bacteria help create nutrient-rich humus. Fewer bacteria are at work in dry climates or in moist climates with long dry seasons.

Invertebrates   Animals without backbones are called invertebrates. They include simple animals, such as worms, and more complex animals, such as wasps and snails. Certain groups of invertebrates must spend part of their lives in water. These types are not found in trees, but in ponds, lakes, and streams, or in pools of rainwater.

Some invertebrates, such as beetles, are well adapted to life in dry tropical forests. They have an external skeleton, a hard shell made from a substance called chitin (KY-tin). Chitin is like armor and is usually waterproof, protecting against the heat of the sun and preventing the animal from drying out. These same invertebrates do not survive as well in temperate forests because many adults die in the cold of winter. Their well-protected eggs or larvae may survive until the spring.

Common deciduous forest invertebrates Invertebrates found in temperate forests include the tent caterpillar, the woolly bear caterpillar, the luna moth, the stag beetle, and the wolf spider. Other common invertebrates include the earthworm, the slug, the forest snail, and the acorn snail.

In tropical climates, many species of invertebrates, including the silkworm, inhabit moist forests. Dry climates have fewer insects; termites and grasshoppers are common, as are many species of caterpillars.

Food Many invertebrates eat plants or decaying animal matter. The larvae of insects, such as caterpillars, are the primary leaf eaters in the deciduous forest. The tent caterpillar, the larvae form of a moth, spins a large, filmy, tent-like cocoon around a tree branch, which it soon picks clean. Weevils drill holes in acorns, which their larvae use for food, thus destroying the seed of the oak. Bees gather pollen and nectar (sweet liquid) from flowers, as do butterflies and moths, helping produce new plants through pollination. Arachnids (spiders), which are carnivores (meat eaters), prey on insects. Larger species may even eat small lizards, mice, and birds.

Reproduction Most invertebrates have a four-part life cycle. The first stage of this cycle is spent as an egg. The egg's shell is usually tough and resistant to long dry spells in tropical climates. After a rain and during a period of plant growth, the egg hatches. The second stage is the larva (such as a caterpillar). This may be divided into several stages between which there is a shedding of the animal's outer skin. Larvae often spend their stage below ground where it is cooler and moister than on the surface. The pupal, or third stage, is spent hibernating within a casing (such as a cocoon). When the animal emerges from this casing, it is an adult.

The Destructive Hitchhiker

In 1996, 2,400 trees in Brooklyn and Amityville, New York, were destroyed when the Asian long-horned beetle turned up in the United States. The 2-inch- (5-centimeter-) long insect lays its eggs just under the bark of maple, ash, elm, and horse chestnut trees. When the larvae hatch and seek food, they cut off vital nutrients to the trees starving them to death. It is believed that the beetle first made its way to this country in the wood packing materials of goods shipped from China.

In 1998 this black and white beetle was discovered in Chicago, Illinois. In an effort to stop the insect's spread, 470 trees had to be cut down and burned. Burning is done during the winter months while the beetle is inactive and cannot escape. Hopefully all the infested trees were identified and destroyed, but there is no guarantee the beetles will not turn up somewhere else in the future.

Hide and Seek

Many animals use camouflage (KAH-mah-flahj; protective coloration) to disguise themselves from predators. Some predators camouflage themselves to lurk among tree leaves, waiting for their prey to pass by. The yellow color of the goldenrod spider, for example, enables it to hide in goldenrod flowers where it can sneak up on an insect sipping the flower's nectar.

Amphibians   Amphibians are vertebrates (animals with backbones) that spend part, if not most, of their lives in water. Frogs, toads, and salamanders live in significant numbers in temperate and moist tropical deciduous forests. Frogs and toads can also be found in dry tropical forests if there is a dependable source of water.

Because amphibians breathe through their skin, and only moist skin can absorb oxygen, they must remain close to a water source. Mating, egg-laying, and young-adulthood all take place in ponds, lakes, or pools of rainwater. Offspring that survive and reach maturity leave the pools for dry land where they feed on both plants and insects. In dry tropical forests, amphibians must find shade during the day or risk dying in the heat of the sun.

Amphibians are cold-blooded animals, which means their bodies are about the same temperature as their environment. They need a warm environment in order to be active. As temperatures get cooler, they slow down and seek shelter. In temperate climates, amphibians hibernate (remain inactive) during winter months. In hot, dry climates, amphibians go through estivation, a similar inactive period. While the soil is still moist from the rain, they dig themselves a foot or more into the ground, where they remain until the rains return. Only their nostrils remain open to the surface.

Common deciduous forest amphibians   Amphibians common in temperate forests include spring peepers (tiny frogs that climb trees), spotted newts, Fowler's toads, and marble salamanders. The African bullfrog is common to dry forests in Africa and the Pipid toad in South America. The flying frog is found in moist forests in India. It has a web of skin on both sides that begins at the wrist and attaches to the ankle. This skin acts as a parachute and enables the frogs to glide from one branch to another.

Food   Adult amphibians are usually carnivorous, feeding on insects, slugs, and worms. Salamanders that live in water suck their prey into their mouths. Those that live on land have long, sticky tongues to capture food. Amphibian larvae are mostly herbivorous (plant eaters), feeding on vegetation. Frogs and toads are omnivores (both plant and meat eating) feeding on algae, plants, and insects such as mosquitoes.

Reproduction   Mating and egg-laying for amphibians must take place in water. Male sperm are deposited in the water, often right on top

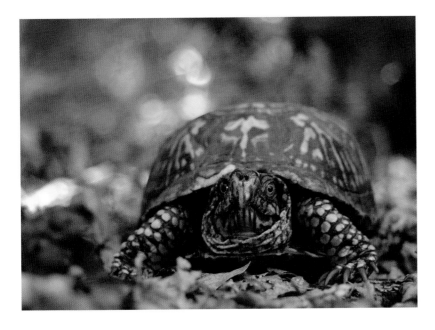

Box turtles are common deciduous forest residents, enjoying insects and nearly all vegetable matter they find on the forest floor. IMAGE COPYRIGHT JAMIE WILSON, 2007. USED UNDER LICENSE FROM SHUTTERSTOCK.COM.

of the female's eggs. As the young develop into larvae and young adults, they have gills for breathing.

Reptiles   Reptiles that live in deciduous forests include many species of snakes, lizards, and turtles. The body temperature of a reptile changes with the temperature of the surrounding environment. Early in the day, they expose as much of their bodies as possible to the sun for warmth. As temperatures climb, they begin to seek shade. During hot, dry periods, they must find shade or a hole in which to wait for cooler weather. During chilly nights, they become sluggish. In temperate climates, snakes may hibernate in burrows during the long winter.

Common deciduous forest reptiles   Temperate forest reptiles in eastern North America include the five-lined skink, eastern box turtle, and garter snake. Reptiles found in dry tropical forests include the night adder, puff adder, Gabonan adder, and the agama lizard. Moist tropical forests are home to pythons and the calot lizard.

Food   A lizard's diet varies, depending upon the species. Some have long tongues with sticky tips and specialize in insects. Many are carnivores that eat small mammals and birds. The water they need is usually obtained from the food they eat.

Blue jays are a familiar, and frequently noisy, deciduous forest resident. IMAGE COPYRIGHT BOB BLANCHARD, 2007. USED UNDER LICENSE FROM SHUTTERSTOCK.COM.

All snakes are carnivores. One large meal (such as a rabbit, rat, or bird) can last them days or weeks. Constrictors squeeze their prey to death, while other snakes kill their prey with venom (poison) injected through the snake's fangs.

Reproduction   Reptile eggs are leathery and tough. Offspring are seldom cared for by the parents. Some females remain with their eggs, but most bury them in a hole and leave. The young are left to hatch by themselves. Once free of the eggs, the babies dig themselves out of the hole and begin life on their own.

Birds   All forests have bird populations. Some species, such as the grosbeak, are migratory, which means they travel from one seasonal breeding place to another. During excessively cold or dry periods, most birds fly to more comfortable regions. Others, such as the blue jay, prefer to stay in the same area year-round.

Feathers protect birds not only from cold winters but from tropical heat. Air trapped between layers of feathers acts as insulation against both climates.

Common deciduous forest birds   In temperate forests, common birds include screech owls, great horned owls, hummingbirds, woodpeckers, nuthatches, woodthrushes, American redstarts, hawks, blue jays, cardinals, scarlet tanagers, chickadees, and turkey vultures.

Wrens, falcons, weaverbirds, and chats are found in dry tropical forests. In the moist deciduous forests of Australia, currawongs build nests of sticks in the eucalyptus trees. Thrush are common in India.

Jay   Most species of jays are found in the Northern Hemisphere but they are also common in South America, Eurasia, and Africa. Their feathers may be drab or brightly colored, such as those of the North American blue jay. Many have crests and long tail feathers. They eat both plant matter and insects, and some species eat the eggs of other birds.

Jays are known for their bold, aggressive behavior and loud, harsh voices. Gangs of jays often harass other birds and even humans.

Falcon   Found all over the world, falcons are birds of prey. They are characterized by long, pointed wings and the ability to fly very fast. Some species fly to a high altitude and then dive on their prey, killing it with the

Falcons have exceptional vision and are adept flyers. IMAGE COPYRIGHT PETER BARRETT, 2007. USED UNDER LICENSE FROM SHUTTERSTOCK.COM.

powerful blow of their clenched talons. A peregrine falcon's dive can reach more than 200 miles (322 kilometers) per hour during an attack.

The sport of falconry (training falcons to hunt other animals) originated in the East with the earliest records dating back to 700 BC in China. Falconry was also popular in Japan, Mongolia, Korea, and Russia.

Food   Birds are found in greater variety and numbers where there is an ample supply of seeds, berries, and insects. Different birds seek food in different layers of the forest. Orioles and tanagers, for example, hunt for food high in the canopy. The white-breasted nuthatch hunts for insects along the trunks of the trees, and towhees dig around on the ground. Some birds that live year-round in temperate climates such as chickadees and blue jays may hide seeds in holes in trees where they can find them during the cold months. This hiding of seeds is called caching.

Reproduction   In dry tropical climates, such as that in most of Australia, birds adapt their breeding habits to periods of rainfall and breeding cycles may be far apart.

Birds are free to fly away from uncomfortable temperatures during the most of the year, but the breeding cycle dictates when they can travel. They must remain in the same spot from the time nest building begins until the fledgling birds can fly, a period of many weeks.

Raccoons eat a varied diet that includes berries, fruits, insects, small mammals, and fish.
IMAGE COPYRIGHT MARKUS JABS, 2007. USED UNDER LICENSE FROM SHUTTERSTOCK.COM.

Parents usually sit on the nest to protect the eggs from heat or cold. During very hot weather, the parents may stand over the nest to give the eggs or the nestlings shade.

Mammals Mammals are vertebrates that have hair and bear live young. Only a few large mammals, such as bear and deer, live in temperate deciduous forests. Several small mammals, including mice, squirrels, woodchucks, and foxes, make their homes there. During the cold winters, many mammals burrow underground or find some other kind of shelter. Squirrels, for example, build nests high in the forest canopy. Some mammals, like bears, hibernate. In dry tropical climates, small mammals, such as rodents, may estivate (be very inactive) during the dry season.

Common deciduous forest mammals Temperate forests are home to shrews, wood-mice, gray foxes, chipmunks, ground squirrels, badgers, black bears, silver-haired bats, raccoons, opossums, weasels, cottontail rabbits, gray squirrels, skunks, flying squirrels, and bobcats.

Dry deciduous forests support grazing animals, such as zebras and gazelles, which feed on the grasses that grow beneath the widely spaced trees. In the moist deciduous forests of Australia, red and gray kangaroos browse on leafy foliage. Wombats, opossums, and koalas live among the trees. Tigers are common in the moist forests of Asia, as are elephants and buffalo.

Raccoon Raccoons are medium-sized furry mammals with stout bodies, short legs, and long, bushy tails. They are perhaps best known for the black "mask" around their eyes and their proficiency as burglars. They prefer living in the woods where they hunt rodents, birds and bird eggs, berries, fruit, and other plant matter. They also love corn, melons and other foods of civilized life, which makes them expert raiders of suburban gardens and garbage cans.

Raccoons live in dens made in hollow trees. This is where they spend the daylight hours, and they go out to hunt at night. They sleep more during cold seasons, but they do not hibernate. Intelligent and curious animals, raccoons are hunted for their fur and meat.

Tiger   The tiger is one of the largest and strongest carnivores. They can grow more than 9 feet (2.7 meters) from nose to tail and weigh as much as 500 pounds (227 kilograms). They are found in the Asia wild, where they prey on hoofed animals, such as wild deer and pigs, as well as fish, birds, leopards and, occasionally, bears. Although tigers are only successful in one or two attacks out of twenty, they sustain themselves by their ability to eat up to 80 pounds (36 kilograms) in one sitting. Only 5,000 to 7,000 specimens of tigers exist. Their population has decreased by 95 percent since the turn of the twentieth century, mostly due to habitat destruction.

Food   Some mammals, such as mice, eat plants and insects. Others, like squirrels and hedgehogs, eat bird and reptile eggs and young. Many smaller mammals do not need to drink water as often because they obtain moisture from the food they eat.

Reproduction   The young of mammals develop inside the mother's body. In this way they are protected from heat, cold, and predators. Mammals produce milk to feed their young. Those that live in dens must remain nearby until the young can survive on their own. In temperate forests, the young are usually born in the spring so they have many warm months ahead in which to grow strong.

Endangered species   In Asia, South America, and Africa, all the big cats, including tigers, leopards, and cheetahs, are endangered as humans encroach on their habitats. In some parts of the United States and Canada, the timber wolf remains threatened. In Australia, the koala and some species of kangaroos are threatened, as is the elephant in Africa and Asia. In some areas the animals are overhunted; in others their habitats are disappearing.

Human Life

Humans are creatures of the forest. Until they learned to hunt, humans ate plant foods such as bark, nuts, and berries. The earliest records of

Nature's Johnny Appleseeds

Johnny Appleseed was the nickname of John Chapman (1774–1845), a man who traveled around North America planting apple trees. Some animals fulfill similar roles, although perhaps not on purpose. Squirrels and chipmunks, for example, prepare for the long winter by burying acorns and other nuts in the ground where they can dig them up later and eat them. They often forget where they buried them, and in the spring the nuts sprout and send up shoots. Thanks to the poor memories of squirrels and chipmunks, forests spread and grow.

humankind show that people and the great forests evolved together. As humans learned to hunt animals for food and clothing, they sought out the forests, which had plenty of animal life.

Impact of the deciduous forest on human life   Forests have an important impact on the environment as a whole. From the earliest times, forests have offered food and shelter, a place to hide from predators, and many useful products.

Environmental cycles   Trees, soil, animals, and other plants all interact to create a balance in the environment from which humans benefit. This balance is maintained in what can be described as cycles.

The oxygen cycle   Plants and animals take in oxygen from the air and use it for their life processes. When animals and humans breathe, the oxygen they inhale is converted to carbon dioxide, which they exhale. This oxygen must be replaced, or life could not continue. Trees help replace oxygen during photosynthesis, when they release oxygen into the atmosphere through their leaves.

The carbon cycle   Carbon dioxide is also necessary to life, but too much is harmful. During photosynthesis, trees and other plants remove carbon dioxide from the air. By doing so, they help maintain the oxygen/carbon dioxide balance in the atmosphere.

When trees die, the carbon in their tissues is returned to the soil. If decaying trees become part of Earth's crust, after millions of years, this carbon becomes oil and natural gas.

The water cycle   Forests shade the snow, allowing it to remain in deep drifts. Root systems and fallen leaves help build an absorbent covering on the ground, allowing rain water and melting snow to soak into the soil and trickle down to feed underground streams and groundwater supplies.

Not only do forests help preserve water, but they also protect the land. Trees act as barriers, or walls, that help to reduce the strong forces of winds and rain. When forests are cut down, this barrier is removed and the topsoil is either blown away, or during heavy rains, the soil washes away. As a result, flooding is more common because there is no absorbent layer to soak up the rain. Since 1997, parts of India and Bangladesh have had severe flooding caused in part by the cutting of forests in the nearby Himalaya Mountains.

Trees take up water through their roots and use it for their own life processes. Extra moisture is released through their leaves back into the atmosphere, where it forms clouds and once again falls as rain or snow, continuing the water cycle.

The Nutrient cycle   Trees get the mineral nutrients they need from the soil. Dissolved minerals are absorbed from the soil by the tree's roots and are sent upward throughout the tree. These mineral nutrients are used by the tree much like humans take vitamins. When the tree dies, these nutrients, which are still contained within parts of the tree, decompose and are returned to the soil. These nutrients are then available for other plants and animals to use.

Food   Since the earliest times, forests have been home to game animals, such as deer, which supply meat for hunters and their families. Forests also supply fruits and seeds, as well as vegetation for livestock, and honey made by bees. Cranberries, gooseberries, strawberries, raspberries, huckleberries, and currants all grow in temperate woodlands.

Shelter   During prehistoric times, humans lived in the forest because it offered protection from the weather and dangerous animals. People of developed countries who continue to live in forested areas usually do so because they enjoy nature's beauty. Some native tribes still live in forests, as their ancestors did many years ago.

Economic values   Forests are important to the world economy. Many products used commercially are obtained from forests, such as wood, medicine, tannis, and dyes.

WORLD TRADE IN TIMBER PRODUCTS (PARTIAL LIST)		
Country	Exports: tons (metric tons)	Imports: tons (metric tons)
United States	12,948 (11,744)	16,778 (15,218)
Canada	17,588 (15,952)	2,938 (2,665)
Great Britain	----	5,484 (4,974)
Russia	16,050 (14,577)	----
China	554 (493)	4,348 (3,944)
Japan	----	31,679 (28,733)
Indonesia	13,961 (12,663)	----
Sweden	4,403 (3,994)	2,023 (1,835)

Healing Saps and Gums

Gums and saps from certain trees have important commercial uses. For example, the sap of the spiny acacia, called gum arabic, was first used by the ancient Egyptians to make inks. It has been used in medicines, adhesives, and is still used in making watercolor paints. These helpful liquids, which usually ooze from wounds in a tree, are produced only by trees that are unhealthy because of dry weather or poor soil and have been infected by microorganisms or fungi. The sap or gum may help the tree heal itself.

Wood   Trees produce one of two general types of wood: hardwood or softwood, based on the trees' cell wall structure. Hardwoods are usually produced by deciduous trees, such as oaks and elms. Most coniferous trees, such as pines, produce softwoods. These names can be confusing because some softwood trees, such as the yew, produce woods that are harder than many hardwoods. Some hardwoods, such as balsa, are softer than most softwoods.

Wood is used for fuel, building structures, and manufacturing other products, such as furniture and paper. Wood used for general construction is usually softwood. In order to conserve trees and reduce costs, some manufacturers have created engineered wood, which is composed of particles of several types of wood mixed with strong glues and preservatives. Engineered woods are very strong and can be used for many construction needs.

Hardwood from deciduous trees is more expensive because the trees grow slowly. It is used primarily for fine furniture and paneling. Most of this hardwood comes from forests in Europe. In the United States, the major commercial hardwoods are sugar maple, red oak, black walnut, and beech.

Farmland   In temperate regions, the soil beneath a deciduous forest is often fertile. For this reason, forestland has often been cleared for agricultural purposes. As the United States was settled, most of the original deciduous forest in the East was cut down to accommodate farms and large plantations. After the land was exhausted and farming became centralized in the plains of the Midwest, the forests gradually grew back. Oaks, maples, and hickories now flourish in the same regions that supported their ancestors 400 years ago.

Medicines   Since the earliest times, plants have been used for their healing properties. The ancient Greeks, for example, used extracts from willow bark to relieve pain, as did certain tribes of Native Americans. During the nineteenth century, scientists discovered the bark's pain-killing ingredient—salicylic acid. This ingredient is a component of the familiar pain-killing medicine, aspirin, made of acetylsalicylic acid.

Tannins and dyes   Tannins are chemical substances found in the bark, roots, seeds, and leaves of many plants. These tannins can be extracted by boiling or soaking plant material. The extract is then used to cure leather, making it soft and supple. Trees used for tannins include oaks, chestnuts, and quebracho.

Dyes used to color fabrics can be obtained from oak, alder, birch, walnut, brazilwood, and logwood. Natural dyes are no longer commonly used commercially, since less expensive dyes can be produced from chemicals.

Recreation   Many people feel the need to escape to natural surroundings on occasion. The beauty and quiet of deciduous forests draw many visitors for hiking, horseback riding, skiing, fishing, hunting, bird watching, or just sitting and listening to nature.

The World's Oldest Tree Species

The ginkgo (*Ginkgo biloba*), or maidenhair tree, is the only remaining survivor of a group of plants that thrived during the Permian period (260 million years ago). Essentially unchanged since prehistoric times, the ginkgo is a smooth-barked tree with fan-shaped leaves and few branches. Although it forms naked seeds, the ginkgo is deciduous; its leaves turn a golden color in fall and drop.

In China the ginkgo is sacred and is planted near temples. It is a popular ornamental plant in the temperate climates of Europe and North America. The seeds and leaves of the ginkgo are valued for their medicinal properties.

Impact of human life on the deciduous forest   Just as the forest has had an effect on human life, human life has had an effect on the forest. About 10,000 years ago, forests covered about half of Earth's land surface. They now cover less than one-third. Nearly 2 billion tons (1.8 billion metric tons) of timber are cut from the world's forests each year. Most of the losses in forest cover occur in developing nations where wood is used for fuel and trees are cleared for farming. The rest of the crop is used commercially.

Use of plants and animals   During the Middle Ages (500–1450) in Europe and the eighteenth and nineteenth centuries in America, it was thought that forests were indestructible. They seemed to go on forever. Eventually, the cutting of trees brought an end to many ancient forests. Only when they were left alone to regrow or were deliberately replanted, did the forests begin to recover.

In the United States, environmentalists are often in disagreement with logging companies over the cutting of old-growth forests. Trees are a renewable resource but old-growth trees may take more than 100 years to be replaced. Oftentimes, the logging companies replace the old trees with seedlings from other species that grow faster, and the original species are never

The Mighty Acorn

It is an old saying that "Mighty oaks from little acorns grow." Acorns are appreciated for more than just turning themselves into oak trees. Many animals use them for food, and, at various times in history, humans have pounded them into a nutritious flour. In recent years a new use has been found: a cure for polluted rivers.

Acorns contain acornic acid, which binds with poisons from heavy metals, such as uranium, allowing these pollutants to be removed from rivers and streams. An estimated 2.2 pounds (4.8 kilograms) of acorns can clean up 3.5 tons (3.9 metric tons) of water.

replanted. The companies sometimes replace only certain species, destroying the forest's diversity, along with plants and animals that depend on it.

Other threats to North American forests include mining operations that want to locate on public forest lands, and the cutting down of trees in order to develop land for homes and businesses.

Conservation laws in many states protect trees on public lands, while other laws protect forest creatures from being overhunted.

In tropical regions, forest land is being lost as populations grow and want the land for farms. Slash and burn agriculture is practiced when trees are cut and burned. The land is then used between one and five years for farming. When the land, which is usually poor, no longer supports crops, it is abandoned and another forest plot is cut down elsewhere. As a result, many animals and plants lose their habitats.

Quality of the environment Destruction of the forests does not just mean loss of their beauty and the products they provide. Soil quality declines. Some soil is washed away by rain, and the loss of plant life means the soil will not be built back up again.

Water quality and supply also suffers. With the loss of trees, rain does not seep into the soil and underground water reserves are not replaced. Soil that is washed away often ends up in streams and rivers. If the quantity of soil is large enough, fish may die.

Air quality is reduced when forests are destroyed. Not only do trees put oxygen back into the air, but soot and dust collect on their leaves. When it rains, the trapped soot and dust are washed to the ground where they enter the soil. In this way, trees help keep the air clean. When trees are cut down, the dust and soot remain, contributing to air pollution.

Carbon dioxide and other undesirable gases have built up in the atmosphere with the popularity of the automobile. Most scientists believe these gases are helping to raise the temperature of Earth's climate by forming an invisible layer in the atmosphere. This layer traps heat instead of letting it escape into the upper atmosphere. This is called the "greenhouse effect." Cutting down forests may be helping cause this global warming because they can no longer remove carbon dioxide from the air. If Earth

COMMON HARDWOODS

North America and Europe	Central and South America	Africa	Asia	Australia
Alder	Aromata	African oak	Aralia	Black bean
Ash	Balsa	African walnut	Bow wood	Cedar
Basswood	Bois gris	Comphorwood	Boxwood	Coconut palm
Beech	Bois lait	Canarium	Canarium	Gum
Birch	Brazilwood	Ebony	Cedar	Ironbark
Boxwood	Chilean laurel	Mahogany	Cinnamon	Peppermint
Cherry	Greenheart	Olive	Ebony	Silky oak
Chestnut	Lancewood	Teak	Elm	Tasmanian oak
Dogwood	Lignum vitae		Gum	Tea tree
Elm	Mahogany		Horse chestnut	Turpentine
Hickory	Pepper		Indian laurel	Walnut
Holly	Rosewood		Japanese alder	Wattle
Hornbeam	Satinwood		Japanese ash	
Lime	Snakewood		Japanese birch	
Magnolia	Teak		Japanese maple	
Maple	Tulipwood		Katsura	
Oak	Yokewood		Rosewood	
Olive			Sandalwood	
Pear			Teak	
Plane			Tree of Heaven	
Poplar			Walnut	
Sycamore			Willow	
Walnut				
Willow				

continues to grow warmer, many species of plants and animals could become extinct.

Air pollution is contributing to forest loss as well. Some forests take on an off-color, or sickly, appearance in polluted environments. Air pollution causes acid rain, which damages some types of trees. Acid rain occurs when certain compounds in polluted air mix with water vapor and fall to Earth in rain. When acid rain is absorbed into the soil, it can destroy nutrients and make the soil too acidic to support some species of trees. Forests in northern Europe, southern Canada, and the eastern United States have been damaged by acid rain.

Off-road vehicles, such as motorbikes and four-wheelers, tear up forest undergrowth, kill flowers, scare away animals, and destroy the peace of the forest.

Forest Management The U.S. National Forest Service was established in 1905 to protect forest resources. More than 193 million acres (78 million hectares) of land are now publicly owned. Most of this acreage is west of the Mississippi. Forests in the eastern half of the United States are managed by state programs. These forests may consist of land that can be used for logging and other commercial purposes; however, certain portions are kept for recreation and conservation.

Other nations, including Great Britain, Japan, China, and India, have established programs to conserve and replant forests.

Native peoples By 1950, native peoples in industrialized parts of the world had abandoned most of their tribal lands and customs. Many went to live in cities but some still live a traditional lifestyle. The Birhor of central India are one example. They live in the forests as nomadic hunter-gatherers and supplement their diet with rice that they trade for with forest products such as bark fiber rope.

Algonquin and Iroquois Tribes Until the European settlers forced them off their ancestral lands, many Native American tribes lived in the deciduous woodlands of the northeastern United States. They included tribes who spoke the Iroquois language—the Cayuga, Erie, Huron, Mohawk, Oneida, Onondaga, Seneca, Tuscarora, and Neutral; and those who spoke Algonquin—the Delaware, Fox, Illinois, Kickapoo, Mohican, Massachuset, Menominee, Miami, Mohegan, Ottawa, Pequot, Sauk, Shawnee, Shinnecock, and Wampanoag.

Long winters in those regions limited farming, so most foods were collected from the wild. These included fish, game, maple syrup, and wild rice.

Nearly all native groups who survived contact with European settlers were forced to move to reservations in Oklahoma during the early nineteenth century.

Ainu The Ainu are native peoples who live on Hokkaido, the northernmost island of Japan, and on the Russian island of Sakhalin in the North Pacific. Originally hunters and gatherers, the men used bow and arrow to hunt bear, deer, fox, otter, and other animals during the winter; in summer they fished. The women gathered roots, berries, mushrooms, and nuts and also did some farming. The men were skilled woodcarvers, and the women wove fabrics and did embroidery. Their chief musical instruments were the drum and flute.

At one time, the Ainu lived throughout the Japanese islands, but gradually, as the Japanese population has moved in and expanded, the Ainu have been pushed to their present territory. As of the last census in 1984, the population was only 24,381 people.

The Food Web

The transfer of energy from organism to organism forms a series called a food chain. All the possible feeding relationships that exist in a biome make up its food web. In the deciduous forest, as elsewhere, the food web consists of producers, consumers, and decomposers. An analysis of the food web shows how energy is transferred within the biome.

Green plants are the primary producers in the forest. They produce organic materials from inorganic chemicals and outside sources of energy, primarily the sun. Trees and other plants turn energy into plant food.

Animals are consumers. Plant-eating animals, such as grasshoppers and mice, are primary consumers in the forest food web. Secondary consumers eat the plant-eaters. Tertiary consumers are predators, like owls, foxes, and tigers. They are carnivores. Humans fall into this category, but they are omnivores, which means they eat both plants and animals.

Decomposers feed on dead organic matter, and include fungi and animals like the turkey vulture. In moist environments, bacteria also help in decomposition. When fallen leaves from deciduous trees carpet the ground forming a thick layer, bacteria feed on the leaves and help decompose them into humus.

The Ainu are native people who live on the northernmost island of Japan. AP IMAGES.

Spotlight on Deciduous Forests

Deciduous forests of Medieval Europe   About 5,000 years ago, birch trees dominated the forests of the Northern Hemisphere. As the climate gradually became warmer other trees started to take over. By Medieval times (500–1450), many hardwood trees, such as beeches and long-lived oaks, ranged over much of central and western Europe north of the Alps and the Pyrenees Mountains, and eastward across Russia to the Ural Mountains. Oaks and beeches usually formed the canopy, with maples and birches in the secondary layer, and dogwoods, hawthorns, and hollies closer to the ground.

The forests were home to falcons, hawks, herons, owls, deer, wolves, boars, otters, squirrels, foxes, badgers, and other wild animals. Many of these were hunted; some for food and others to protect crops and domesticated animals.

The people who lived there depended on forests as a source of timber for building livestock houses, vines and leaves for feeding, and game animals for hunting. Bees, prized for their honey, were often kept within the forest, and the fruits and nuts of many trees, such as the hazel, were used as food. Pigs were kept in the forest where they could feed on acorns. Valued for these nuts, oaks were allowed to grow old. Wood was prized as fuel, not only as logs but as charcoal, which is created when wood is partially burned. Charcoal produces a very hot fire and was used in beer brewing and forging iron. Wood ash, a by-product of burning wood, was needed for making glass and soap. Wood was used to build boats, carts, furniture, and even shoes.

Open land was used for farming but as populations grew, more and more forests were cut down and used for planting crops. By the eleventh century, the heavy plow came into use. It worked the soil more efficiently than previous methods and increased the amount of land that could be used for agriculture.

Deciduous forests of Japan   Japan is a series of islands, and deciduous forests cover at least half of the largest island, Honshu, and the lower-lying parts of southern Hokkaido.

Beeches are the dominant trees, but many other species are mixed in, including oaks, chestnuts, maples, and limes. Oaks and chestnuts are cultivated on privately owned tree plantations. Much of the land in Japan is intensely cultivated because it is a small country in terms of available land. This has led to the production of miniature trees that can be planted in small gardens.

The climate of Japan's deciduous forests is temperate but cool. Rain is plentiful, as is snow in winter. The stately beeches, which have bright green leaves in summer, turn a rich gold-brown in autumn.

Forests of Medieval Europe
Location: Northern and western Europe
Classification: Temperate

Deciduous forests of Japan
Location: Northern Japan
Classification: Temperate

Few trees are planted in Japan for timber. Most commercially grown trees, such as the beautiful Japanese maple and the flowering cherry, are sold for ornamental purposes.

Deciduous forests of China   China is the third largest country in the world based on acreage, and its forested land stretches over many hundreds of thousands of square miles. In the north, the climate is cool temperate, while in the south the climate is warm temperate. Oak, ash, birch, and poplar forests predominate in the northeast. No single species predominates in the southeast, and even the canopy shows a mixture of trees, including oak, maple, poplar, boxwood, and sweetgum.

The world's first artificial forest was located in China, and is currently 115 million acres large (46 million hectares). It accounts for 26 percent of the world's artificial forests and covers 16.5 percent of China's land mass—more than double the 8.6 percent China had in 1950.

Deciduous forests of North America   Deciduous forests are found in North America in portions of southern Canada, New England, the upper Midwest, the Appalachian region, along the Mississippi, and in the southeastern states.

When European settlers arrived in America in the 1600s, these forests were thick with oak, beech, and chestnut trees. Many trees were at least 100 feet (31 meters) tall and shaded a wide variety of other plants. Wild turkeys, passenger pigeons, moose, cougars, bison, beavers, otters, bears, and wolves were present. By 1970 most of the deciduous forests had been cut down, sacrificed to the building of houses and the need for farmland. Only in remote areas where the land was too steep to allow easy access did the original forest survive.

In some areas, deciduous forests are recovering. New England, for example, has more forest now than there was 100 years ago. Deciduous trees, such as sugar maple, birch, beech, and hemlock, mingle with coniferous forests. From Minnesota and Michigan eastward toward New England, the land is now being reclaimed by oak, beech, maple, aspen, and other species. In the southern and southeastern United States, the land was once covered primarily by deciduous trees, such as oaks, which were cut for timber and to clear the land for farms. Coniferous trees now predominate in some areas. If the land remains undisturbed, deciduous trees will once again take over.

Deciduous Forests of China
Location: Eastern China
Classification: Temperate

Deciduous Forests of North America
Location: Southern Canada and eastern United States
Classification: Temperate

Deciduous forests of Australia   Only about 15 percent of the total area of Australia has enough rainfall to support forests. Its central region is primarily desert mixed with grassland, and its forests grow in bands on the outer fringes of the continent. Although most of these trees are evergreen, moist deciduous forests can be found along the north and northeast coasts. Along the southern edge of the continent are open woodlands and dry tropical forest mixed with grasslands.

In the more humid upland and coastal areas of southwestern and eastern Australia, eucalyptus, angophora, and sheoaks predominate, mixed with beeches in some areas and shrubs having leathery leaves. In the south, acacia, or wattle, trees are common.

Woodland animals are varied and include many poisonous snakes. One interesting species, the carpet snake, is not poisonous but suffocates its victims by wrapping itself around them. A climber, the carpet snake is often turned loose in barns by farmers who want it to catch rats and mice.

Forest birds include budgerigars, currawongs, honey-eaters, and laughing kookaburras.

Mammals are predominantly marsupials, such as wombats and kangaroos, that carry their young in a pouch. Kangaroos range through the open woodlands of eastern Australia.

The native peoples of Australia are the Aborigines, who live in dry regions.

Deciduous forests of Central India   Central India, in the general area between the cities of Delhi and Nagpur, is a dry tropical region with dry and mixed deciduous forests. Trees found here include teak, mango, mohwa, jamun, gardenia, sal, and palm. Much of the area is grassland, and bamboo is common.

The region supports many parks and nature preserves, including Kanha Tiger Reserve and Taroba and Shivpuri National Parks.

Animals in this region include jays, peacocks, demoiselle cranes, wild boar, sambar and chital deer, gazelles, jackals, leopards, and tigers.

Forests account for only about 10 percent of India's land area, and forests are not accessible for commercial development. The government is attempting to increase the forested area by outlining three key goals—reduce soil erosion, supply wood product industries, and supply the needs of the rural population.

Deciduous forests of Australia
Location: Along the coastlines of the continent
Classification: Moist tropical and dry tropical

Deciduous forests of Central India
Location: Central India between Delhi and Nagpur
Classification: Dry tropical

Deciduous forests of Southern India Several regions at the southern tip of India support moist tropical deciduous forest and mixed forests with many evergreens. Trees include teak, ebony, and bejal. Except for areas devoted to the cultivation of teak, undergrowth tends to be thick. Open areas are covered by grasses and bamboo.

Several reserves and national parks are located here, including the Mudumalai Sanctuary, the Nagarhole Sanctuary, and the Bandipur Tiger Reserve.

The animal population is rich and varied. Termite nests can be seen along the roadways. Pythons, cobras, and monitor lizards are common. Birds include peacocks, parrots, pigeons, hornbills, and drongos. Giant squirrels, elephants, gaurs, lipped bears, leopards, and tigers also make their homes in the forest.

Deciduous forests of Tanzania and Kenya In Tanzania, the forest is called *miombo*. As of 2000, 41 percent of the Tanzanian land mass was covered in forests. Their trees are short with flat tops. During the dry season, which may last as long as seven months, the trees shed their leaves. Grasses and other plants die off, and the forest looks brown and scorched. When new leaves begin to appear, they signal the start of the rains, which give new life to the region.

Tree seedlings often develop large tap roots used to store water. During this time there is little development of the tree above the ground. Trees may take as long as seven years to grow more than 1 foot (30 centimeters) in height.

In Kenya, acacia woodlands are common, although baobab is predominant. Seasonal droughts cause vegetation to die. Many trees store water in tap roots or, like the baobab, in their trunks. A single baobab trunk can contain up to 25,000 gallons (94,625 liters) of water.

Common animals include the buffalo, elephant, leopard, lion, rhinoceros and wildebeest. Lions are the largest predator.

For More Information
BOOKS

Allaby, Michael. *Biomes of the Earth: Temperate Forests*. New York: Chelsea House, 2006.

Allaby, Michael. *Temperate Forests*. New York: Facts on File, 2007.

Braun, E. Lucy. *Deciduous Forests of Eastern North America*. Caldwell, NJ: Blackburn Press, 2001.

Deciduous forests of Southern India
Location: The tip of India, south of Bangalore
Classification: Moist tropical

Deciduous forests of Tanzania and Kenya
Location: Eastern Africa
Classification: Dry tropical

Hurtig, Jennifer. Deciduous Forests. New York: Weigl Publishers, 2006.

Jacke, Dave. *Edible Forest Gardens.* White River Junction, VT: Chelsea Green Publishing Co., 2005.

Johansson, Philip. The Temperate Forest: A Web of Life. Berkely Heights, NJ: Enslow Publishers, 2004.

Yahner, Richard H. *Eastern Deciduous Forest, Second Edition: Ecology and Wildlife Conservation.* Minneapolis, MN: University of Minnesota Press, 2000.

PERIODICALS

Bright, Chris, and Ashley Mattoon. "The Restoration of a Hotspot Begins." in *World Watch* 14.6 Nov-Dec 2001: p. 8–9.

Kessler, Rebecca. "Spring Back." in *Natural History* 115.9 November 2006: p 18.

Shefrin, Russell. "An Optimistic Look at Falling Leaves." in *New York State Conservationist* 62.2 October 2007: p32.

ORGANIZATIONS

Environmental Defense Fund, 257 Park Ave. South, New York, NY 10010, Phone: 212-505-2100; Fax: 212-505-2375, Internet: http://www.edf.org

Environmental Protection Agency, 401 M Street, SW, Washington, DC 20460, Phone: 202-260-2090, Internet: http://www.epa.gov

Friends of the Earth, 1717 Massachusetts Ave. NW, 300, Washington, DC 20036, Phone: 877-843-8687; Fax: 202-783-0444, Internet: http://www.foe.org

Global ReLeaf, American Forests, PO Box 2000, Washington, DC 20013, Phone: 202-737-1944, Internet: http://www.amfor.org

Greenpeace USA, 702 H Street NW, Washington, DC 20001, Phone: 202-462-1177, Internet: http://www.greenpeace.org

Izaak Walton League of America, 707 Conservation Lane, Gaithersburg MD, 20878, Phone: 301-548-0150, Internet: http://www.iwla.org

Sierra Club, 85 2nd Street, 2nd Fl., San Francisco, CA 94105, Phone: 415-977-5500; Fax: 415-977-5799, Internet: http://www.sierraclub.org

The Wilderness Society, 1615 M St. NW, Washington, DC 20036, Phone: 800-the-wild, Internet: http://www.wilderness.org

World Wildlife Fund, 1250 24th Street NW, Washington, DC 20090, Internet: http://www.wwf.org

WEB SITES

National Geographic Magazine. http://www.nationalgeographic.com (accessed August 22, 2007).

National Park Service. http://www.nps.gov (accessed August 22, 2007).

Nature Conservancy. http://www.tnc.org (accessed August 22, 2007).

Scientific American Magazine. http://www.sciam.com (accessed August 22, 2007).

USDA Forest Service. http://www.fs.fed.us (accessed August 22, 2007).

The World Conservation Union. http://www.iucn.org (accessed August 22, 2007).

World Wildlife Fund. http://www.wwf.org (accessed August 22, 2007)

Desert

All deserts have two things in common: they are dry, and they support little plant and animal life. If a region receives an average of fewer than 10 inches (25 centimeters) of rain each year, it is classified as a desert. Contrary to what most people believe, not all deserts are hot. Some deserts near the North and South Poles are so cold that all moisture is frozen—these are called polar deserts. Tropical desert areas are near the equator. Temperate desert areas are between the tropics and the North and South Poles.

True deserts cover about one-fifth of the world's land area. With the addition of polar deserts, the total rises to 30 percent. Another 25 percent of Earth's land surface possesses desertlike characteristics. In all, deserts constitute 33 million square miles (86 million square kilometers). Most deserts lie near the tropic of Cancer and the tropic of Capricorn, two lines of latitude about 25 degrees from the equator. The area between these two lines is called the Torrid Zone (*torrid* means very hot).

How Deserts Are Formed

Deserts are generally caused by the presence of dry air. The average humidity (moisture in the air) is between 10 and 30 percent. In some cases, mountain ranges prevent moisture-laden clouds from reaching the area. Mountains can cause heavy, moisture-filled clouds to rise into the colder atmosphere. There, the moisture condenses and falls in the form of rain, leaving the air free of moisture as it crosses the range. In other cases, certain wind patterns along the equator bring air in from dry regions. Cold-water ocean currents can cause moist air to drop its moisture over the ocean. The resulting dry air quickly evaporates (dries up) ground moisture along the coastal regions as it moves inland.

Deserts have always existed, even when glaciers covered large portions of Earth during the great Ice Ages. Although geological evidence is scarce,

WORDS TO KNOW

Arroyo: The dry bed of a stream that flows only after rain; also called a wash or a *wadi*.

Butte: A small hill.

Deforestation: The cutting down of all the trees in a forest.

Desertification: The changing of fertile lands into deserts through destruction of vegetation (plant life) or depletion of soil nutrients. Topsoil and groundwater are eventually lost as well.

Dormant: A suspension of growing (plants) or activity (animals) when conditions are harsh.

Estivation: An inactive period experienced by some animals during very hot months.

Mesa: A flat topped hill.

Oasis (plural is oases): A fertile area in the desert having a water supply that enables trees and other plants to grow there.

Wadi: The dry bed of a stream that flows after a rain; also called a wash, or an *arroyo*.

Xeriscaping: Landscaping method that uses drought tolerant plants and efficient watering techniques.

---

scientists tend to agree that some desert areas have always been present, but they were probably smaller than those of today. Fossils, the ancient remains of living organisms that have turned to stone, can reveal the climatic history of a region. For example, scientists believe that the Arabian Desert, which covers most of the Arabian Peninsula to the east of North Africa, once included wetlands because fossils of a small species of hippopotamus have been found there. In the Sahara Desert of North Africa, rock paintings made 5,000 years ago show pictures of elephants, giraffes, and herds of antelope that are no longer present.

Desertification (DES-aurt-ih-fih-KAY-shun; desert formation) occurs continuously, primarily on the edges of existing deserts. It is caused by a combination of droughts (rainless periods) and human activity such as deforestation (cutting down forests) or overgrazing of herd animals. When all the grass is used and rain is scarce, plants do not grow back. Without plants to hold the soil in place, wind blows away the smaller and finer particles of soil, exposing the less compacted layer of sand. This leaves a barren, unprotected surface. Eventually, even groundwater disappears.

Kinds of Deserts

Scientists measure a region's aridity (dryness) by comparing the amount of precipitation (rain, sleet, or snow) to the rate of evaporation.

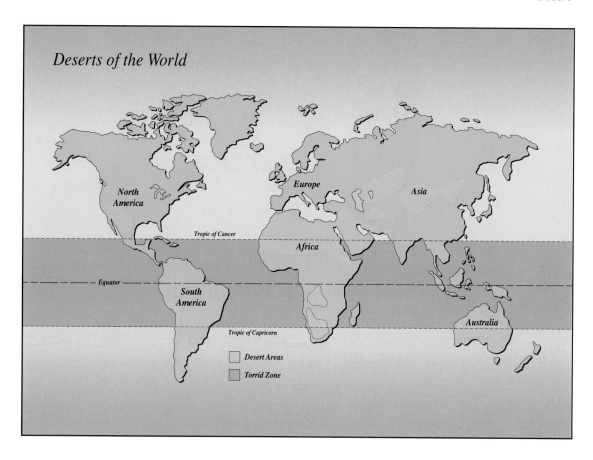

Deserts of the World

North America

Europe   Asia

Tropic of Cancer

Africa

Equator

South America

Australia

Tropic of Capricorn

☐ Desert Areas

☐ Torrid Zone

Evaporation always exceeds precipitation. Deserts can be classified as hyperarid (less than 1 inch [2.5 centimeters] of rain per year); arid (up to 10 inches [25 centimeters] of rain per year); and semiarid (as much as 20 inches [50 centimeters] of rain per year, but are so hot that moisture evaporates rapidly). Most true deserts receive fewer than 4 inches (10 centimeters) of rain annually.

Except for those at the North and South Poles, which are special cases, deserts are classified as hot or cold. Daytime average temperatures in hot deserts are warm during all seasons of the year, usually above 65°F (18°C). Nighttime temperatures are chilly and sometimes go below freezing. Typical hot deserts include the Sahara and the Namib Desert of Namibia. Cold deserts have hot summers and cold winters. At least one month during the year the mean temperature is below 45°F (7°C). Cold deserts include Turkestan in Kazakhstan and Uzbekistan, Gobi (GOH-bee)

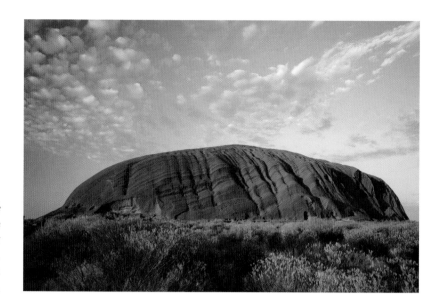

in China and Mongolia, and the Great Salt Lake Desert in Utah. These deserts usually get some precipitation in the form of snow.

Deserts can be further characterized by their appearance and plant life. They may be flat, mountainous, broken by gorges and ravines, or covered by a sea of sand. Plants may range from nearly invisible fungi to towering cacti and trees.

Climate

Although desert climates vary from very hot to very cold, they are always arid (dry).

Temperature   In hot deserts, days are usually sunny and skies are cloudless. During the summer, daytime air temperatures between 105° and 110°F (43.8° and 46.8°C) are not unusual. A record air temperature of 136.4°F (62.6°C) was measured in the Sahara Desert, in a place called El Azizia, on September 13, 1922. The absence of vegetation exposes rocks and soil to the sun, which may cause ground temperatures in the hottest deserts to reach 170°F (77°C). Nights are much cooler. The lack of cloud cover allows heat to escape and the temperature may drop 25 degrees or more after the sun sets. At night, temperatures of 50°F (10°C) or less are common, and they may even drop below freezing.

The Sands of Time

When living things die, moisture in the air aids the bacteria that cause decay. Before long, tissues dissolve and eventually disappear. Desert air is so dry that decay does not take place or occurs extremely slowly. Instead, tissues dry out and shrink, turning an animal or human being into a mummy.

In ancient Egypt around 3000 BC, the dead were buried in shallow graves in the sand. The very dry conditions mummified the bodies, preserving them. Later, for those who could afford it, Egyptian burials became more complex. Internal organs were removed, and the bodies underwent special treatments designed to preserve them. They were then placed into tombs dug into rocky cliffs or, in the case of certain pharaohs (kings), placed within huge pyramids of stone. In most cases, bodies of the ancient Egyptians are so well preserved that much can still be learned about

what they ate, how they lived, and what caused their deaths.

Graves discovered in the Takla Makan (TAHK-lah mah-KAN) Desert of China have also given scientists important information. (The name Takla Makan means "the place from which there is no return.") Well-preserved mummies as much as 3,800 years old have been found in the graves. The mummies have European features and some are dressed in fine woolens woven in tartan (plaid) patterns commonly used by the ancient Celts and Saxons of Northern Europe. Scientists believe these mummies were the first Europeans to enter China, which was officially closed to outsiders for thousands of years. Evidence exists that these people rode horses using saddles as early as 800 BC, and they may have introduced the wheel to China. Their descendants, who have intermarried with the Chinese, still live in the Takla Makan.

Winters in cold deserts at latitudes midway between the polar and equatorial regions can be bitter. In the Gobi Desert, for example, temperatures below freezing are common. Blizzards and violent winds often accompany the icy temperatures.

Precipitation   Rainfall varies from desert to desert and from year to year. The driest deserts may receive no rainfall for several years, or as much as 17 inches (43 centimeters) in a single year. Rainfall may be spread out over many months or fall within a few hours. In the Atacama Desert of Chile, considered the world's driest desert, more than half an inch (1.3 centimeters) of rain fell in one shower after four years of drought. Such conditions often cause flash floods, which sweep vast quantities of mud, sand, and boulders through dry washes, gullies, and dry river beds (called *wadis* or *arroyos*). The water soon evaporates or disappears into the ground. The Atacama Desert is the site of the world's longest known drought; no rain fell for 400 years (from 1571 until 1971).

In coastal deserts, fog and mist may be common. Fog occurs when cold-water ocean currents cool the air and moisture condenses. The Atacama Desert lies in a depression behind mountains, so most of its precipitation is received in fog form.

Some deserts, such as the polar deserts, experience snow rather than rain or fog.

Geography of Deserts

The geography of deserts involves landforms, elevation, soil, mineral resources, and water resources.

Landforms   Desert terrain may consist of mountains, a basin surrounded by mountains, or a high plain. Many desert areas were once lake beds that show the effect of erosion and soil deposits carried there by rivers. Wind

Sandstone formations are seen in Monument Valley, Utah. IMAGE COPYRIGHT SIGEN, 2007. USED UNDER LICENSE FROM SHUTTERSTOCK.COM.

helps shape the desert terrain by blowing great clouds of dust and sand that break down rock, sometimes sculpting it into strange and magnificent shapes. In the Australian Desert, unusual pinnacles (tall mountain shapes) of limestone rock, formed over thousands of years by the wind, stand on the desert floor. These limestone rock formations may be divided into two types. A mesa, the Spanish word for plateau, is a steep-sided, flat-topped hill. The mesa may be reduced to a butte (BYUT), the French word for hill or knoll, by erosion.

Sand dunes   Bare rock, boulders, gravel, and large areas of sand appear in most desert landscapes. Vast expanses of sand dunes, sometimes called ergs, are not very common. Sand dunes make up less than 2 percent of deserts in North America, only 20 percent of the Sahara, and 20 percent of the Arabian Desert. The Empty Quarter (*Rub' al-Khali*) in the Arabian Desert is the largest sandy desert in the world, covering about 250,000 square miles (647,500 square kilometers).

Unless anchored by grass or other vegetation, sand dunes migrate constantly. Their rate of movement depends upon their size—smaller dunes move faster—and the speed of the wind. Some dunes may move over 100 feet (30 meters) in a year and can bury entire villages. In the Sahara, dunes created by strong winds can achieve heights of 1,000 feet (300 meters). Scientists estimate that dunes in the Namib Desert are the largest in the world.

Dunes take different shapes, depending upon how they lie in respect to prevailing winds. When the wind tends to blow in one direction, dunes often form ridges. The ridges may lie parallel to the wind forming seif (SAFE), or longitudinal dunes; or at right angles forming transverse dunes. Seif dunes are the largest, with some in the Sahara approaching 100 miles (160 kilometers) in length. At desert margins where there is less sand, dunes may assume crescent shapes having pointed ends. These are called barchan (bahr-KAN) dunes, and the wind blows in the direction of their "points." In the Sahara, stellar (star-shaped) dunes are commonly found. Stellar dunes form when the wind shifts often, blowing from several directions.

Disappearance of *Lady Be Good*

Becoming lost in the desert can often end in tragedy. In 1943, an American bomber, called *Lady Be Good*, went off course and crashed in the Sahara Desert. The surviving crew saw a line of hills in the distance and mistook them for the hills around the Mediterranean, where they hoped to find human settlements. At night they walked and they rested by day, covering 75 miles (120 kilometers) in a week. As it turned out, the hills were not those around the Mediterranean, and the crewmen were still 375 miles (600 kilometers) from the sea. The entire crew died from sun exposure and lack of food and water. Their bodies were not found until 1960—seventeen years later.

Soil   Desert soils tend to be coarse, light colored, and high in mineral content. They contain little organic matter because there is little vegetation. If the area is a basin or a catch-all for flash-flood waters, mineral salts may be carried to the center where concentrations in the soil become heavy. If the area was once an inland sea, like the Kalahari (kah-lah-HAHR-ee) Desert of Botswana, eastern Namibia, and northern South Africa, exposed bottom sediments (matter deposited by water or wind) are very high in salt.

Most desert sand is made of tiny particles of the mineral quartz. Placed under pressure for long periods, grains of sand may stick together forming a type of rock called sandstone.

Some deserts have little soil, exposing bare, wind-polished, pebbly rock, called desert pavement. Rocks are often broken due to contraction and expansion caused by extreme temperature variations. Basin areas scoured by winds show surfaces of gravel and boulders, and on steep slopes, whipping winds may leave little soil.

Dust devils, columns of dust that spin over the desert landscape, are carried by whirlwinds. Dust storms can produce clouds thousands of feet high. In the Sahara, up to 200 million tons (180 million metric tons) of dust is created each year. Saharan dust has occasionally crossed the Atlantic to the United States. It has been known to travel as far north as Finland.

Two long-lasting chemical reactions affect desert rocks and soil. One, called desert varnish, gives rocks, sand, and gravel a dark sheen. Desert varnish is believed to be caused by the reaction between the moisture from overnight dew and minerals in the soil. The second reaction is the formation of duricrusts—hard, rocklike crusts that form on ridges when dew and minerals such as limestone combine, creating a type of cement.

Desert soils offer little help to plant life because they lack the nutrients provided by decaying vegetation and are easily blown away, exposing plant roots to the dry air. Some deep-rooted plants can exist on rock, where moisture accumulates in cracks. Other plants remain dormant during the driest periods, thriving and blooming after brief rains.

Soil reveals much about a desert's geological history. In Jordan, a Middle-Eastern country, the Black Desert takes its name from black basalt, a rock formed from volcanic lava.

Elevation   Deserts exist at many altitudes. North American deserts are partly mountainous, but Death Valley, a large basin in California, is 282 feet (86 meters) below sea level at its lowest point. The main plateau of

The land is very flat in the Thar Desert. IMAGE COPYRIGHT CHRIS HOWEY, 2007. USED UNDER LICENSE FROM SHUTTERSTOCK.COM.

the Gobi is 3,000 feet (914 meters) above sea level, and the Sahara extends from 436 feet (130 meters) below to 10,712 feet (3,265 meters) above sea level. Temperature, plant, and animal life, are all influenced by elevation.

Mineral resources   Valuable minerals like gold and oil (petroleum) are often found in desert regions. In the Great Sandy Desert of Australia, miners hunt for gold nuggets. "Black gold," as oil is often called, is found beneath the desert regions of the Middle East, where it formed over time from the sediment of prehistoric oceans. Iron ore is mined in portions of the Sahara. Borax—a white salt used in the manufacture of such products as glass and detergent—was once mined in Death Valley, California.

Water resources   Water sources in the desert include underground reserves and surface water.

Groundwater   In addition to occasional rainfall, deserts may have reserves of underground water. These reserves, often trapped in layers of porous rock called aquifers, were formed over thousands of years when rainwater seeped underground. Reserves close to the surface may create an oasis, a green, fertile haven where trees and smaller plants thrive. The presence of water may allow a completely different biome to form like an island in the desert.

People who live in the desert dig wells into aquifers and other underground water sources to irrigate crops and water their animals. As

WELL-KNOWN DESERTS OF THE WORLD

Name	Type	Location	Approximate Size
Arabian	Hot; extremely arid and arid	Arabian Peninsula	900,000 square miles (2,330,000 square kilometers)
Atacama	Hot; extremely arid and arid	Chile	70,000 square miles (181,300 square kilometers)
Australian	Hot; arid and semiarid	Australia	529,346 square miles (1,371,000 square kilometers)
Death Valley	Hot; arid	California (United States)	3,012 square miles (7,800 square kilometers)
Gobi	Cold; arid and semiarid	China, Mongolia	500,000 square miles (1,300,000 square kilometers)
Kalahari	Hot; arid	Southern Africa	10,038 square miles (260,000 square kilometers)
Mojave	Hot; arid	California and Nevada (United States)	25,000 square miles (65,000 square kilometers)
Namib	Hot; arid	Botswana, eastern Namibia, and northern South Africa	52,000 square miles (135,000 square kilometers)
Negev	Hot; arid	Israel	4,700 square miles (12,170 square kilometers)
Patagonian	Cold; arid	Argentina	260,000 square miles (673,000 square kilometers)
Sahara	Hot; extremely arid and arid	North Africa	35,600 square miles (92,200 square kilometers)
Thar	Hot; extremely arid	India and Pakistan	92,163 square miles (238,700 square kilometers)

desert populations grow, water sources shrink and cannot be replaced fast enough. There is a real danger that groundwater reserves will one day be depleted.

Surface water   Water may be found in desert areas in the form of rivers or streams. Some streams form only after a rain, when water sweeps along a dry river bed in a torrent (violent stream) then quickly sinks into

A herd of wild horses run in the Mongolian desert. IMAGE COPYRIGHT PICHUGIN DMITRY, 2007. USED UNDER LICENSE FROM SHUTTERSTOCK.COM.

the ground or evaporates. Moisture sometimes remains under the surface, and plants can be seen growing along the path of streams.

Permanent rivers are found in desert regions. The Colorado River is one example. Over a million years ago, the Colorado River began cutting a path into the plateau of limestone and sandstone rock in northern Arizona, ultimately forming the Grand Canyon, which is 1.2 miles (1.9 kilometers) deep and 277 miles (446 kilometers) long. Perhaps the most famous desert river is the Nile, which bisects Egypt. Since ancient times, Nile floods have brought enough rich soil from countries farther south to turn Egypt's river valley into fertile country well known for its agricultural products, such as cotton.

Permanent lakes rarely occur in desert regions. Two exceptions are the Great Salt Lake of Utah, which is all that remains of what once was a great inland sea, and the Dead Sea of Israel and Jordan. The Dead Sea is actually a salt lake that was once part of the Mediterranean.

Plant Life

One of the most important characteristics of any biome is its plant life. Not only do plants provide food and shelter for animals, they recycle gases in the atmosphere and add beauty and color to the landscape. Deserts support many types of plants, although not in large numbers.

Algae, fungi, and lichens   Algae (AL-jee), fungi (FUHN-ji), and lichens (LY-kens) do not fit neatly into either the plant or animal categories.

Algae   Most algae are single-celled organisms; a few are multicellular. Like plants, nearly all algae have the ability to make their own food by means of photosynthesis (foh-toh-SIHN-thuh-sihs). Photosynthesis is the process by which plants use the energy from sunlight to change water and carbon dioxide into the sugars and starches they use for food. Other algae absorb nutrients from their surroundings. Although most algae are water plants, the bacteria known as blue-green algae do appear in the desert. They survive as spores during the long dry periods and return to life as soon as it rains. (Spores are single cells that have the ability to grow into a new organism.)

Fungi   Fungi are commonly found in desert regions wherever other living organisms are found. Fungi cannot make their own food by means of photosynthesis. Some species, like molds and mushrooms, obtain nutrients from dead or decaying organic matter. They assist in the decomposition (breaking down) of this matter, releasing nutrients needed by other desert plants. Fungi that attach themselves to living plants are parasites. Parasites can be found wherever green plants live, and may weaken the host plant so that it eventually dies. Other parasitic fungi actually help their host absorb nutrients more effectively from the soil. All fungi reproduce by means of spores.

Lichens   Lichens are actually combinations of algae and fungi living in cooperation. The fungi surround the algal cells. The algae obtain food for themselves and the fungi by means of photosynthesis. It is not known if the fungi aid the algal organisms, but they may provide them with protection and moisture.

Lichens are among the longest living organisms. Some lichens in polar deserts are believed to have survived at least 4,000 years. Although lichens grow slowly, they are very hardy and can live in barren places under extreme conditions, such as on bare desert rock or arctic ice. Crusty types colored gray, green, or orange, often cover desert rocks and soil. During very dry periods, they remain dormant. When it rains, they grow and make food.

Green plants   Most green plants need several basic things to grow: light, air, water, warmth, and nutrients. In the desert, light, air, and warmth are abundant, although water is always scarce. The nutrients—primarily nitrogen, phosphorus, and potassium—obtained from soil may be in short supply.

Earth's Balancing Act

Many scientists recognize the many links among all life forms living on our planet. One biologist, James Lovelock, has theorized that life itself is responsible for changes in the land, water, and air. For example, until about 2 billion years ago, there was almost no oxygen in the atmosphere. Then blue-green bacteria, also called blue-green algae, began using energy from the sun for photosynthesis (a food-making process), which produces oxygen as a by-product. After enough blue-green algae and later plants got to work, the atmosphere eventually became, and is still maintained at, 21 percent oxygen, which is ideal for animal life. Lovelock believes that living things somehow work together in this way, instinctively providing a comfortable environment for themselves and one another.

To test his theory, Lovelock has produced a computer model. (Computer models enable scientists to more quickly study processes that take very long periods of actual time to show a result.) Suppose, for example, there are two species of flowers, one white and one dark blue. The white flowers reflect the sun's heat and can survive in warm climates. The dark blue flowers absorb heat and do better in cooler climates. According to Lovelock's model, the flowers help control the environment. The presence of blue flowers in a cool environment means heat is absorbed and the surrounding temperature is prevented from being too cool. The white flowers, on the other hand, reflect the heat and help keep a warm environment from being too warm.

Desert plants must protect against water loss and wilting, which can damage their cells. Large plants require strong fibers or thick, woody cell walls to hold them upright. Even smaller plants have a great number of these cells, which makes them fibrous and tough. Their leaves tend to be small and thick, with fewer surfaces exposed to the air. Outer leaf surfaces are often waxy to prevent water loss. Pores in the surface of green leaves allow the plant to take in carbon dioxide and release oxygen. The leaves of some desert plants may have grooves to protect their pores against the movement of hot, dry air. Other leaves curl up or develop a thick covering of tiny hairs for protection. Still others have adjusted to the dry environment by adapting the shape of their leaves. For, example cactus leaves are actually spines (needles). These spines have less surface area from which water can evaporate. As a result, more water is stored within the plant.

Common desert plants   Several species of plants grow in the desert, including cacti, shrubs, trees, palms, and annuals.

Cacti   Cactus plants originated in southern North America, Central America, and northern South America. Instead of leaves, a cactus has spines, which come in many forms from long, sharp spikes to soft hairs.

Photosynthesis takes place in the stems and trunk of the plant. Nectar, a sweet liquid that appeals to insects, birds, and bats, is produced in the often spectacular flowers.

One of the largest plants in the desert is the giant saguaro (sah-GWAH-roh) cactus. Its large central trunk can grow as tall as 65 feet (20 meters) and have a diameter of 2 feet (60 centimeters). Ninety percent of its weight is water, which it stores in its soft, spongy interior. During very dry conditions, as the plant uses up this stored water, the trunk shrinks in size.

Like many desert plants, the saguaro has a wide, shallow root system designed to cover a large area. After a long dry period, its roots can take up as much as 1 ton (1 metric ton) of water in 24 hours. The trunk expands as it absorbs and stores the new supply.

Pores run in deep grooves along the saguaro's stems. These pores open during the cooler nighttime hours to take in carbon dioxide and release oxygen. For protection from wind and animals, long, sharp spines run along the grooves. These spines reduce air movement, which conserves water and keeps grazing animals away.

Birds and bats love the nectar produced in saguaro flowers, and bats help to pollinate the saguaro. A bat's head fits the shape of the flowers almost perfectly. As the bat drinks the nectar, its head gets heavily dusted with pollen grains, which it then carries to the next plant.

Woody shrubs and trees   Small, woody perennials that flourish in the desert climate include sagebrush, salt-brush, creosote, and mesquite (meh-SKEET). They have small leaves and wide-ranging root systems. Most shrubs have spines or thorns to protect them against grazing animals.

The mesquite is a tree with roots that may grow 80 feet (24 meters) deep, with most of the root system in the upper 3 feet (1 meter). The long roots find a constant supply of water and it remains green all year. The mesquite produces long seedpods with hard, waterproof coverings. When the pods are eaten by desert animals, the partially digested seeds pass out of the animal's body and begin to grow.

Joshua trees, a form of yucca plant, live for hundreds of years in the Mojave Desert of California. They can grow to 35 feet (11 meters) tall. Yuccas and treelike aloes store water in their leaves, not their stems. One

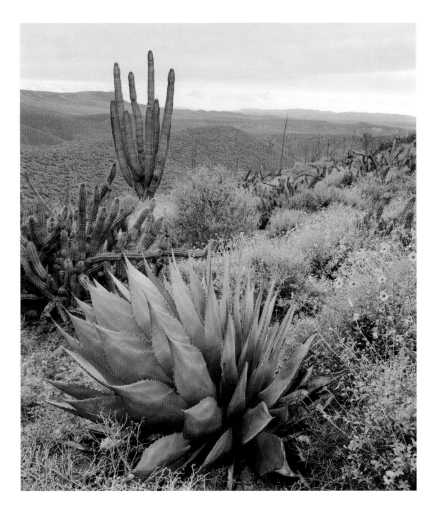

Several species of cactus including agave, candelabra, and cardon thrive in the desert climate. IMAGE COPYRIGHT DAVID M. SCHRADER, 2007. USED UNDER LICENSE FROM SHUTTERSTOCK.COM.

type of aloe, the kokerboom tree of southwest Africa, can survive several years without rain.

Palms Date palms, found at many oases in the Sahara and Arabian Deserts, can grow in soil with a high salt content. Only female trees produce dates, and only a few male trees are necessary for cross-pollination. The dates can be eaten raw, dried, or cooked and are an important food source for desert dwellers.

The Washingtonian fan palm is the largest palm in North America. Native to California, it requires a dependable supply of water to survive and sends out a thick web of tiny roots at its base. When its fronds (branches) die, they droop down around the trunk and form a "skirt," where animals like to live. The fan palm produces a datelike fruit that is eaten by many desert inhabitants.

Annuals   Long grasses, such as alpha or esparto grass, often flourish in the desert after seasonal rains. Their stems can be used to make ropes, baskets, mats, and paper. Tufts of grasses sometimes become so entwined they form balls that drop their seeds as they spin across the landscape in the wind.

Almost every desert has its share of blooming annuals that add masses of color after a rain. Primroses and daisies adorn the California desert, while daisies, blue bindweed, dandelions, and red vetch beautify the Sahara.

Growing season   The growing season in deserts is limited to the brief periods of rain that, in some cases, do not occur for several years. In some coastal deserts, certain plants absorb mist from the nearby ocean through their leaves. Where the soil is rich and rain is more regular and dependable, desert plants may flourish.

In cold deserts where real winters occur, plants are much like those in temperate climates. The portion above ground dies off, but the root system goes deep and is protected from freezing by layers of snow.

Deserts are home to both annuals and perennials. Annuals live only one year or one season, and they require at least a brief rainy period that occurs regularly. Their seeds seem to sprout and grow overnight into a sea of colorful, blossoming plants. This period of rapid growth may last only a few weeks. When the rains disappear, the plants die and the species withdraws into seed form, remaining dormant (inactive) until the next period of rain.

Unlike annuals, perennials live at least two years or two growing seasons, appearing to die in-between but reviving when conditions improve. Those that live many years must be strong and have several survival methods. As young plants, they devote most of their energy to developing a large root system to collect any available moisture. Plants are often many yards apart, because their roots require a large area of ground in order to find enough water. The above-ground portion of young perennials is small in comparison to the root system because their leaves do not have to compete for sunlight or air as they do for water. Some perennials are succulents (SUHK-yoo-lents), which are able to store water during long dry periods. Some, like the century plant, store water in their leaves, while others store it in their stems or in large roots.

Water supply Except for occasional rivers and oases, water in the desert comes from the brief rains. Plants may grow in greater numbers in arroyos or wadis where moisture may remain beneath the surface. In coastal deserts, some plants absorb moisture from fog and mists that condense on their leaves. In cold deserts, spring thaws provide water from melting snow.

Reproduction Pollination (the transfer of pollen from the male reproductive organs to the female reproductive organs of plants) is often a problem in deserts. The wind may carry pollen from one plant to another, but this

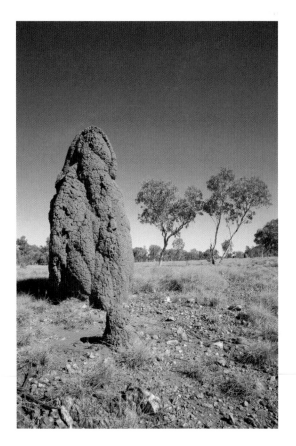

Termite mounds can get surprisingly tall, 6 to 9 feet (2 to 3 meters) is very common.
IMAGE COPYRIGHT COLIN & LINDA MCKIE, 2007. USED UNDER LICENSE FROM SHUTTERSTOCK.COM.

method is not efficient because plants usually grow far apart. Insect pollination is rare because there are fewer insects than in other biomes. As a result, many plants have both male and female reproductive organs and pollinate themselves.

Endangered species   Many desert plants, such as the candy cactus, saguaro cactus, and the silver dollar cactus, are threatened because of their popularity as house plants and for landscaping. They are available for sale in nurseries, but some people take them from the wild. Desert plants are sparse to begin with, so removal from their native home upsets the delicate balance of their reproduction.

Animal Life

All animals face the same problems in adapting to the desert. They must find shelter from daytime heat and nighttime cold, as well as food and water, which are often scarce. In spite of these extreme conditions, many animal species are represented in the desert environment, even some typically associated with temperate or wet surroundings.

Invertebrates   Animals lacking backbones are called invertebrates. They include simple desert animals such as worms, and more complex animals such as the locust. Certain groups of invertebrates must spend part of their lives in water. These types are usually not found in deserts. One exception is the brine shrimp, an ancient species that lives in desert salt lakes. Other exceptions are certain species of worms, leeches, midges, and flies that live in the fresh water of oases and waterholes.

Most invertebrates are better adapted to desert life than vertebrates. Many have an exoskeleton (an external skeleton, or hard shell, made from a chemical substance called chitin [KY-tin]). Chitin is like armor and is usually waterproof. It protects against the heat of the desert sun, preventing its owner from drying out.

Common desert invertebrates   Termites, spiders, locusts and scorpions are all invertebrates found in the desert.

Termites   Termites, found all over the world, build the skyscrapers of the desert. Their mounds, often more than 6 feet (2 meters) tall, are erected over a vast underground system of tunnels. These tunnels go as deep as the groundwater, providing a water supply readily available to the termite colony. The mounds, which are made of dirt, decaying plants, and termite secretions that dry rock-hard in the sun, have many air ducts. As the sun warms the mounds, they grow very hot. The hot air inside the mounds rises, drawing cooler air through the tunnels, creating a type of air-conditioning system.

Termites eat plant foods, especially the cellulose (substance making up a plant's cell walls) found in woody plants.

Termites have an elaborate social structure. A single female—the queen—lays all the eggs and is tended to by workers. Soldier termites, equipped with huge jaws, guard the entrances to the mound. Soldiers cannot feed themselves, and the workers must tend to them, as well.

Locusts   Locusts are found in the deserts of northern Africa, the Middle East, India, and Pakistan. As members of the grasshopper family, they have wings and can fly, as well as leap, considerable distances. For years they live quietly, nibbling on plants and producing a modest number of young. Then, for reasons not completely understood, their numbers increase dramatically. Great armies of locusts suddenly emerge, hopping or flying through the desert in search of food. Eating every plant in sight, these swarms may travel thousands of miles before their feeding frenzy ends. In a short time, the hordes die off and locust life returns to normal. The devastated landscape they leave behind may take years to recover. The most destructive species, the desert locust, lives wherever the average rainfall is less than 8 inches (20 centimeters). A swarm may contain as many as 40 million to 80 million insects.

Food and water   Many invertebrates are winged and can fly considerable distances in search of food. They eat plant foods or decaying animal matter. Some invertebrates are parasites, like the Guinea worm, that lurk at waterholes waiting for an unsuspecting animal to wander by.

Living Juice Boxes

Honeypot ants, which live in Africa, Australia, and the Americas, take the business of food very seriously. They maintain herds of aphids, insects that suck the juices of plants and then secrete a sugar-rich "honey." Worker ants collect this honey and bring it back to the nest, where they feed it to a second group of workers. This second group takes in so much aphid honey that their stomachs swell and it is difficult for them to move. They then suspend themselves from the ceiling of the nest and wait. Later, when food becomes scarce, they spit the honey back up for other ants to eat. Some desert peoples like eating honeypot ants and seek out their nests.

Parasites attach themselves to the animal's body or are swallowed and invade the animal from the inside.

Arachnids (spiders and scorpions), which are carnivores (meat eaters), seem well suited to desert life. They prey on insects and, if they are large enough, small lizards, mice, and birds. Scorpions use their pinchers to catch prey, then inject it with venom (poison) from the stinger in their tails. Their venom can be lethal, even for large animals and humans. Arachnids do not usually drink water but get what they need from their prey.

Shelter   Most desert spiders live on the ground rather than on webs, hiding in holes or under stones to escape the heat. The large, hairy camel spiders are nocturnal, which means they rest during the daytime hours and hunt at night.

Scorpions hunt at night to avoid the heat of the day, taking shelter beneath rocks or burying themselves in sand or loose gravel. Several American and Australian species dig burrows more than 3 feet (1 meter) below the surface.

Reproduction   Some invertebrates, such as the scorpion, go through a mating ritual. Male and female scorpions appear to dance with their pinchers clasped together, as they do a two-step back and forth. After mating, the males hurry away to avoid being killed and eaten by the female.

Insects, the largest group of invertebrates, have a four-part life cycle that increases their ability to survive in an unfavorable environment. The first stage of this cycle is the egg. The egg's shell is usually tough and resistant to long dry spells. After a rain and during a period of plant growth, the egg hatches. The second stage is the larva, which may be divided into several stages between which there is a shedding of the outer covering, or skin, as the larva increases in size. Larvae have it the easiest of all in the desert, often being able to spend a portion of their life cycle below ground where it is cooler and more moist than on the surface. Some larvae store fat in their bodies and do not have to seek food. The third stage of development is the pupal stage. During this stage, the animal often lives inside a casing, in a resting state, which may offer as much protection as an egg. Finally, the adult emerges.

Amphibians   Amphibians are vertebrates (animals with backbones) that usually spend part, if not most, of their lives in water. Unlikely as it seems, such animals can be found in a desert. Frogs and toads manage to survive in significant numbers in desert environments.

The short, active portion of their lives occurs during and immediately after the seasonal rains, when pools of water form. Mating, egg-laying, and young adulthood all take place in these pools. Offspring that survive into maturity leave the pools and take their chances on the desert floor, where they spend a few weeks feeding on both plants and insects. They must find shade or risk dying in the heat of the sun.

Common amphibians Frogs may spend up to ten months out of the year in their burrows, which are usually 3 feet (1 meter) under the desert floor. The Australian water frog can wait up to seven years for rain in a burrow made of its own shed skin. The Sonoran Desert toad is poisonous to predators and the largest toad in Arizona.

Food Frogs and toads feed on algae, plants, and freshwater crustaceans such as tiny shrimps that manage to survive in egg or spore form until brought to life by the rains. Frogs that eat the meat of crustaceans while they are tadpoles often become cannibals as they mature, eating their smaller, algae-eating brothers and sisters. If the rainy season is short, the cannibals have a better chance of survival because they have more food choices. If the rainy season lingers, the smaller tadpoles have a better chance because the cannibals cannot see their prey as well in muddy waters churned up by the rains, and the plant-eaters receive an increased supply of algae.

Shelter During the hottest, driest seasons, amphibians go through estivation (ess-tih-VAY-shun), an inactive period. While the soil is still moist from the rain, they dig themselves a foot or more into the ground. Only their nostrils remain open to the surface. Normally, their skin is moist and soft and helps them absorb oxygen. During estivation the skin hardens and forms a watertight casing. All the animal's bodily processes slow down to a minimum, and it remains in this state until the next rainfall, when it emerges. When water is scarce, Australian Aborigines (native peoples) dig up estivating frogs or toads and squeeze the animal's moisture into their mouths.

Reproduction Mating and egg-laying for amphibians takes place in water; the male's sperm is deposited in the water on top of the female's jellylike eggs. As the young develop into larvae and young adults, they often have gills and require a watery habitat. If there is not enough rain for pools of water to form, amphibian populations may not survive.

Avoiding Hot Sand

Several species of lizards have evolved methods for traveling over hot sand without burning their toes. The agamid lizard has long legs and keeps one foot raised and swinging in the breeze to cool it off while the other three support the animal. It does this in rotation, so that all its feet get an equal chance to cool off.

**HOW TEMPERATURES GROW
COOLER UNDERGROUND**

Burrowing animals escape the heat by going underground, where it can be up to twice as cool as above ground.

Surface land temperature	165°F (74°C)
1 foot (31 centimeters) down	105°F (41°C)
2 feet (61 centimeters) down	95°F (36°C)
3 feet (91 centimeters) down	85°F (29°C)
4 feet (122 centimeters) down	83°F (28°C)

Reptiles   Of all the animals, reptiles are perhaps most suited to living in the desert. Snakes, lizards, and some species of tortoises are the most common. The scaly, hard skin of reptiles prevents water loss, and their urine is almost solid, so no water is wasted.

Reptiles are cold-blooded, which means their body temperature changes with the temperature of the surrounding air. Early in the day, they expose as much of their bodies as possible to the sun for warmth. As the temperature climbs, they expose less and less of their bodies. During the hottest period of the day, they find shade or a hole in which to wait for cooler temperatures. During the chilly nights they become sluggish, because they do not have to use energy keeping their body temperatures up as do warm-blooded mammals and birds.

Besides being cold-blooded, some species of lizards have specially developed clear membranes in their lower eyelids that cover the entire eye and protect it from losing moisture.

Snakes have no legs. They move using special muscles that flex their flat belly scales forward and backward. Ridges on their scales grip the ground and pull them along. Some rattlesnakes, like the sidewinders of North American deserts, manage to move diagonally by coiling into a kind of S-shape, and propel themselves by pushing with the outside back portion of each S-shaped curve.

Common desert reptiles   Snakes are less common in deserts than lizards. Common desert snakes include the gopher snake, horned viper, Gaboon viper, rattlesnake, and cobra. The Egyptian cobra can grow up to 8 feet (2.5 meters) long and is found in Africa. The Western diamondback rattlesnake, the most dangerous American snake, can grow to 6.5 feet (2 meters).

Common lizards include the gecko, the skink, the bearded dragon, the iguanid lizard, and the monitor lizard. The only two species of venomous lizards, the Gila monster and the bearded lizard, are related to the monitor. They are found in the southwestern United States and western Mexico.

Food and water   The diet of lizards varies, depending upon the species. Some have long tongues with sticky tips good for catching insects.

Many are carnivores that eat small mammals and birds. The water they need is usually obtained from the food they eat. Geckos can survive long periods without food by living on stored fat.

While most lizards hunt food during the day, the Gila monster, found in the southwestern United States, looks for reptile eggs and baby animals after dark. Making the most of its opportunities, the lizard stuffs itself. During periods when food is scarce, its body draws on extra nutrients stored as fat in its tail, which can double in size after a big meal.

All snakes are carnivores, and one decent-sized meal will last them days or weeks. In the desert, they use their eyes to hunt during the cool nights when their prey is most active. Snakes cannot close their eyes because they have no eyelids. A transparent covering protects their eyes from the dry air, dust, and sand. Snakes often hunt underground and they have adapted to detecting ground vibrations. Many desert snakes bury themselves in the sand so that only their eyes and flickering tongues are visible. Some snakes kill their prey with venom (poison).

Although commonly thought of as jungle dwellers, boa constrictors and pythons (a species of constrictor) live in the desert. Constrictors strike their prey, hold it with a mouthful of tiny teeth, and then wrap their body around it like a coil. The prey suffocates and the constrictor swallows its meal whole, gradually working it into its stomach with its hinged lower jaw and strong throat muscles.

Shelter   Lizards and snakes hide in the shade during the hottest hours of the day to escape the sun. Only a few make their own burrows. Most take over the abandoned burrows of other animals, find shelter in rock crevices, or bury themselves in the sand.

Desert tortoises obtain some shade from the sun with their thick outer shells. Most of the time they escape the heat of the day by retreating to burrows they dig. In the spring and autumn, when the days are not excessively warm, the tortoise ventures out during the day to forage for food. During the summer they forage for food at night when it is cooler, remaining in burrows during the day. In the winter, tortoises hibernate (become dormant) in a second burrow they have dug.

Reproduction   The eggs of reptiles are leathery and tough and do not dry out easily. Some females remain with the eggs, but most bury

A Living Funnel

Most lizards obtain water from the food they eat. The thorny devil, a small lizard from Australia, is an exception. During the cool nights, dew condenses in the creases and folds of its skin. Most of these folds lead toward the lizard's mouth, and the lizard is able to lap up the moisture.

Secret Weapons

Rattlesnakes and other pit vipers have small pits on both sides of their face. These pits detect the body heat of prey, just like heat-seeking missiles. Pit vipers hunt at night, and their secret weapon allows them to find small animals hidden in the dark.

them in a hole. Offspring are seldom coddled and are left to hatch by themselves. Once free of the eggs, the offspring dig themselves out of the hole and begin life on their own.

Birds All deserts have bird populations. Tropical and subtropical deserts are visited twice each year by hundreds of species of migratory birds traveling from one seasonal breeding place to another. These migrators include small birds such as wheat-ears, as well as larger species such as storks and cranes. Some species know the route and where to find food or water. Others fly at night, when it is cool. Migrators are not true desert birds. They cannot survive for long periods in the desert as can birds for which the desert is home.

Birds have the highest body temperature of any animal—around 104°F (40°C). They do not need to lose body heat until the desert temperature is greater than their own. This makes desert life easier for them than for mammals, which must lose heat regularly during the warmest months, usually by panting or sweating.

Feathers protect birds not only from the cold in winter but from the sun and heat. Air trapped between layers of feathers acts as insulation. Birds do

This spitting cobra is ready to attack defending itself near its home in the Kalahari Desert.
IMAGE COPYRIGHT LUCIAN COMAN, 2007. USED UNDER LICENSE FROM SHUTTERSTOCK.COM.

not sweat but, by flexing certain muscles, can make their feathers stand erect. This allows them to direct cooling breezes to their skin. Those having broad wing spans, such as eagles and buzzards, can soar at high altitudes and find cooler temperatures.

Common desert birds Common desert birds include ground birds and birds of prey.

Ground birds Ground birds are not hunters or scavengers (animals that eat decaying matter) but obtain most of their food from plants and insects. They have strong legs that enable them to dart around on the ground without tiring.

In Asia, Africa, Australia, and the Arabian Peninsula, families of thrushes, called chats, are common. Varieties of chats live at many different altitudes, including those over 13,000 feet (4,000 meters). They are found in both arid and semiarid regions, and their diets and habits vary according to their location.

Wrens are common in desert habitats all over the world. They eat insects, and species in North American deserts eat seeds and soft fruits. Cactus wrens, as their name implies, live among prickly desert plants where they build their nests among the spines.

A small desert bird that is a popular pet is the parakeet. Originally from Australia, parakeets live in huge flocks containing tens of thousands of birds. During years when food is plentiful, a flock may number in the millions. Parakeets prefer seeds and are nomads, often traveling from habitat to habitat in search of the seeds of annuals that bloom after a rainfall.

The largest ground birds found in deserts are members of the bustard family. The houbara bustard is found in the Sahara and the deserts of central Asia. It is about 2 feet (60 centimeters) tall and weighs as much as 7 pounds (3 kilograms). Houbaras depend primarily upon plants for food, but will eat invertebrates and small lizards. Houbaras can run fast—up to 25 miles (40 kilometers) per hour—and seldom fly. Other birds include the pale crag martin and the swallow.

Birds of prey Birds of prey are hunters and meat eaters. They soar high in the air on the lookout for small animals to eat. Their eyesight and

The Flying Sponge

The sandgrouse, found in the deserts of Africa and Asia, is a water-drinking bird. Most members of this species live near waterholes, except during nesting periods, when they may be forced to remain in an area experiencing drought (extreme dryness). Male sandgrouse have evolved an unusual method of overcoming this problem. They fly to the nearest waterhole, perhaps 20 miles (35 kilometers) away, and turn themselves into sponges. They wade into the water and let their special belly feathers absorb the liquid—as much as twenty times their own weight. Then they fly back to the nest where the nestlings drink by squeezing the water out with their beaks.

The Eyes Have It

The eyes of all birds are large in relation to their body size. Some of the largest are the eyes of owls, which take up about one-third of the space in the skull. Owl eyes are specially adapted to see better at night. They have more rods, the cells that are most sensitive to low light levels, and fewer cones, the cells sensitive to bright light. An owl's eyes are pear shaped and face forward, which gives the owl a kind of binocular vision and superior judgment of distances. An owl's eyes cannot turn in their sockets because of their size and shape. To look around, the owl must swivel its entire head.

hearing are usually very sensitive and enable them to see and hear creatures scurrying on the ground far below.

The roadrunner, found in the southwestern United States, can scurry over the desert floor for long stretches at speeds of about 13 miles (20 kilometers) per hour. Roadrunners are carnivores and are known to come running at the sound of a creature in trouble.

Several species of falcons live in semiarid regions; one of the true desert falcons is the prairie falcon of North America. Prairie falcons hunt for other birds such as larks and quail, and small mammals such as rabbits and prairie dogs. When food is scarce, they eat insects and reptiles. A falcon attacks its prey by diving at the head and trying to seize the head in its talons. Prairie falcons do not build their own nests. Instead, they move into the abandoned nests of other birds or use a hollow in a rock.

Owls live on the edges of deserts. The eagle owl is the largest, measuring 27 inches (68 centimeters) in length with a wingspan of over 6.5 feet (2 meters). They have the power to attack small deer. The smallest owl, the elf owl, hunts invertebrates, mainly insects. This owl is about 5 to 6 inches (12 to 15 centimeters) long and weighs 1.25 to 1.75 ounces (35 to 55 grams). Most owls hunt in the evening or at night when their extraordinary eyes and superior hearing allow them to find their prey.

The bird most often pictured in the desert is the vulture, waiting patiently while a creature dies of thirst. Most vultures are not really desert birds, although they do spend much time hunting in desert regions. They soar high in the air, circling and looking for carrion (dead animals), which their excellent eyesight allows them to easily see. When one bird spots a potential food source it begins to descend, and the other vultures follow.

Food and water Birds are found in greater variety and numbers around oases and waterholes where there is an ample supply of water, seeds, and insects. Some, like the Australian scarlet robin, often drink water. Birds that live in the desert itself are able to fly long distances in search of food or water. Some birds become nomads, following the rains from habitat to habitat. Birds usually require less than 10 percent of the amount of water needed by mammals. For this reason, many birds, like shrikes and some wheatears, can obtain enough moisture from the seeds, plants, and insects that they eat and do not need an additional water source. The same is true of vultures and birds of prey, which obtain water from the flesh of animals. Birds have kidneys that are very efficient in their ability to extract water, and their urine is not liquid but jellylike.

> ## Commensalism
>
> Sometimes animals are involved in relationships in which one animal is helped and the other is not affected. This is called commensalism. One example is a desert snake that takes over the abandoned burrow of a prairie dog.

Shelter   During the hottest part of the day, most desert birds rest by roosting in the shade or in underground burrows. During excessively hot or dry periods, birds fly to more comfortable regions. It has been estimated that one-third of Australian birds are constantly on the move to escape the heat.

Many desert birds build nests in rock crevices, in abandoned burrows, or on the ground in the open because there are few trees in the desert. Those that build on the ground may put walls of pebbles around the nest that act as insulation and reduce the force of the wind.

Reproduction   Except in Australia, desert birds appear to breed as other birds do—according to the seasons. In Australia, they adapt their breeding habits to periods of rainfall, and breeding cycles may be years apart.

Birds are free to fly away from the heat most of the year, but during the breeding cycle they must remain in the same spot from the time nest building begins until the young birds can fly. This is usually a period of many weeks.

Normally, the parents sit on the nest to protect the eggs from heat or cold. During very hot weather, the parents may stand over the nest to give the eggs or the nestlings shade.

Mammals   Many mammals live in the desert. More than 70 species live in North American deserts alone. Among all of these species, only monkeys and apes are rarely seen.

Mammals must prevent the loss of moisture from their bodies in the desert. The urine and feces of many desert mammals are concentrated, containing only a small amount of water. Small desert mammals, such as rodents, do not sweat. They manage to lose enough heat through their skin. During the hottest times, they burrow underground. Some estivate in summer months.

No Need for Sunscreen

The naked mole rat, sometimes called the sand puppy, is an animal that seems poorly designed for desert life. It has no fur, just its wrinkly skin for protection, and it is almost blind. To make matters worse, unlike most mammals, it cannot maintain a steady body temperature. Its name gives a clue as to how it survives in the Sahara Desert; it burrows. Naked mole rats are tunneling experts, and a clan of rats will create an entire apartment complex of nurseries, storage chambers, and bedrooms. They dig so fast with their sharp buck teeth most predators cannot catch them and get just a face full of dirt for their trouble. The clan leader is always a female. She is the only one who breeds. Other females do not mature sexually until the queen dies or they decide to leave the den to create their own clan elsewhere.

Medium-sized mammals, such as rabbits and hares, do not burrow or estivate; but they will use another animal's burrow to escape from immediate danger. They have no sweat glands and cannot keep cool by sweating, although some heat escapes from their large ears. Hares and rabbits stay in whatever shade they can find during the hottest time of day. The quokka, a rabbitlike marsupial (a mammal that carries new offspring in a pouch) from Australia, copes with the heat by producing large amounts of saliva and licking itself. It is not known how the quokka makes up for this water loss.

Larger grazing animals, such as gazelles, can sweat, which helps them tolerate the heat. Some carnivores, such as coyotes, release body heat by panting (breathing rapidly through their mouths). This results in lost moisture. True desert dwellers, like the mongoose, the meerkat, and the hyena, avoid the midday heat by retiring to underground dens.

The Desert fox is one of the mammal residents of the desert. IMAGE COPYRIGHT MICHAEL SCHOFIELD, 2007. USED UNDER LICENSE FROM SHUTTERSTOCK.COM.

Common desert mammals   Other mammals commonly found in deserts include the kangaroo, the camel, and the hyena.

Kangaroos   A well-known grazing animal of Australia is the red kangaroo. The kangaroo will hop long distances in search of food. Water is less of a problem as they get much of the moisture they need from grasses. They have efficient kidneys and produce a concentrated urine.

The kangaroo's strong legs allow them to move as fast as 20 miles (30 kilometers) an hour. Each hop can carry them as far as 25 feet (8 meters). Kangaroos are marsupials, which means that females carry their young, called a joey, in a pouch on their abdomen. Females with young in their pouches are seldom able to travel fast. If the female is in danger and the joey is too heavy, the mother will dump the young out in order to escape. This may seem cruel, but if she is caught the joey will die anyway. If she escapes, she will breed again.

Camels   Camels are the mammals most people associate with the desert. The Bactrian camel has two humps and lives in the deserts of central Asia. The one-humped Arabian camel, called a dromedary, lives in the Arabian and Sahara Deserts. Camels are well adapted for desert life. They can travel almost 100 miles (160 kilometers) a day, for as long as four days, without drinking. When they do drink, they can take in more than 20 gallons (100 liters) in just a few minutes.

At one time it was believed that camels stored water in their humps. This is not true. The hump contains fat, which is used up during long journeys and may shrink in lean times. Camels have strong teeth and the membranes that line the insides of their mouths are tough, allowing them to eat almost anything that grows in the desert, even the thorniest plants. They can drink bitter, salty water that other animals cannot tolerate.

Camels have thick fur that molts (falls out) during the hottest seasons and is replaced by new, thinner hair. Camels can sweat to reduce body temperature, but their body temperature is not constant and varies depending upon surrounding air temperatures. Their eyes have long protective lashes, and their nostrils can be closed to keep out blowing sand. Their padded, two-toed feet are well insulated against the hot desert floor.

The Rabbit Plague

In the nineteenth century, English settlers introduced rabbits into the Australian Desert and grasslands. A few soon multiplied into half a billion strong. They ate everything growing in the pasturelands and then, when there was no more grass to supply moisture, the rabbits mobbed the water holes. Scientists got rid of vast numbers by introducing rabbit diseases in 1950. Some hardy animals survived and are still multiplying.

Packing it Away

Packrats are rodents that collect almost anything—seeds, bones, rocks—and store it away in their dens. Some of those dens need housecleaning so badly that, over the years, the stuff becomes glued together. Many generations of packrats often live in the same spot, and the piles can grow for thousands of years. The packrats' messy lifestyle may actually help scientists. When the burrows are studied, scientists can find out what an area looked like thousands of years ago.

Camels can no longer be considered wild animals. It is doubtful any wild groups still exist. They have been thoroughly domesticated (tamed) and are used by humans for transportation and other needs. Their ability to travel long distances and carry up to 600 pounds (270 kilograms) makes them useful.

Hyenas   Hyenas are members of the dog family and have one of the strongest sets of jaws of any animal. They range over the deserts of Africa and Arabia, hunting in packs for antelope and other game, or stealing the meals of other carnivores. They also eat carrion and, occasionally, plant foods. Hyenas are not particularly fast, but they do not give up easily and may simply wear out their prey, which collapses beneath the snarling pack. Hyenas live as part of a clan in dens they dig themselves.

Food and water   Some small mammals eat plant foods and insects; others, like the desert hedgehog, eat bird and reptile eggs and young. In Australia, a tiny mole no more than 8 inches (20 centimeters) long eats at least its own weight in insects and young lizards every day. Many small mammals do not need to drink water as often because they obtain moisture from the food they eat.

Large grazing animals need to drink and require a water source to replace the moisture lost in sweating. A few, such as the Arabian gazelle and the Nubian ibex, seldom drink water. They obtain what they need from the plants they eat. Grazing animals can travel to areas where rain has recently fallen. In temperate climates, most grazing animals live in large herds. The desert food supply will not support such numbers, and desert groups are usually very small.

Carnivores, such as mountain lions and coyotes, do not live in the deep desert but remain on the desert fringes where a supply of water is more readily found. Carnivores obtain much of their moisture requirements from the flesh of their prey, but they still need to drink.

Shelter   Small mammals remain in burrows during the day. The air inside a burrow is up to five times more humid than the outside air. This helps the animal prevent moisture loss.

Medium-sized hares and rabbits do not live in burrows but seek shelter in the shade of plants or rocks and in shallow depressions. Grazing animals look for shade during the midday heat. Young animals may lie on the ground in the shade created by the adults.

Carnivores dig their own dens, which may consist of many tunnels to accommodate a family clan. The males mark their territories with scent, usually that of urine.

Reproduction Young mammals develop inside the mother's body where they are protected from heat, cold, and predators. The extra weight can make it difficult for the pregnant females themselves to escape danger. Female mammals produce milk to feed their young. In the desert this presents a problem in lost moisture. Those that live in dens must remain nearby until the young can survive on their own, making survival for both mother and young during drought conditions more difficult.

Endangered species   As in other biomes, many desert animal species are threatened.

A wombat is a squirrel-like or rabbit-like mammal found in Australia. IMAGE COPYRIGHT TIMOTHY CRAIG LUBCKE, 2007. USED UNDER LICENSE FROM SHUTTERSTOCK.COM.

The addax, a desert antelope with beautiful horns, has been greatly reduced in numbers by Saharan nomads who believe its stomach contents have healing powers. Its skin is valuable, for it is believed to have the power to ward off attacks from snakes and scorpions.

After World War II (1939–45), when dichlorodiphenyl-trichloroethane (DDT) and other dangerous pesticides were in common use, aplomado falcons shrank in number. These small falcons lived in desert areas of Mexico, Texas, and Arizona, but are no longer found north of Mexico. The poisons were used to kill grasshoppers that were devouring grasses and other vegetation. Grasshoppers are part of the falcons' diet, and as the birds ate the contaminated insects, the poison killed the falcons. The number of falcons will hopefully increase now that DDT is banned.

The California condor is one of the world's rarest birds. When early settlers slaughtered deer herds for food, they reduced the condor's food supply. Later, cattle ranchers set out poison baits to kill wolves and coyotes. The poison also killed the condors who ate the dead animals. California

The Web of Life: Natural Balance

Balance is important to every biome. Changes made by humans with even the best of intentions can create serious problems. During the nineteenth century, early settlers brought the American prickly pear cactus to Australia because they liked the plant's appearance. In America the prickly pear is a useful desert shrub, often serving as fencing for livestock. In Australia, where it had no natural enemies, it was a disaster. By 1925, prickly pear cacti covered more than 100,000 square miles (260,000 square kilometers) of the Queensland and Victoria provinces.

Nobody wanted the job of cutting down all those plants. Instead, a natural predator, a little moth that in caterpillar form loves to munch on prickly pears, was brought to Australia. Five years later, there were no more prickly pears.

condors are now protected. As a result of captive breeding in 2008 there were about 300 condors, with about half of those in captivity.

The beautiful spiral horns of the Arabian oryx are prized by hunters looking for trophies. By 1960 the Arabian oryxes were reduced to only about a dozen animals. In 1961 they became protected and several hundred were bred in zoos. After 1982 many of the zoo-bred animals were reintroduced into the wild.

Human Life

Human beings are able to adapt to many unfriendly environments. It is no surprise that they have learned to live in the desert and make it their home. Ten percent of the world's population lives on arid (dry) land; they include a large variety of native peoples of all races. This number is growing because most desert inhabitants live in developing countries with high rates of population growth.

Impact of the desert on human life   Humans are able to maintain a safe body temperature in the desert by sweating. Under extreme heat, a human being may lose as much as 5 pints (3 liters) of moisture in an hour and up to 21 pints (12 liters) in a day. This water must be replaced or the person will die from dehydration. Dehydration occurs when tissues dry out, depleting the body of fluids that help keep it cool. Unlike the kidneys of many desert animals, human kidneys cannot concentrate urine to conserve water. The loss of salt through sweating is also a problem. Humans need a certain amount of salt to maintain energy production. If too much salt is lost, painful muscle cramps occur.

Humans can change very little physically to adapt to desert conditions, so they must change their behavior. This has been done in many ways, from the choice of lifestyle to the development of technologies such as irrigation (watering of crops).

Food and water   Until the mid-1900s, many native desert dwellers were nomads—either hunter-gatherers, like the Bushmen of the Kalahari and Namib, or herders, like the Bedouin of the Middle East. They moved regularly, usually along an established route, in order to seek food and shelter for themselves or their herds of animals. Most nomads return year after year to the same areas within a given territory. They know when the rains usually come, where to find food or pastures, and where a water supply is located. By the late twentieth century less than 3 percent of desert peoples lived nomadic lives, having been driven from their lands by ranchers or mining companies looking for mineral, gas, and oil resources. Since 1950, many nomadic peoples have moved to cities where they often live in poverty.

> ### Reverse Desertification
>
> In some cases it might be possible to reverse desertification because nature fights back. Grasslands in Northern Uganda, Africa, had been lost when herds of cattle were allowed to overgraze the area. Then tsetse flies moved in and attacked the cattle. When the cattle herders moved to avoid the flies, the plants returned.

The diet of hunter-gatherers consists primarily of plant foods and game animals, although meat is usually scarce. Some, like the Aborigines of Australia, eat the grubs (larvae) of certain insects, which provide a source of protein.

Herding tribes depend primarily upon their animals for food, but they may also raise grains or trade for them. In the Sahara, dates from the date palm are an important food.

Many Native Americans found important uses for desert plants. The leatherplant, also called sangre de drago (blood of the dragon), contains a red juice used as a medicine for eye and gum diseases. Wine and jelly were made from the fruit of the saguaro cactus, the fruit of the prickly pear was made into jam, and ocotillo branches were useful as building materials.

Shelter   The homes of hunter-gatherers tend to be camps, not houses. The Bushmen of the Kalahari, for example, make huts from tree branches and dry grass.

Traditionally, the nomadic tribes of the Sahara, whose shelters had to be portable, used tents made from the hides or hair of herd animals such as goats. The tents of the Bedouin are an example. Village houses in the desert are often made of mud bricks dried in the sun. The bricks do not need to be waterproof because there is so little rain.

In the desert country of Mongolia, desert dwellers commonly live in yurts—tentlike structures made from felt created from sheep's wool. The felt is stretched over a wood frame, and a hole at the top of the yurt allows smoke from cooking fires to escape.

Some Native Americans of the southwestern desert, such as the Hopi and Zuni tribes, built homes called pueblos from mud, wood, and stone.

The thick walls and small windows kept the interior cool. The Anasazi, who lived around 1100 AD, built their homes in the sides of cliffs. The homes were reached by ladders, which could be pulled up for defense. The Navajos made hogans—houses of logs and mud. Modern-day Native Americans live in the same kinds of homes as other Americans.

Clothing   One advantage humans have over other animals is clothing, which is a substitute for fur. Unlike fur, clothing can be put on or taken off at will. Most traditional desert peoples wear layers of loose-fitting garments that protect the body from the heat. A naked person absorbs twice as much heat as a person in lightweight clothes. Loose clothing absorbs sweat and, as the air moves through, it produces a cooling effect. As a result, the person sweats less, conserving water. Many desert tribes, especially in the Middle East, have at least partially adopted western clothing styles.

The only desert peoples to go naked were the Bushmen of the Kalahari and the Aborigines of Australia. When nights were chilly they occasionally wore "blankets" made from bark, but more often their warmth came from a campfire. Those Bushmen and Aborigines who still live a traditional lifestyle continue to go without clothes.

Some kind of headgear is usually worn by people in the desert to shield their face from the sun and blowing sand. The Fulani, who live on the edge of the Sahara in West Africa, wear decorated hats made from plant fibers and leather.

Economy   For traditional hunter-gatherers, possessions are almost meaningless. If they favor a particular stone for sitting on, they might carry it along. However, a stone, as well as other possessions, gets very heavy after a few miles. Their economy tends to be simple and little trading is done.

A century ago, desert herders were self-sufficient. Their wealth moved with them in the form of herd animals, jewelry, tents, and other possessions. Commerce usually involved selling goats, camels, or cattle. In the Middle East, the discovery of oil made important changes in the economy. In some cases, sweeping modernization made irrigation and food production more stable. Nomads settled in one spot and became farmers. In other cases, the wealth fell into the hands of a few people, while the large majority lived in poverty.

Impact of human life on the desert   The fact that the desert is so unfriendly to human life has helped preserve it from those who could destroy its ecological balance.

Use of plants and animals   As long as traditional lifestyles remained in effect, the human impact on the desert was not severe. Desert dwellers understood the need to maintain balance between themselves and their environment. While animals and plants were used for food, they were not exploited (overused), and their numbers could recover. Since the introduction of firearms and the rapid growth of human populations, however, many plants and animals have become threatened.

Desertification, the deterioration of land until it becomes desertlike, continues in spite of efforts by conservationists (people who work to preserve the environment) to stop it. Several popular desert plants such as cacti, and animals such as lizards, are sold at high prices to collectors. Many of these species are threatened as a result.

Natural resources   Overpopulation has diminished many natural resources. The digging of wells has caused the water table (the level of ground water) to drop in many desert regions. Supplies of oil and minerals are being removed from beneath the desert surface and cannot be replaced.

For thousands of years, crops have been grown in desert soil with the aid of irrigation (mechanical watering systems). Furrows were dug between rows of plants, and water pumped from wells was allowed to run along the furrows. In modern times, dams and machinery are used to control the rivers or pump groundwater for irrigation, allowing many

Xeriscaping

Green lawns and many popular trees and shrubs require constant watering in the summer. This puts a strain on water supplies. Some desert communities ask residents to forget the lawns and xeriscape instead. Xeriscaping is a kind of landscaping using desert plants that need less water.

former nomads to become settled farmers. To irrigate large cotton farms in the Kara Kum Desert of central Asia, water is brought from the Amu Darya River by means of a canal 500 miles (800 kilometers) long.

Irrigation must be controlled. If too much groundwater is pumped, it may be used up faster than it can be replaced. When the water table drops in regions near the ocean, the land may slump. Salt water may enter aquifers (underground layers of earth that collect water), destroying the fresh water. Another problem caused by irrigation is an accumulation of salt in the soil. All soils contain some salts and, if irrigation water is used without proper drainage, the salt builds up within the surface layers and prevents plant growth.

Quality of the environment People have impacted the desert environment in several ways. Drilling for oil and mining for other resources requires roads. The people who operate the drills need houses. Most of these changes have occurred along the Mediterranean in mineral-rich countries on the edges of the desert. However, the deep centers of deserts have usually not been disturbed. Roads remain tracks and have escaped being blacktopped.

The world's climate may be changing because of human activity. If so, the climate of the desert will change with unknown consequences to the plant and animal life.

Desert peoples The Bushmen and the Tuareg are two groups of desert peoples commonly found living in the desert.

Bushmen The Bushmen of the Kalahari and Namib Deserts of Africa live in clans consisting of several families. A clan's territory is about 400 square miles (1,036 square kilometers). Clans move according to the rains or the seasons, returning to familiar campgrounds year after year. Their territory includes good waterholes. Bushmen live off the land, eating berries, roots, and wild game. Plants, which make up the greatest share of their diet, are gathered by the women. Bushmen are expert trackers and use these skills to hunt game for food with bows and poisoned arrows. The meat is cut into strips and dried so that it will not spoil. Bushmen are not tall, ranging between 55 and 63 inches (140 and 160 centimeters) in height. This may be partially due to a diet deficient in some nutrients.

Overnight shelters built from grass and branches provide protection from the wind. In the winter, clans may break up into smaller groups and build stronger huts to keep out the rains. The Bushmen population numbers approximately 20,000. Probably fewer than half of those still live as hunter-gatherers.

The Tuareg The northern Tuareg of the Sahara depend upon the camel for their livelihood, grazing their animals on what little pasture exists on the desert fringes. Camels may be killed for meat or their milk used to make butter and cheese. They are also the primary means of transportation. Since the Tuareg are traders, camels are essential to carry goods such as cloth and dates.

The southern Tuareg tribes are more settled. As a result of modern technology that allows the digging of deep wells, the Tuareg have established cattle ranches on the edges of the Sahara. Unfortunately, the land is often overgrazed, and more territory is lost to the desert every year.

Tuareg men wear a characteristic blue veil wound into a turban (head covering) on their heads. Both men and women wear loose robes for protection against the sun. An indigo (blue) dye is used to color some clothing. The Tuareg have been known as the "blue men" because the dye often rubs off on the skin.

Homes are usually low tents made of animal hides dyed red. The tent roof is supported by poles and the sides are tied to the ground with ropes to keep out the wind and sand. During the hottest parts of the year, the Tuareg build a *zeriba,* a large, tall hut made from grasses attached to a wooden frame.

The Tuareg are known for their ability to fight. Before firearms were introduced during the eighteenth century, they made impressive weapons such as daggers and swords. They now prefer high-powered rifles. Historically, the Tuareg have had a tendency to raid other tribes, and wars between one tribe and another may last for years.

It is estimated that the Tuareg number as many as 1 million people. This figure is only approximate, since about 700,000 of the Tuareg are nomads and rarely remain in one place long enough for a reliable count to be made.

Expert Trackers

The Bushmen and the Aborigines are excellent huntsmen and trackers. Bushmen can follow animal signs over the hardest ground and can distinguish the signs of one individual animal from those of another. During World War II (1939–45), when pilots whose planes had crashed were lost in the Australian deserts, Aborigines could find them by following footprints no one else could see.

A Tuareg man draws water from a well, with help from his camel, to irrigate crops on his oasis plot. AP IMAGES.

The Food Web

The transfer of energy from organism to organism forms a series called a food chain. All the possible feeding relationships that exist in a biome make up its food web. In the desert, as elsewhere, the food web consists of producers, consumers, and decomposers. The following shows how these three types of organisms transfer energy to create the food web within the desert.

Green plants are the primary producers. They make organic materials from inorganic chemicals and outside sources of energy, primarily the sun. Desert annuals and hardy perennials, such as cacti and palms, turn energy into plant matter.

Animals are consumers. Plant-eating animals, such as locusts, gazelles, and rabbits, are primary consumers in the desert food web. Secondary consumers eat plant-eaters. They include the waterhole tadpoles that consume smaller, plant-eating family members. Tertiary consumers are meat-eating predators, like mongooses, owls, and coyotes. They will eat any prey small enough for them to kill. Humans, like the Bushmen, fall into this category. Humans are omnivores, which means they eat both plants and animals.

Decomposers feed on dead organic matter and include fungi and animals like the vulture. In moister environments, bacteria aid in decomposition, but they are less effective in the desert's dry climate.

Spotlight on Deserts

The Gobi Desert
Location: Mongolia and western China
Area: 500,000 square miles (1,300,000 square kilometers)
Classification: Cold; arid and semiarid

The Gobi Desert In the eastern part of central Asia, extending into Mongolia and western China, is the great Gobi Desert. It is part of a chain of deserts, including the Kara-Kum, the Kyzyl-Kum, the Takla Makan, the Alashan, and the Ordos. *Gobi* is a Mongolian word meaning "waterless place."

Surrounded by mountains—the Pamirs in the west, the Great Kingan in the east, the Altai, Khangai, and Yablonoi in the north, and the Nan

Shan in the south—the Gobi is a high, barren, gravelly plain where few grasses grow. It is so flat that a person can see for miles in any direction.

Except for the polar deserts, the Gobi is the coldest because of its altitude—about 3,000 feet (900 meters) in the east and about 5,000 feet (1,500 meters) in the south and west. Arctic winds blow down from the north so that, in the winter, some areas become snow covered. Any rainfall occurs in the spring and fall. Temperatures average between 27°F (-3°C) in January to 86°F (30°C) in July.

Several rivers flow into the Gobi from the surrounding mountains, but the desert has no oases (waterholes). Dry river beds and signs of old lakes indicate that water once existed here. The only surface water that remains is alkaline (containing too many undesirable minerals). Fresh water is obtained primarily from wells.

The few trees found here are willow, elm, poplar, and birch. In general, the largest plants are the tamarisk bush and the saxoul. Grass, thorn, and scrub brush survive, and bush peas, saltbush, and camel sage are abundant. During the brief spring, annuals (plants that live only one season) flourish.

Few reptiles are present because they do not favor the cold winters, but several species of snakes live in the Gobi. Many birds, including sand grouse, bustards, eagles, hawks, and vultures, thrive here. Many of these are migrators (animals that have no permanent home). Small mammals include jerboas, hamsters, rats, and hedgehogs. Larger mammals include gazelles, sheep, and rare Mongolian wild horses.

The Mongolian people living in the Gobi include settled farmers, who cultivate grains on its fringes, and herders who prefer life on the windy plain. Herders tend to be nomads (wandering tribes) who raise horses, donkeys, camels, sheep, goats, cattle, and, in upland areas, yaks. The two groups often trade; the farmers provide grain and the herders supply meat. Since the 1940s, irrigation has been used to make cotton and wheat crops possible, and many nomadic peoples have settled on farms.

Famous Venetian explorer Marco Polo (1254–1324) reached the Gobi during his travels in the thirteenth century. Modern explorers, including archaeologists and anthropologists, still visit in search of dinosaur bones and eggs commonly found there. Such fossils are evidence that the Gobi was once a friendlier environment supporting diverse animal life.

The Thar Desert   The Thar (TAHR) Desert (also called the Great Indian Desert) begins near the Arabian Sea and extends almost to the base of the Himalaya Mountains. It contains a variety of landforms and differing climates. It is considered an arid, lowland desert characterized by extreme temperature variations. January temperatures average 61°F (16°C), while June temperatures average 99°F (37°C).

The plain of the Thar slopes gently from more than 1,000 feet (305 meters) in the southeast to fewer than 300 feet (91 meters) in the northwest near the Indus River, broken only by areas of sand dunes—primarily seif (SAFE) dunes that run parallel to the wind. Some more or less permanent dunes may soar to heights of 200 feet (61 meters). Several salt lakes lie on the desert's margins. The salt covering the lake beds is mined and sold.

Rainfall is unreliable and drops to about 4 inches (100 millimeters) a year in the west. In the summer, the Thar benefits from seasonal monsoons (rainy periods) that arrive in July and August. During monsoon season, the largest salt lake may cover 90 square miles (35 square kilometers) and be 4 feet (1.22 meters) deep, only to disappear during the dry period.

Wheat and cotton have been grown on the irrigated Indus plain in the northeast since the 1930s, but most areas support only grass, scrub, jujube, and acacia, which are eaten by domesticated camels, cattle, goats, and sheep. Birds, such as the great bustard and quail, are found here. Wild

The Thar Desert
Location: India and Pakistan
Area: 77,000 square miles (200,000 square kilometers)
Classification: Cold; arid

mammals live in or on the fringes of the Thar, including hyenas, jackals, foxes, wild asses, and rabbits.

Nomads raise sheep, cattle, and camels. Villages are located in areas where grass will grow after a rain and support herds of livestock. Small industries are based on wool, camel hair, and leather.

About 5,000 years ago, the Indus Valley was home to the great Indus civilization. The decline and disappearance of this civilization is a mystery, but it may be partly due to climatic changes that caused the Thar to spread.

The Australian Desert   About three-quarters of the Australian continent is desert or semiarid land, a mixture of stone, rock, sand, and clay. January temperatures average 79°F (26°C), and July temperatures average 53°F (12°C). The central region is a basin, the western area a high plateau. The Australian desert region is composed of six different deserts—the Simpson, the Great Victoria, the Sturt Stony, the Gibson, the Great Sandy, and the Tanami. They blend into one another and are part of the same whole.

The basin region is a flat land, where a visitor can gaze for miles without the view being interrupted by hills. This makes it a difficult place in which to navigate, for there are no landmarks. The terrain varies, changing from semiarid grassland to rocky stretches, to areas with sandy dunes. Strange, massive, solitary rock formations have spiritual meaning to the Aborigines, such as Ayers Rock or the Olgas.

The lowest point of the Australian Desert is near Lake Eyre, which lies 60 feet (18 meters) below sea level. The lake, situated close to sand dunes, is about 50 miles (80 kilometers) long and so salt-encrusted that during dry periods it appears white. It fills with water only once or twice during a ten-year period. When full, it supports abundant wildlife, including birds, frogs, and toads.

Mulga, a type of thorny acacia bush, and mallee, a species of eucalyptus, grow in the most arid regions of the Australian Desert. At the desert's edges, spinifex grass grows.

Australia is home to a number of animals found nowhere else in the world, but their ways of adapting to the desert are the same as animals elsewhere. Insects, such as locusts and termites; snakes, such as the bandy bandy and the brown snake; and lizards, such as the blue-tongued skink are commonly found in the Australian Desert. Birds include the emu, a large, flightless bird that resembles an ostrich, parrots, quail, cockatoos, and kookaburras.

The Australian Desert
Location: Australia
Area: 600,000 square miles (1,500,000 square kilometers)
Classification: Hot; arid and semiarid

Kangaroos are Australia's largest mammals. They prefer to live in grasslands but can travel long distances in the desert without water. Kangaroos are marsupials and carry their young in a pouch. Other marsupials unique to Australia are the wallaby and the wombat.

Until the middle of the twentieth century, most Aborigines of Australia still lived as hunter-gatherers. Traveling in small groups, or clans, they moved over an established territory. They gathered plant roots, bulbs, termites, and grubs; and hunted kangaroos and wallabies with spears and boomerangs. When young Aborigine men attained a certain age, they went on a "walkabout." During this time they had to leave their clan to wander in the desert, perhaps for years, learning about life and survival.

The Arabian Desert The Arabian Desert covers most of the Arabian Peninsula, from the coast of the Red Sea to the Persian Gulf. It measures 900,000 square miles (2,330,000 square kilometers). Except for fertile spots in the southeast and southwest, the peninsula is all desert. During prehistoric times, volcanic cones and craters formed along its western edge. On the eastern side, sedimentary rocks and prehistoric sea life formed the world's richest oilfields. Inside some of these same rocks are vast supplies of underground water, captured during ages past when the area included wetlands.

The desert plateau consists of bare rock, gravel, or sand having a characteristically golden color, with the exception of deep ravines in the south. Wind and occasional flooding has carved the rocks into fantastic shapes. The Empty Quarter—about one-third of the southern part of the peninsula—is a vast sea of sand dunes. Treacherous quicksand is found here, its particles so smooth they act like ballbearings, drawing unwary creatures below the surface to their deaths. Another area of dunes, the Great Nafud, is found farther north and contains so few waterholes even camels find it difficult to cross. Along the coasts, changing sea levels have resulted in large salt flats, some as much as 20 miles (30 kilometers) wide.

A monsoon season (rainy period) occurs along the southeast; rainfall elsewhere is only 1.4 inches (35 millimeters) per year. Flash floods are common during the infrequent rains, and hailstorms sometimes occur. Droughts may last several years. January temperatures average 65°F (18°C).

In the southern portion of the Arabian Desert annuals spread a colorful blanket over the soil right after a rain; otherwise hardy perennials

The Arabian Desert
Location: The Arabian Peninsula
Area: 900,000 square miles (2,300,000 square kilometers)
Classification: Hot; extremely arid

are the most common plant life, including mimosas, acacias, and aloe. Oleanders and some species of roses also thrive. Few trees can survive. The tamarisk tree helps control drifting sand, and junipers grow in the southwest. Date palms grow almost everywhere except at high elevations, and coconut palms are found on the southern coast. Plants that can be cultivated with the aid of irrigation include alfalfa, wheat, barley, rice, cotton, and many fruits, including mangoes, melons, pomegranates, bananas, and grapes.

Swarms of locusts move over the land periodically, causing much destruction. Other common invertebrates include ticks, beetles, scorpions, and ants. Horned vipers and a special species of cobra make their home in the Arabian Desert, as do monitors and skinks. Ostriches are now extinct there, but eagles, vultures, and owls are common. Seabirds, such as pelicans, can be seen on the coasts. Wild mammals include the gazelle, oryx, ibex, hyena, wolf, jackal, fox, rabbit, and jerboa. The lion once lived there but has long been extinct in the area.

For centuries, the Arabian Desert has been home to nomadic tribes of Bedouin. The camel makes life in the desert possible for them. A camel's owner can live for months in the desert on the camel's milk. The camel is also used for meat, clothing, and muscle power, and its dung (solid waste) is burned for fuel. Domestic sheep and goats are raised, as well as donkeys and horses.

The Sahara Desert   The Sahara Desert ranges across the upper third of Africa, from the Atlantic Ocean to the Red Sea, and is about 1,250 miles (2,000 kilometers) wide from north to south. It is the world's largest hot desert, covering an area of 3.5 million square miles (9 million square kilometers). Its landforms, which tend to have a golden color, range from rocky mountains and highlands (some as high as 10,712 feet [3,265 meters]) to stretches of gravel and vast sand dunes. Erosion has shaped the sandstone rocks in some areas into unusual shapes and deep, narrow canyons.

Millions of years ago, volcanic activity occurred here. The region was the site of shallow seas and lakes, which contributed to the vast reserves of oil deposits found there. Around 150 BC when the Romans controlled North Africa, the northern Sahara was a rich agricultural area. Over the centuries sand has claimed the once fertile landscape.

The Sahara is the hottest desert, with a mean annual temperature of 85°F (29°C). Nights are cool and occasionally fall below freezing in the winter months. Except along the southern fringe, rain is not dependable

The Sahara Desert
Location: North Africa
Area: 3,500,000 square miles (9,000,000 square kilometers)
Classification: Hot; extremely arid

and may be absent for as many as 10 years in succession. When it does rain, it tends to fall in sudden storms.

In some areas, such as the Tanezrouft region, nothing appears to grow. In other areas, annuals bloom after the unpredictable rains and provide food for camels and wild animals. At one time, the only perennial vegetation at oases were tamarisks and oleander bushes. The date palm has since been introduced and now citrus fruits, peaches, apricots, wheat, barley, and millet are all cultivated.

Animals such as gazelles, oryx, addax, foxes, badgers, and jackals live in the wild. Domesticated animals include camels, sheep, and goats.

Three main groups of people now live in the Sahara: the Tuareg, the Tibbu, and the Moors. Two-thirds of the population live at oases, where they depend upon irrigation and deep wells that tap underground water.

The Patagonian Desert   Along the entire length of Argentina, between the Andes Mountains in the west and the Atlantic Ocean in the east, lies the Patagonian Desert, which is 300,000 square miles (777,000 square kilometers). It owes its existence to a cold ocean current and the Andes Mountains, both of which cause dry air to form. The terrain is a series of plateaus, some as high as 5,000 feet (900 meters) near the Andes, which slope toward the sea. Deep, wide valleys made by ancient rivers have created clifflike walls, but only a few streams remain. These are usually formed by melting snow from the Andes.

In some areas, the soil is alkaline or covered by salt deposits and does not support plant life. Elsewhere it is primarily gravel. Mineral resources, including coal, oil, and iron ore, have been found in several places but quantities are too small to be important.

Rainfall, which occurs in the summer, is usually less than 10 inches (25 centimeters) annually. Although arid, the Patagonian Desert does not experience extremes of temperature, primarily because it is so close to the ocean. Temperatures range from 45°F (7°C) to 78°F (26°C). During the colder months, subzero temperatures and snow are common. Mean annual temperatures range from 43° to 78°F (6° to 26°C). Winds of 70 miles (112 kilometers) per hour are not uncommon.

Plants, mostly saltbushes and other members of the amaranth family, cover 15 percent of the desert. In moister areas, cushion plants, shrubs, feather grass and meadow grass cover almost half the ground.

Many reptiles are found here, but small mammals are the most numerous animals. Rabbits and hares are widespread. The rhea, an

The Patagonian Desert
Location: Argentina
Area: 300,000 square miles (777,000 square kilometers)
Classification: Cold; arid

American ostrich, lives throughout the region. Other common animals are the mara and the guanaco, a llamalike animal prized for its long, fine hair. The guanaco was hunted almost to extinction because of the fine quality of its coat.

The most unusual animal of the Patagonian Desert is the armadillo. Its skin consists of plates of tough armor, including one that covers its face. It can travel very fast on its short legs and, when threatened, digs a hole to escape.

Patagonia means "big feet," and refers to the Tehuelche Indians when they were first seen by Portugese explorer Ferdinand Magellan (c. 1480–1521) in 1520. The Tehuelche were nomadic hunters whose size and vigor caused Europeans to consider them giants. After the Europeans introduced the Tehuelche to horses, their ability to seek new territory and intermarry with other tribes increased. By 1960, the race was virtually extinct. Modern settlements in and around the Patagonian Desert were established during the twentieth century after oil was discovered on the coast.

The Atacama Desert   The Atacama Desert is a long, narrow, coastal desert 600 miles (965 kilometers) long, parallel to the coast of Chile. The Pacific Ocean lies to the west, where sheer cliffs about 1,475 feet (450 meters) high rise from the sea. Beyond these cliffs lies a barren valley that runs along the foothills of the Andes Mountains.

Cold ocean currents are responsible for the dry conditions that make the Atacama the world's driest desert. Droughts may persist for many years, and there is no dependable rainy season. Although it is classified as a hot desert, mean temperatures seldom exceed 68°F (20°C).

Much of the Atacama consists of salt flats over gravelly soil. Sand dunes have formed in a few areas. In the south, a raised plateau nearly 3,300 feet (1,006 meters) high and broken with volcanic cones takes on an otherworldly appearance. In the southeast, a plateau bordering the Andes reaches a height of 13,100 feet (4,000 meters).

The area is rich in boron, sodium nitrate, and other minerals, which contaminate any underground water, making it unusable both by plants and animals. Plant life consists primarily of coarse grasses, mesquite, and a few cacti.

Animal life is rare. The most commonly found animals are lizards, but even they are not numerous. The rather timid giant iguanas, some growing over 6 feet (2 meters) long and resembling dragons prowling, are

The Atacama Desert
Location: Chile and parts of Peru
Area: 54,000 square miles (140,000 square kilometers)
Classification: Hot; extremely arid

scavengers. Huge Andean condors that feed on carrion can be seen soaring overhead. Wherever cacti are found, cactus wrens feed and breed. Ovenbirds build their own little adobe (mud) huts instead of nests, and live in the less arid regions. The only mammals living in the Atacama are small rodents, such as the chinchilla, with guanaco and vicuña inhabiting higher elevations.

Indians may have lived in or on the fringes of the Atacama at one time; however, they may have been killed by European settlers during the eighteenth century. Those people who still live in the area are descendants of the European immigrants.

The Atacama was once important to the fertilizer industry for which sodium nitrate was mined. Another fertilizer, bird droppings called guano (GWAN-oh), was collected on the offshore islands, where seabirds would breed. In the 1920s synthetic fertilizers became popular, and the mining settlements in the Atacama were abandoned.

The Namib Desert   A coastal desert, the Namib is part of the vast tableland (flat highland) of southern Africa. Although it borders the Kalahari Desert to the east, the two are very different. Some scientists do not consider the Kalahari a true desert, while the Namib certainly is one. The desert is dry, but not very hot, with temperatures between 66°–75°F (19°–24°C). It has been nick-named the world's oldest desert, dating back 55,000,000 years. The terrain is gravelly in the north, a rich area for gemstones, particularly diamonds. Sand prevails in the south, creating enormous dunes as much as 980 feet (300 meters) high in some areas.

Rain is rare and years may pass between showers. When rain does come, it creates flash floods and then disappears as quickly as it came. The winds that blow in from the Atlantic do not bring storms. Instead, dense fog rolls in almost nightly, creating very humid air.

Unusual life forms exist in the Namib, particularly in the southern dunes where plant life depends upon the fog and has evolved to draw moisture from it. The strange welwitschia plant is an example.

The Hartmann's zebra that lives in the Namib is able to sniff out small pools of water that may lie in gullies or dry stream beds. The zebras dig, sometimes 2 or 3 feet (0.6 or 1 meter), into the ground until the water is uncovered. The Namib is also inhabited by elephants, rhinos, giraffes, and lions.

Bushmen live principally in the Kalahari, but they occasionally frequent the Namib.

The Namib Desert
Location: Eastern Namibia
Area: 52,000 square miles
(135,000 square
kilometers)
Classification: Hot; arid

The Mojave Desert   Deserts in North America are all part of the Great Basin, a vast territory stretching from just north of the Canadian border into parts of Mexico. In the north, cold semiarid deserts have formed, ringed by the Sierra Nevada and Rocky Mountains. Further south lie the hot deserts, the Mojave and the nearby Sonora Desert.

The Mojave Desert, named for the Mojave Indians who once lived along the Colorado River, consists of salt flats, barren mountains, deep ravines, high plateaus, and wide, windy plains of sand. Elevations range from 2,000 to 5,000 feet (600 to 1,500 meters), and it measures 25,000 square miles (65,000 square kilometers). During prehistoric times the Pacific Ocean covered the area until volcanic action built the mountain ranges, leaving saltpans and mudflats as the only remaining signs. The desert is rich in minerals. Borax, potash, salt, silver, and tungsten are mined here.

Annual rainfall is less than 5 inches (13 centimeters). Frost is common in the winter, and snow occasionally falls. One major river, the Mojave, crosses the desert, running underground for part of its length. Summer temperatures often rise above 100°F (38°C), and winter temperatures often drop below freezing.

Vegetation characteristic of North American deserts includes different species of cacti such as organ pipe, prickly pear, and saguaro. Although nothing grows on the salt flats, plants, such as the creosote bush, can find a foothold in other areas. Joshua trees are protected in the Joshua Tree National Park. On the highest mountains, piñon and juniper grow.

A wide variety of invertebrates, amphibians, reptiles, birds, and smaller mammals make a home in this region. The rare Mojave ground squirrel may spend nine months estivating (being dormant in hot weather) in its burrow. Larger mammals include the puma, jaguar, peccary, prong-horned antelope, and bighorn sheep.

Death Valley   Death Valley is a basin in the Mojave Desert of which approximately 550 square miles (1,430 square kilometers) of the total 5,313 square miles (13,813 square kilometers) lie below sea level. Near its center is the lowest point in North America, 282 feet (86 meters) below sea level. Prehistoric salt flats exist in the lowest areas where nothing grows.

Death Valley is the hottest place on the continent. Average summer temperatures are 117°F (47°C) with a record temperature of 134°F (57°C) on July 10, 1913. Rainfall is seldom more than 2 inches (50 millimeters) per year. Many species of plants are found here. Annuals,

The Mojave Desert
Location: Southeastern California, Nevada, Arizona, Utah
Area: 25,000 square miles (65,000 square kilometers)
Classification: Hot; arid

Death Valley
Location: California
Area: 5,312 square miles (13,812 square kilometers)
Classification: Hot; arid

such as poppies, appear in late winter and early spring; perennials, such as cacti and mesquite, survive all year. Lizards, foxes, rats, mice, squirrels, coyotes, bighorn sheep, wild burros, and rabbits live here, as well as many birds, such as ravens.

The name Death Valley came from the numbers of gold-seekers who died there during the gold rush in the mid-1800s. Although gold, silver, lead, and copper have been mined in the area, Death Valley became known for borax (compound used as an antiseptic and cleanser), discovered in 1873 and brought out by mule teams. Mining ghost towns now draw tourists. Death Valley became a national monument in 1933 and a national park in 1994.

Walter Edward Scott (1872–1954), known as "Death Valley Scotty," was a cowboy in Buffalo Bill's Wild West Show. A mansion approximately 32,000 square feet (2,973 square meters) was built in 1927 by Albert Johnson, a wealthy Chicago executive, in the Grapevine Canyon of Death Valley. Johnson met Scott at one of his shows and the two become friends. Through their friendship, the ranch became known as Scotty's Castle, and is one of the most popular tourist attractions in Death Valley National Park.

The Antarctic Desert Polar deserts are like other deserts only in the dryness of the air. Here, all moisture is frozen. During the warmest season in the polar desert, temperatures never rise above 12.8°F (-3°C), with the mean temperature ranging from -30° to -4°F (-34° to -20°C). In the cold season, the mean temperature is -52.9°F (-47.2°C) and ranges between -94° and -40°F (-70° to -40°C).

Scientists know very little about the landforms in Antarctica because they are buried beneath such deep ice—over 14,000 feet (4,270 meters) deep in places. It is believed that the area is a series of islands connected by great ice sheets. Western Antarctica is mountainous, and eastern Antarctica is a plateau (high, flat land). It measures approximately 360,000 square miles (936,000 square kilometers). The Antarctic desert is the largest desert in the world, followed by the Sahara.

Tiny communities of microbes (microorganisms) have been found in the ice desert of Antarctica. During the summer, the sun warms little pockets of dirt and grit and turns them to slush. In the dim light, bacteria suspended in the slush can photosynthesize.

Plant growth is limited to the bordering tundra regions where lichens and mosses are the largest plant forms. Algae, yeasts, fungi, and bacteria

The Antarctic Desert
Location: Antarctica
Area: Approximately 360,000 square miles (936,000 square kilometers)
Classification: Polar

are found in some areas. Grasses and a few other seed plants may grow on the fringes. The driest areas support no known plant life.

The only land animals are about 100 species of invertebrates, half of which appear to be parasites that live on birds and mammals. These include lice, mites, and ticks.

Seabirds, such as petrels and terns, frequent the coast where they feed on fish. The only true Antarctic bird is the penguin, and about eighteen species populate the area. Penguins live in large flocks and nest in the autumn, living on fish they catch in the coastal waters. They range in size from the fairy penguin, which is 16 inches (41 centimeters), to the emperor penguin, which is about 4 feet (1.2 meters) tall. Leopard seals, the largest of all seals, are 10 feet (3 meters) long and weigh 770 pounds (300 kilograms). They inhabit the Antarctic waters and are the natural predators of penguins.

Marine mammals, such as whales and seals, live in the coastal waters, but they do not enter desert areas. (Polar bears live only at the North Pole; they do not live in Antarctica.)

Temporary year-round human settlements were established in Antarctica around 1900, primarily for exploration purposes. Any industry is centered on the surrounding sea, primarily whaling and seal hunting.

For More Information

BOOKS

Allaby, Michael. *Biomes of the Earth: Deserts.* New York: Chelsea House, 2006.

Hodgson, Wendy C. *Food Plants of the Sonoran Desert.* Tucson: University of Arizona Press, 2001.

Irish, Mary. *Gardening in the Desert: A Guide to Plant Selection & Care.* Tucson: University of Arizona Press, 2000.

Johnson, Mark. *The Ultimate Desert Handbook: A Manual for Desert Hikers, Campers and Travelers.* Camden, Maine: Ragged Mountain Press/McGraw Hill, 2003.

Oliver, John E., and John J. Hidore. *Climatology: An Atmosperic Science.* Upper Saddle River, NJ: Prentice Hall, 2nd ed. 2004.

Sowell, John B. *Desert Ecology.* Salt Lake City: University of Utah Press, 2001.

PERIODICALS

El-Bagouri, Ismail H.M. "Interaction of Climate Change and Land Degradation: the Experience in the Arab Region." *UN Chronicle.* 44. 2 June 2007: 50.

Greer, Carrie A. "Your local desert food and drugstore." *Skipping Stones.* 20. 2 March-April 2008: 34.

Lancaster, Pat. "The Oman experience." *The Middle East.* 384 December 2007: 55.

Levy, Sharon. *New Scientist: Last Days of the Locust.* February 21, 2004, 48-49.

ORGANIZATIONS

Chihuahuan Desert Research Institute, PO Box 905, Fort Davis, TX 79734, Phone: 432-364-2499; Fax: 432-364-2686, Internet: http://www.cdri.org

Desert Protective Council, Inc., PO Box 3635, San Diego, CA 92163, Phone: 619-342-5524, Internet: http://www.dpcinc.org/environ_issues.shtml

Environmental Defense Fund, 257 Park Ave. South, New York, NY 10010, Phone: 212-505-2100; Fax: 212-505-2375, Internet: http://www.edf.org

Environmental Protection Agency, 401 M Street, SW, Washington, DC 20460, Phone: 202-260-2090, Internet: http://www.epa.gov

Friends of the Earth, 1717 Massachusetts Ave. NW, 300, Washington, DC 20036-2002, Phone: 877-843-8687; Fax: 202-783-0444; Internet: http://www.foe.org

Greenpeace USA, 702 H Street NW, Washington, DC 20001, Phone: 202-462-1177; Fax: Internet: http://www.greenpeace.org

Sierra Club, 85 2nd Street, 2nd fl., San Francisco, CA 94105, Phone: 415-977-5500; Fax: 415-977-5799, Internet: http://www.sierraclub.org

World Wildlife Fund, 1250 24th Street NW, Washington, DC 20090-7180, Phone: 202-293-4800; Internet: http://www.wwf.org

WEB SITES

National Center for Atmospheric Research. http://www.ncar.ucar.edu (accessed on August 17, 2007).

World Meteorological Organization. http://www.wmo.ch (accessed on August 17, 2007).

Where to Learn More

Books

Allaby, Michael. *Biomes of the Earth: Deserts.* New York: Chelsea House, 2006.

Allaby, Michael. *Biomes of the Earth: Grasslands.* New York: Chelsea House, 2006.

Allaby, Michael. *Biomes of the Earth: Temperate Forests.* New York: Chelsea House, 2006.

Allaby, Michael. *Biomes of the Earth: Tropical Forests.* New York: Chelsea House, 2006.

Allaby, Michael. *Temperate Forests.* New York: Facts on File, 2007.

Angelier, Eugene, and James Munnick. *Ecology of Streams and Rivers.* Enfield, New Hampshire: Science Publishers, 2003.

Ballesta, Laurent. *Planet Ocean: Voyage to the Heart of the Marine Realm.* National Geographic, 2007.

Batzer, Darold P., and Rebecca R. Sharitz. *Ecology of Freshwater and Estuarine Wetlands.* Berkeley: University of California Press, 2007.

Braun, E. Lucy. *Deciduous Forests of Eastern North America.* Caldwell, NJ: Blackburn Press, 2001.

Brockman, C. Frank. *Trees of North America: A Guide to Field Identification,* Revised and Updated. New York: St. Martin's Press, 2001.

Burie, David, and Don E. Wilson, eds. *Animal.* New York: Smithsonian Institute, 2001.

Carson, Rachel L. *The Sea Around Us*, Rev. ed. New York: Chelsea House, 2006.

Cox, C.B., and P.D. Moore. *Biogeography and Ecological and Evolutionary Approach*, 7th ed. Oxford: Blackwell Publishing, 2005.

Cox, Donald D. *A Naturalist's Guide to Seashore Plants: An Ecology for Eastern North America.* Syracuse, NY: Syracuse University Press, 2003.

Day, Trevor. *Biomes of the Earth: Lakes and Rivers.* New York: Chelsea House, 2006.

Day, Trevor. *Biomes of the Earth: Taiga.* New York: Chelsea House, 2006.

Fisher, William H. *Rain Forest Exchanges: Industry and Community on an Amazonian Frontier.* Washington DC: Smithsonian Institution Press, 2000.

Fowler, Theda Braddock. *Wetlands: an Introduction to Ecology, the Law, and Permitting.* Lanham, MD: Government Institutes, 2007.

Gaston, K.J., and J.I. Spicer. *Biodiversity: An Introduction*, 2nd ed. Oxford: Blackwell Publishing, 2004.

Gleick, Peter H., et al. *The World's Water 2004-2005: The Biennial Report on Freshwater Sources.* Washington DC: Island Press, 2004.

Gloss, Gerry, Barbara Downes, and Andrew Boulton. *Freshwater Ecology: A Scientific Introduction.* Malden, MA: Blackwell Publishing, 2004.

Grzimek, Bernhard. *Grizmek's Animal Encyclopedia*, 2nd ed. Vol 7. *Reptiles*, edited by Michael Hutchins, James B. Murphy, and Neil Schlager. Farmington Hills, MI: Gale Group, 2003.

Hancock, Paul L., and Brian J. Skinner, eds. *The Oxford Companion to the Earth.* New York: Oxford University Press, 2000.

Harris, Vernon. *Sessile Animals of the Sea Shore.* New York: Chapman and Hall, 2007.

Hauer, Richard, and Gary A. Lamberti. *Methods in Stream Ecology*, 2nd ed. San Diego: Academic Press/Elsevier, 2007.

Hodgson, Wendy C. *Food Plants of the Sonoran Desert.* Tucson: University of Arizona Press, 2001.

Houghton, J. *Global Warming: The Complete Briefing.* 3rd ed. Cambridge: Cambridge University Press, 2004.

Humphreys, L.R. *The Evolving Science of Grassland Improvement.* Cambridge, UK: Cambridge University Press, 2007.

Hurtig, Jennifer. Deciduous Forests. New York: Weigl Publishers, 2006.

Irish, Mary. *Gardening in the Desert: A Guide to Plant Selection & Care.* Tucson: University of Arizona Press, 2000.

Jacke, Dave. *Edible Forest Gardens.* White River Junction, VT: Chelsea Green Publishing Co., 2005.

Johansson, Philip. The Temperate Forest: A Web of Life. Berkely Heights, NJ: Enslow Publishers, 2004.

Johnson, Mark. *The Ultimate Desert Handbook: A Manual for Desert Hikers, Campers and Travelers.* Camden, Maine: Ragged Mountain Press/McGraw Hill, 2003.

Jose, Shibu, Eric J. Jokela, and Deborah L. Miller *The Longleaf Pine Ecosystem: Ecology, Silviculture, and Restoration.* New York: Springer, 2006.

Luhr, James F., ed. *Earth.* New York: Dorling Kindersley in association with The Smithsonian Institute, 2003.

Marent, Thomas, and Ben Morgan. *Rainforest.* New York: DK Publishing, 2006.

McGonigal, D., and L. Woodworth. *Antarctica: The Complete Story.* London: Frances Lincoln, 2003.

Miller, James H., and Karl V. Miller. *Forest Plants Of The Southeast And Their Wildlife Uses.* Athens: University of Georgia Press, 2005.

Mitsch, William J., and James G. Gosselink. *Wetlands*, 4th ed. Hoboken, NJ: Wiley: 2007.

Moore, Peter D. *Biomes of the Earth: Tundra.* New York: Chelsea House, 2006.

Moore, Peter D. *Wetlands.* New York: Chelsea House, 2006.

Moul, Francis. *The National Grasslands: A Guide to America's Undiscovered Treasures.* Lincoln: University of Nebraska Press, 2006.

National Oceanic and Atmospheric Administration *Hidden Depths: Atlas of the Oceans.* New York: HarperCollins, 2007.

Ocean. New York: DK Publishing, 2006.

O'Shea, Mark, and Tim Halliday. *Smithsonian Handbooks: Reptiles and Amphibians.* New York: Dorling Kindersley, 2001.

Oliver, John E., and John J. Hidore. *Climatology: An Atmosperic Science*, 2nd ed. Upper Saddle River, NJ: Prentice Hall, 2004.

Peschak, Thomas P. *Wild Seas, Secret Shores of Africa.* Cape Town: Struik Publishers, 2008.

Postel, Sandra, and Brian Richter *Rivers for Life: Managing Water For People And Nature.* Washington, DC: Island Press, 2003.

Preston-Mafham, Ken, and Rod Preston-Mafham. *Seashore.* New York: HarperCollins Publishers, 2004.

Primack, Richard B., and Richard Corlett. *Tropical Rain Forests: An Ecological and Biogeographical Comparison.* Hoboken, NJ: Wiley-Blackwell, 2005.

Romashko, Sandra D. *Birds of the Water, Sea, and Shore.* Lakeville, MN: Windward Publishing, 2001.

Scientific American, ed. *Oceans: A Scientific American Reader.* Chicago: University Of Chicago Press: 2007.

Scrace, Carolyn. *Life in the Wetlands.* New York: Children's Press, 2005.

Shea, John F., et al. *Wetlands, Buffer Zones and Riverfront Areas: Wildlife Habitat and Endangered Species.* Boston: MCLE, 2004.

Sowell, John B. *Desert Ecology.* Salt Lake City: University of Utah Press, 2001.

Sverdrup Keith A., and Virginia Armbrust. *An Introduction to the World's Oceans.* Boston: McGraw-Hill Science, 2006.

Swarts, Frederick A. *The Pantanal: Understanding and Preserving the World's Largest Wetland.* St. Paul, MN: Paragon House Publishers, 2000.

Vandermeer, John H., and Ivette Perfecto *Breakfast Of Biodiversity: The Political Ecology of Rain Forest Destruction.* Oakland, CA: Food First Books, 2005.

Vogel, Carole Garbuny. *Shifting Shores (The Restless Sea).* London: Franklin Watts, 2003.

Voshell, J. Reese, Jr. *A Guide to Common Freshwater Invertebrates of North America.* Blacksburg, VA: McDonald and Woodward Publishing Company, 2002.

Woodward, Susan L. *Biomes of Earth: Terrestrial, Aquatic, and Human Dominated.* Westport, CT: Greenwood Press, 2003.

Worldwatch Institute, ed. *Vital Signs 2003: The Trends That Are Shaping Our Future.* New York: W.W. Norton, 2003.

Yahner, Richard H. *Eastern Deciduous Forest, Second Edition: Ecology and Wildlife Conservation.* Minneapolis, MN: University of Minnesota Press, 2000.

Zabel, Cynthia, and Robert G. Anthony. *Mammal Community Dynamics: Management and Conservation in the Coniferous Forests of Western North America.* New York: Cambridge University Press, 2003.

Periodicals

"Arctic Sea Ice Reaches Record Low." *Weatherwise.* 60. 6 Nov-Dec 2007: 11.

Bischof, Barbie. "Who's Watching Whom?" *Natural History.* 116. 10 December 2007: 72.

Bright, Chris, and Ashley Mattoon. "The Restoration of a Hotspot Begins." *World Watch* 14.6 Nov-Dec 2001: p. 8–9.

Carwardine, Mark. "So Long, and Thanks for All the Fish: If the Yangtze River Dolphin isn't Quite Extinct Yet, It Soon Will Be." *New Scientist.* 195. 2621 September 15, 2007: 50.

Coghlan, Andy. "Earth Suffers as We Gobble Up Resources." *New Scientist.* 195. 2611 July 7, 2007: 15.

Cunningham, A. "Going Native: Diverse Grassland Plants Edge Out Crops as Biofuel." *Science News.* 170. 24 December 9, 2006: 372.

Darack, Ed. "Death Valley Springs Alive." *Weatherwise.* 58. 4 July-August 2005: 42.

Darack, Ed. "The Hoh Rainforest." *Weatherwise.* 58. 6 Nov-Dec 2005: 20.

De Silva, José María Cardoso, and John M. Bates. "Biogeographic Patterns and Conservation in the South American Cerrado: A tropical Savanna Hotspot." *BioScience* 52.3 March 2002: p225.

El-Bagouri, Ismail H.M. "Interaction of Climate Change and Land Degradation: the Experience in the Arab Region." *UN Chronicle.* 44. 2 June 2007: 50.

Ehrhardt, Cheri M. "An Amphibious Assault." *Endangered Species Bulletin.* 28. 1 January-February 2003: 14.

Flicker, John. "Audubon view: Grassland Protection." *Audubon.* 107. 3 May-June 2005: 6.

Greer, Carrie A. "Your Local Desert Food and Drugstore." *Skipping Stones.* 20. 2 March-April 2008: 34.

Gunnard, Jessie, Andrew Wier and Lynn Margulis. "Mycological Maestros: in the Ecuadorean Rainforest, a 'Missing Link' in the Evolution of Termite Agriculture?" *Natural History.* 112. 4 May 2003: 22.

Haedrich, Richard L. "Deep Trouble: Fishermen Have Been Casting Their Nets into the Deep Sea After Exhausting Shallow-water Stocks. But Adaptations to Deepwater Living Make the Fishes There Particularly Vulnerable to Overfishing—and Many are Now Endangered." *Natural History.* 116. 8 October 2007: 28.

Hansen, Andrew J., et al. "Global Change in Forests: Responses of Species, Communities, and Biomes." *BioScience.* 51. 9 September 2001: 765.

Johnson, Dan. "Wetlands: Going, Goings … Gone?" *The Futurist.* 35. 5 September 2001: 6.

"Katrina Descends." *Weatherwise.* 58. 6 November-December 2005: 10.

Kessler, Rebecca. "Spring Back." *Natural History* 115.9 November 2006: p 18.

Kloor, Keith. "Fire (in the Sky): In Less than an Hour, Flames had Reduced Nearly 8,000 acres of Grasslands to Smoldering Stubble and Ash." *Audubon.* 105. 3 September 2003: 74.

Lancaster, Pat. "The Oman experience." *The Middle East.* 384 December 2007: 55.

Levy, Sharon. *New Scientist: Last Days of the Locust.* February 21, 2004, p. 48–49.

Marshall, Laurence A. "Sacred Sea: A Journey to Lake Baikal." *Natural History.* 116. 9 November 2007: 69.

Maynard, Barbara. "Fire in Ice: Natural Gas Locked Up in Methane Hydrates Could Be the World's Next Great Energy Source—If Engineers Can Figure Out How to Extract it Safely." *Popular Mechanics.* 183. 4 April 2006: 40.

Mohlenbrock, Robert H. "Wetted Bliss: in a Louisiana Refuge, Different Degrees of Moisture Create Distinctive Woods." *Natural History.* 117. 2 March 2008: 62.

Morris, John. "Will the Forest Survive?" *Wide World.* 13. 1 September 2001: 15.

Payette, Serge, Marie-Josee Fortin, and Isabelle Gamache. "The Subarctic Forest—Tundra: The Structure of a Biome in a Changing Climate." *BioScience.* 51. 9 September 2001: 709.

Pennisi, Elizabeth. "Neither Cold Nor Snow Stops Tundra Fungi." *Science.* 301. 5,638 September 5, 2003: 1,307.

Petty, Megan E. "The Colorado River's Dry Past." *Weatherwise.* 60. 4 (July-August 2007): 11.

Pollard, Simon D, and Robert R. Jackson. "Vampire Slayers of Lake Victoria: African Spiders get the Jump on Blood-filled Mosquitoes. (*Evarcha culicivora*)." *Natural History.* 116. 8 October 2007: 34.

Shefrin, Russell. "An Optimistic Look at Falling Leaves." *New York State Conservationist.* 62.2 October 2007: p32.

"Siberia Sees the Wood from the Trees." *Geographical.* 73. 1 January 2001: 10.

Springer, Craig. "Leading-edge Science for Imperiled, Bonytail." *Endangered Species Bulletin.* 27. 2 March-June 2002: 27.

Springer, Craig. "The Return of a Lake-dwelling Giant." *Endangered Species Bulletin.* 32. 1 February 2007: 10.

Sterling, Eleanor J, and Merry D. Camhi. "Sold Down the River: Dried Up, Dammed, Polluted, Overfished—Freshwater Habitats Around the World are Becoming Less and Less Hospitable to Wildlife." *Natural History.* 116. 9 November 2007: 40.

Stone, Roger D. "Tomorrow's Amazonia: as Farming, Ranching, and Logging Shrink the Globe's Great Rainforest, the Planet Heats Up." *The American Prospect.* 18. 9 September 2007: A2.

Tucker, Patrick. "Growth in Ocean-current Power Foreseen: Florida Team Seeks to Harness Gulf Stream." *The Futurist.* 41. 2 March-April 2007: 8.

Wagner, Cynthia G. "Battles On the Beaches." *The Futurist.* 35. 6 November 2001: 68.

Weir, Kirsten L. "Don't Tread on It." *Natural History.* 110. 9 November 2001: 37.

Yalden, Derek. "Managing moorland." *Biological Sciences Review.* 18. 2 November 2005: 14.

Organizations

African Wildlife Foundation, 1400 16th St. NW, Suite 120, Washington, DC 20036. Phone: 202-939-3333, Fax: 202-939-3332, Internet: http://www.awf.org.

American Cetacean Society, PO Box 1391, San Pedro, CA 90733. Internet: http://www.acsonline.org.

American Littoral Society, Sandy Hook, Highlands, NJ 07732. Phone: 732-291-0055, Internet: http://www.alsnyc.org.

American Oceans Campaign, 2501 M St., NW Suite 300, Washington DC 20037-1311. Phone: 202-833-3900. Fax: 202-833-2070, Internet: http://www.oceana.org.

American Rivers, 1101 14th St. NW, Suite 1400, Washington, DC 20005. Phone: 202-347-7550, Fax: 202-347-9240, Internet: http://www.americanrivers.org.

Canadian Lakes Loon Survey, PO Box 160, Port Rowan, ON, Canada N0E 1M0. Internet: http://www.bsc-eoc.org/cllsmain.html.

Center for Environmental Education, Center for Marine Conservation, 1725 De Sales St. NW, Suite 500, Washington, DC 20036.

Center for Marine Conservation, 1725 DeSales St., NW, Suite 600, Washington, DC 20036. Phone: 202-429-5609, Fax: 202-872-0619, Internet: http://www.cmc-ocean.org.

Chihuahuan Desert Research Institute, PO Box 905, Fort Davis, TX 79734. Phone: 432-364-2499, Fax: 432-364-2686, Internet: http://www.cdri.org.

Coast Alliance, PO Box 505, Sandy Hook, Highlands, NJ 07732. Phone: 732-291-0055, Internet: http://www.coastalliance.org.

Desert Protective Council, Inc., PO Box 3635, San Diego, CA 92163. Phone: 619-342-5524, Internet: http://www.dpcinc.org/environ_issues.shtml.

Envirolink, PO Box 8102, Pittsburgh, PA 15217. Internet: http://www.envirolink.org.

Environmental Defense Fund, 257 Park Ave. South, New York, NY 10010. Telephone: 212-505-2100, Fax: 212-505-2375, Internet: http://www.edf.org.

Environmental Network, 4618 Henry St., Pittsburgh, PA 15213. Internet: www.environlink.org

Environmental Protection Agency, 401 M St., SW, Washington DC 20460. Telephone:202-260-2090, Internet: http://www.epa.gov.

The Freshwater Society, 2500 Shadywood Rd., Navarre, MN 55331. Phone: 952-471-9773, Fax: 952-471-7685, Internet: http://www.freshwater.org.

Friends of the Earth, 1717 Massachusetts Ave. NW 300, Washington, DC 20036. Telephone:877-843-8687, Fax:202-783-0444, Internet: http://www.foe.org.

Global ReLeaf, American Forests, PO Box 2000, Washington, DC 20013. Telephone: 202-737-1944, Internet: http://www.amfor.org.

Global Rivers Environmental Education Network (GREEN), 2120 W. 33rd Avenue, Denver, CO 80211. Internet: http://www.earthforce.org/green.

Greenpeace USA, 702 H St. NW, Washington, DC 20001. Telephone:202-462-1177, Internet: http://www.greenpeace.org.

International Joint Commission, 1250 23rd St. NW, Suite 100, Washington, DC 20440. Phone: 202-736-9024, Fax: 202-467-0746, Internet: http://www.ijc.org.

Izaak Walton League of America, 707 Conservation Ln., Gaithersburg, MD 20878. Telephone: 301-548-0150; Internet: http://www.iwla.org

National Wetlands Conservation Project, The Nature Conservancy, 1800 N Kent St., Suite 800, Arlington, VA 22209. Phone: 800-628-6860, Internet: http://www.tnc.org.

Nature Conservancy, Worldwide Office, 4245 North Fairfax Dr., Arlington, VA 22203-1606. Phone: 800-628-6860, Internet: http://www.nature.org.

North American Lake Management Society, PO Box 5443, Madison, WI 53705-0443. Phone: 608-233-2836, Fax: 608-233-3186, Internet: http://www.nalms.org.

Olympic Coast Alliance, PO Box 573 Olympia, WA 98501. Phone: 360-705-1549, Internet: http://www.olympiccoast.org.

Project Wet, 1001 West Oak, Suite 210, Bozeman, MT 59717. Phone: 866-337-5486, Fax: 406-522-0394, Internet: http://projectwet.org.

Rainforest Alliance, 665 Broadway, Suite 500, New York, NY 10012. Phone: 888-MY-EARTH, Fax: 212-677-1900, Internet: http://www.rainforest-alliance.org.

Sierra Club, 85 St., 2nd Fl., San Francisco, CA 94105. Telephone: 415-977-5500, Fax: 415-977-5799, Internet: http://www.sierraclub.org.

The Wilderness Society, 1615 M St. NW, Washington, DC 20036. Telephone: 800-the-wild, Internet: http://www.wilderness.org.

World Meteorological Organization, 7-bis, avenue de la Paix, Case Postale No. 2300 CH-1211, PO Box 2300, Geneva 2, Switzerland. Phone: 41 22 7308111, Fax: 41 22 7308181, Internet: http://www.wmo.ch.

World Wildlife Fund, 1250 24th St. NW, Washington, DC 20090. Internet: http://www.wwf.org.

Web sites

"America's Wetlands." Environmental Protection Agency. http://www.epa.gov/OWOW/wetlands/vital/what.html (accessed July 13, 2007).

Arctic Studies Center.http://www.nmnh.si.edu/arctic (accessed August 9, 2007).

Blue Planet Biomes. http://www.blueplanetbiomes.org (accessed September 14, 2007).

CBC News Indepth: Oceans. http://www.cbc.ca/news/background/oceans/part2.html (accessed September 1, 2007).

Discover Magazine. http://www.discovermagazine.com (accessed September 12, 2007).

Distribution of Land and Water on the Planet. http://www.oceansatlas.com/unatlas/about/physicalandchemicalproperties/background/seemore1.html (accessed September 1, 2007).

Envirolink. http://www.envirolink.org (accessed September 14, 2007).

FAO Fisheries Department. http://www.fao.org/fi (accessed September 5, 2007).

"The Grassland Biome." University of California Museum of Paleontology. http://www.ucmp.berkeley.edu/exhibits/biomes/grasslands.php (accessed September 14, 2007).

Journey North Project. http://www.learner.org/jnorth (accessed August 14, 2007).

Long Term Ecological Research Network. http://lternet.edu (accessed August 9, 2007).

Monterey Bay Aquarium. http://www.mbayaq.org (accessed September 12, 2007).

National Center for Atmospheric Research. http://www.ncar.ucar.edu (accessed September 12, 2007).

National Geographic Magazine. http://www.nationalgeographic.com (accessed September 14, 2007).

National Oceanic and Atmospheric Administration. http://www.noaa.gov(accessed September 1, 2007).

National Park Service. http://www.nps.gov (accessed September 14, 2007).

National Park Service, Katmai National Park and Preserve. http://www.nps.gov/katm/ (accessed August 9, 2007).

National Science Foundation. http://www.nsf.gov (accessed August 9, 2007).

Nature Conservancy. http://www.nature.org (accessed September 5, 2007).

The Ocean Environment. http://www.oceansatlas.com/unatlas/about/physicaland chemicalproperties/background/oceanenvironment.html (accessed September 1, 2007).

Oceana. http://www.americanoceans.org (accessed August 14, 2007).

"On Peatlands and Peat." International Peat Society. http://www.peatsociety.fi (accessed July 13, 2007).

Ouje-Bougoumou Cree Nation. http://www.ouje.ca (accessed August 25, 2007).

Scientific American Magazine. http://www.sciam.com (accessed September 5, 2007).

"Status and Trends of Wetlands of the Counterminous United States from 1998 to 2004:" U.S. Fish & Wildlife Service. http://wetlandsfws.er.usgs.gov/status_trends/National_Reports/trends_2005_report.pdf (accessed July 13, 2007).

Swedish Environmental Protection Agency. http://www.internat.naturvardsverket.se (accessed August 25, 2007).

Thurston High School: Biomes. http://ths.sps.lane.edu/biomes/index1.html (accessed August 9, 2007).

Time Magazine. http://time.com (accessed August 14, 2007).

"The Tundra Biome." University of California, Museum of Palentology. http://www.ucmpberkeley.edu/exhibits/biomes/tundra.php (accessed August 9, 2007).

U.N. Atlas of the Oceans. http://www.cmc-ocean.org (accessed September 12, 2007).

UNESCO. http://www.unesco.org/ (accessed September 5, 2007).

University of California at Berkeley. http://www.ucmp.berkeley.edu/glossary/gloss5/biome/index.html (accessed July 13, 2007).

U.S. Fish and Wildlife Services. http://www.fws.gov/

USDA Forest Service. http://www.fs.fed.us (accessed August 22, 2007).

"Wind Cave National Park." The National Park Service. http://www.nps.gov/wica/ (accessed September 14, 2007).

Woods Hole Oceanographic Institution. http://www.whoi.edu (accessed May 14, 2008).

The World Conservation Union. http://www.iucn.org (accessed August 22, 2007).

World Wildlife Fund. http://www.wwf.org (accessed August 22, 2007)

World Meteorological Organization. http://www.wmo.ch (accessed August 17, 2007).

Index

Numerals in italic type indicate volume number. Bold type indicates a main entry. Graphic elements (photographs, tables, illustrations) are denoted by (ill.).

A

Aborigines (Australia)
    clothing, *1:* 156
    Kakadu region, *3:* 503
    overview, *1:* 164
    tracking abilities, *1:* 159
Abyssal plains, *2:* 268
Abyssopelagic zones, *2:* 259
Acacia trees, *1:* 98, 110; *2:* 185, 185 (ill.), 188
Academy of Applied Science, *2:* 234
Acadia National Park, *3:* 419–20
Accidents
    plane crashes, *1:* 129, 159
    shipwrecks, *2:* 286
Acid rain
    coniferous forests, *1:* 36
    deciduous forests, *1:* 113
    lakes and ponds, *2:* 242
    wetlands, *3:* 494–95
Acornic acid, *1:* 112
Acorns, *1:* 112
Acquired immune deficiency syndrome (AIDS), *2:* 326
Active continental margins, *1:* 55
Active layers (tundra soil), *3:* 430–31
Addaxes, *1:* 153
"Adopt a Wetland" programs, *3:* 495
Africa
    grassland dwellers, *2:* 199–200
    hardwood trees, *1:* 113t

rain forests, *2:* 331–32
savannas, *2:* 175, 176
softwood trees, *1:* 7t
See also specific countries
African catfish, *3:* 361
African lungfish, *3:* 487
The African Queen (film), *3:* 370
African running frogs, *2:* 190
African weaverbirds, *2:* 192
Agama lizards, *1:* 27 (ill.), 143; *2:* 190
Age
    rivers and streams, *3:* 339–40, 340 (ill.)
    trees, *1:* 11, 96; *2:* 310
Agent Orange, *3:* 501–2
Agriculture. *See* Farming and farmland
Agulhas Current, *2:* 290
AIDS (acquired immune deficiency syndrome), *2:* 326
Ainu people, *1:* 114–15, 115 (ill.)
Air quality and pollution
    deciduous forests, *1:* 112, 113
    rain forests, *2:* 328
    tundra regions, *3:* 451–52
    See also Acid rain
Air temperatures
    boreal forests, *1:* 9
    coniferous forests, *1:* 10
    deserts, *1:* 124, 126–27
    grasslands, *2:* 179
    hurricanes and typhoons, *2:* 261
    ocean effect on, *2:* 258, 264

Fragmentation reproduction, *2:* 269, 291–92; *3:* 436

France
Normandy beach invasion of WWII, *3:* 392
truffles, *1:* 94

Franklin, Benjamin, *2:* 264

Freezing
lakes and ponds, *2:* 234
mosquitoes and, *3:* 439
tundra soil, *3:* 430, 432
See also Ice

Freshwater. *See* Rivers and streams; Wetlands

Freshwater lakes and ponds, defined, *2:* 216

Freshwater marshes, *3:* 471–73

Freshwater swamps, *3:* 471

Friction, river/stream velocity and, *3:* 343

Fringing reefs, *1:* 59

Frogfish, *2:* 259 (ill.)

Frogs
coniferous forests, *1:* 25
deciduous forests, *1:* 102
deserts, *1:* 142–43
grasslands, *2:* 189, 190, 203
lakes and ponds, *2:* 232, 232 (ill.)
rain forests, *2:* 315–16, 316 (ill.)
rivers and streams, *3:* 358
wetlands, *3:* 484

Fulani people, *1:* 156; *2:* 215

Fungi
coniferous forests, *1:* 15
deciduous forests, *1:* 94–95, 94 (ill.), 99–100
deserts, *1:* 134
grasslands, *2:* 183
lakes and ponds, *2:* 227
rain forests, *2:* 307–8
rivers and streams, *3:* 353
seashores, *3:* 400
tundra regions, *3:* 434
wetlands, *3:* 478–79

Fur
chinchillas, *3:* 447
musk oxen, *3:* 447
tundra mammals, *3:* 444

G

Gagnan, Emile, *2:* 288

Galls, tree, *2:* 188

Ganges River
ancient civilizations, *3:* 366
delta, *3:* 350
elevation, *3:* 351
overview, *3:* 377–78

Gases, atmospheric. *See* Atmosphere

Gaspé Peninsula, *3:* 460–61

Geese, Greenland white-fronted, *3:* 491

"General Sherman" (tree), *1:* 8

Geography
coniferous forests, *1:* 11–14
continental margins, *1:* 54–60
deciduous forests, *1:* 91–93
deserts, *1:* 126 (ill.), 128–33, 128 (ill.), 131 (ill.)
grasslands, *2:* 180–83
lakes and ponds, *2:* 222–25
ocean floor, *2:* 265–68
rain forests, *2:* 305–6
rivers and streams, *3:* 346–51, 347 (ill.), 349 (ill.), 350 (ill.), 351 (ill.)
seashores, *3:* 394–99, 398 (ill.)
tundra regions, *3:* 430–33, 431 (ill.), 432 (ill.)
wetlands, *3:* 476–77

Geothermal energy, *2:* 218

Germany
Normandy beach invasion of WWII, *3:* 392
peat loss, *3:* 494

Geysers, *2:* 218

Giant anteaters, *2:* 202

Giant armadillos, *2:* 202

Giant otters, *3:* 374

Giant redwood trees, *1:* 7–8

Giant saguaro cacti, *1:* 136

Giant sequoia trees, *1:* 7–8, 11

Giant tubeworms, *2:* 274

Giant water bugs, *2:* 231

Gila monster lizards, *1:* 144, 145

Ginkgo trees, *1:* 111

Girdling, trees, *1:* 35

M

O